CIA's Analysis of the Soviet Union, 1947-1991: A Documentary Collection

Editors
Gerald K. Haines
Robert E. Leggett

Center for the Study of Intelligence
Central Intelligence Agency
Washington, DC
2001

TABLE OF CONTENTS

Preface

Controversy over the performance of the Central Intelligence Agency during the Cold War has raged since the fall of the Berlin Wall and the subsequent collapse of the Soviet Union. From its origins in 1947, the Agency had, as one of its major missions, the responsibility of analyzing and explaining the intentions and capabilities of the Soviet Union to US policymakers. It was a daunting task. A tightly controlled society, the Soviet Union presented CIA analysts with major challenges as they struggled to make sense of its political, economic, military, and scientific developments. CIA was not always correct in its analysis but the Agency, over the decades, made a unique contribution in helping US policymakers understand America's major adversary. As a long time intelligence analyst, then Deputy Director for Intelligence, and finally Director of Central Intelligence, I spent much of my career watching and analyzing the Soviet Union. In my judgment, overall, the CIA performed admirably in meeting the challenges of assessing Soviet strengths and weaknesses. Others disagree.

I have always believed that the record of actual intelligence assessments represents the best defense of CIA's and the Intelligence Community's analytical performance vis-à-vis the USSR – the good, the bad and the ugly. Thus, as DCI, I began the systematic process of declassifying intelligence assessments from the Cold War, beginning with all National Intelligence Estimates on the USSR. My successors have continued this process. This latest compilation of key documents from CIA's files and the related declassification and release of a large amount of new material on CIA analysis of the USSR will further help scholars and the public assess for themselves CIA's analytical performance during the Cold War. Making these materials available to everyone is a major step in furthering the dialogue. Researchers may now judge the accuracy of CIA forecasts and with that judgment gain deeper insight into the impact of CIA analysis on US policymakers. As a strong believer in government openness, I applaud this effort and look forward to continuing declassification and release programs by the Agency.

Robert M. Gates,
former Director of Central Intelligence

Introduction

The global contest between the United States and the Soviet Union dominated international relations for some 46 years (1945-1991). The Cold War confrontation shaped the foreign policies of the United States and the Soviet Union, deeply affecting their societies and their foreign policies. They engaged in a costly arms race, built devastating nuclear arsenals, and confronted each other in a tense political and military face-off in a divided Europe and in the Third World. The Soviet-American rivalry ended with the collapse of the USSR and the disintegration of the Soviet empire in 1991.

The Central Intelligence Agency (CIA), along with other agencies in the US Intelligence Community, helped American policymakers understand events in the Soviet Union throughout the Cold War. CIA's major analytic component, the Directorate of Intelligence (DI), focused much of its attention on Soviet developments. It tried not only to discern Moscow's intentions, but also to gauge the state of the Soviet economy, the USSR's technological base, the readiness and plans of Soviet military forces, and the internal workings of the Kremlin.

Measuring the degree to which US policymakers read, understood, and acted upon the intelligence assessments they received from the Agency is a difficult task. Each administration formed its foreign policy in different ways. The well-staffed, military-like national security process of the Eisenhower administration, for example, contrasted with the more informal process of the Kennedy administration. On many issues, moreover, the Agency had to compete for the attention of policymakers with the State Department's Bureau of Intelligence and Research (INR), the Defense Intelligence Agency (DIA), the military intelligence organizations, and a wide array of academics, businessmen, and journalists.

A Critical View of the Analysis

Critics of the Agency have argued that CIA provided little accurate and useful information to US policymakers regarding actual conditions within the Soviet Union. Former Senator Daniel Patrick Moynihan (D-NY), for example, in his most recent book, *Secrecy: The American Experience*, contends that CIA overestimated Soviet military strength and failed to predict the collapse of the USSR in 1991. From the 1960s to the 1980s, he argues, American policymakers were led—erroneously—by CIA and other US intelligence organizations to believe that Soviet military forces and the Soviet economy were fundamentally strong and that the USSR was politically stable. This viewpoint dated at least from the Gaither Report of 1957, which compared US and Soviet military capabilities and portrayed the Soviet Union as a modern, vibrant, and powerful industrial-military power.

Senator Moynihan further maintains that he and others noted as early as 1975 that the Soviet emperor had no clothes, as well as "no shoes, butter, meat, living space, heat, telephones, or toilet paper." His countervailing view at the time was that the Soviet Union was so weak economically, as well as so divided ethnically, that it could not survive for long. Moynihan claims that by 1984 he believed, and so stated, that the Soviet Union was dying and that the Soviet idea of Communism was a spent force. The economy was collapsing, rising ethnic consciousness was inciting virulent (and often violent) nationalism, and history was moving rapidly away from the Communist model.

Nevertheless, according to the Senator, CIA and the rest of the US Intelligence Community continued to overestimate Soviet strength and to portray the USSR as a despotism that worked:

> It was as though two chess grandmasters had pursued an interminable, and highly sophisticated, strategy of feint and counter-feint, not noticing that for the past 40 or 50 moves, one side not only had been in checkmate, but . . . had his queen, his rooks, his bishops, and knights all taken from the board. Only nuclear weapons, however, kept the game from being completely boring.[1]

In essence, Senator Moynihan charges that CIA failed in one of its main missions—to accurately assess the political, economic, and military state of the Soviet Union.

---

[1]Daniel P. Moynihan, *Secrecy, The American Experience*, (New Haven: Yale University Press, 1998). See also Gary Wills, "Honorable Man: The Gentleman From New York: Daniel Patrick Moynihan," *New York Review of Books*, Vol. XLVII, No. 18, November 16, 2000, p. 15. For Secretary of State George Shultz's criticism of the Agency and its intelligence effort see George P. Shultz, *Turmoil and Triumph My Years as Secretary of State* (New York: Charles Scribner's Sons, 1993), pp. 864-869. See also Melvin Goodman, "The Politics of Getting It Wrong," *Harper's Magazine*, November 2000, pp. 74-80.

A Vigorous Rejoinder

Former CIA officials and some outside scholars have disputed the claims by Senator Moynihan and other critics and defended the Agency's analytical record. In their view, CIA—and the US Intelligence Community as a whole—accurately tracked and foreshadowed key trends and developments, including the decline and ultimate collapse of the Soviet empire. They argue that, throughout the 1980s, CIA warned of the weakening Soviet economy and later of the impending failure of Mikhail Gorbachev.[2] According to Bruce Berkowitz, for example, the CIA "was right on the mark" in its analysis. He concludes that the Agency performed well in anticipating the Soviet collapse.[3]

Recent Retrospective Conferences

CIA's Center for the Study of Intelligence (CSI) has sponsored several public conferences in recent years to examine the record of the Intelligence Community's analysis of the Soviet Union during the Cold War. The first such gathering, "Estimating Soviet Military Power, 1950-1984," was co-sponsored with the John F. Kennedy School of Government and held at Harvard University in December 1994. The CIA declassified and released a series of National Intelligence Estimates (NIEs) for the conference and published them in a 1996 volume *Intentions and Capabilities: Estimates on Soviet Strategic Forces, 1950-1983*.[4]

A second conference, "Assessing the Soviet Threat: The Early Cold War Years, 1946-1950," took place at CIA Headquarters in Virginia in October 1997 in conjunction with CIA's 50th anniversary. For this event, the Agency

---

[2]See Richard Kerr, "CIA's Record Stands Up to Scrutiny," *New York Times*, October 24, 1991, p.A4; Robert Gates, "The CIA and the Collapse of the Soviet Union: Hit or Miss?" Speech to the Foreign Policy Association, New York, May 20, 1992; and Kirsten Lundberg, "The CIA and the Fall of the Soviet Empire: The Politics of Getting It Right," Harvard Case Study C16-94-12510, Harvard University. Douglas J. MacEachin, former Director of the DI's Office of Soviet Analysis (SOVA), and Bruce Berkowitz, former CIA analyst, both reach similar conclusions. See Douglas MacEachin, *CIA Assessments of the Soviet Union: The Record Versus the Charges*, (Washington, DC: Center for the Study of Intelligence, CIA, 1996) and Bruce Berkowitz and Jeffrey T. Richelson, "The CIA Vindicated: The Soviet Collapse Was Predicted," *The National Interest*, (No. 41, Fall 1995).

[3]Berkowitz, *ibid.*

[4]See Donald P. Steury, ed., *Intentions and Capabilities: Estimates on Soviet Strategic Forces, 1950-1983* (Washington, DC: Center for the Study of Intelligence, CIA, 1994).

and released some of the current intelligence items that had been sent to President Truman on the Soviet threat in Europe, the Middle East, and Asia.[5]

CSI co-sponsored two conferences in 1999. The first, "On the Front Lines of the Cold War, 1946-1961," was held in September in Berlin and was co-sponsored and hosted by the Allied Museum of Berlin. CSI compiled and edited a volume of operational and analytical documents ranging from NIEs to assorted Station cables for the conference.[6] In November 1999, CSI and the George Bush School of Government and Public Service at Texas A&M University co-sponsored a conference, "At Cold War's End." At this event, held at the Bush School, the focus was on the Intelligence Community's National Intelligence Estimates on the Soviet Union and Eastern Europe during the final crisis of the Soviet Bloc from 1989 through 1991. Panelists paid particular attention to the question of how effective US intelligence was in tracking the collapse of Communism in the Soviet Union and Eastern Europe. As was the case with the earlier conferences, CIA released a compendium of newly declassified NIEs and other assessments.[7]

Analysis During 1947-1991: A Multidisciplinary Review

Continuing its quest to build as complete and accurate a public record of the Agency's analytical role as possible during the Cold War, CSI will co-sponsor another retrospective conference with the Center of International Studies at Princeton University in March 2001. The conference will examine the Agency's analytic record and performance from the early Cold War years through the collapse of the Soviet Union, making use of a large body of recently declassified CIA analytical documents.[8] Scholars at the conference also will draw upon the sizable collection of previously released documents on Soviet economics, political developments, military programs, scientific and technological progress, published between 1947 and 1991.

---

[5]See Woodrow J. Kuhns, ed., *Assessing the Soviet Threat: The Early Cold War Years, 1946-1950* (Washington, DC: Center for the Study of Intelligence, CIA, 1997).
[6]See Donald Steury, ed., *On the Front Lines of the Cold War: Documents on the Intelligence War in Berlin, 1946-1961* (Washington, DC: Center for the Study of Intelligence, CIA, 1999).
[7]See Benjamin Fischer, ed., *At Cold War's End: US Intelligence on the Soviet Union and Eastern Europe, 1989-1991* (Washington, DC: Center for the Study of Intelligence, CIA, 1999).
[8]"Analysis" in this context is defined as papers reflecting in-depth or long-term research and, in many cases, also containing conclusions, estimates, and forecasts.

The Production of Intelligence Analysis

CIA's analytic work began in a small Central Reports Staff (CRS) created in 1946 as part of the Central Intelligence Group (CIG), a forerunner of the Central Intelligence Agency, which was established in September 1947. The CIG inherited some operational elements from the Strategic Services Unit, an organization husbanded by the War Department that had kept intact key personnel and facilities from the wartime Office of Strategic Services (OSS) after it was disbanded in September 1945. The analytic elements of OSS's Research and Analysis Branch, however, had been transferred to the State Department, where they were allowed to be dispersed over the next few years. Thus, while CIA eventually acquired some analysts who had been in OSS, it did not inherit a functioning analytic organization or infrastructure.

CRS quickly became an important intelligence link to the White House. President Harry Truman wanted to ensure that all relevant information available to the US Government on any given national security issue was correlated and evaluated centrally and a daily summary provided to him. He was determined that the country would never again suffer a devastating surprise attack as it had at Pearl Harbor.[9] With presidential backing, CRS quickly grew into the Office of Reports and Estimates (ORE), which Truman's foreign policy advisers apparently hoped would produce national intelligence estimates by drawing on information available in the established intelligence agencies, the military services, and the State Department. The President himself, however, preferred the daily intelligence summary that ORE prepared for him over more formal estimates.

The mission of CIA's analysts expanded swiftly. In addition to the estimates and current intelligence tasks, they were asked to take on wide-ranging basic research work on such topics as economics, transportation and geography. In many regards, their work and their organizational structure naturally fell within normal academic disciplines and thus it seemed logical to sort it in this fashion. Also, bureaucratic opportunism played a role. The State Department and military services held that political and military analysis were rightfully theirs and should not be tasked to CIA. At the same time, they left scientific and, increasingly, economic subjects for the Agency's analysts.

Meanwhile, a debate over whether CIA had the right to "produce" (as opposed to "correlate" information supplied by others) analysis gradually was

---

[9]Kuhns, *op. cit.*, p. 3.

resolved in favor of CIA because the work was not being done elsewhere. CIA also inherited from the wartime Manhattan Project the function of providing intelligence on foreign atomic energy matters. To do nuclear-related scientific and technical work, some CIA analysts were given special clearances, and this led in part to the founding of CIA's Office of Scientific Intelligence in 1948. In addition, some CIA analysts were given COMINT clearances for the purposes of producing current intelligence, and thus another important and growing source of information was created. In all of these developments, analysis on the USSR was the dominant task occupying CIA analysts.

Criticism of ORE's work grew in the late 1940s. More than one policymaker and intelligence officer complained that ORE was not producing the kind of "national" estimates many had hoped for. After the Korean War broke out in June 1950, a new Director of Central Intelligence with greater status in Washington than his predecessors, Lieutenant General Walter Bedell Smith, was brought in to improve CIA's performance. Within days of taking office in October 1950, he abolished ORE and replaced it with the Office of National Estimates (ONE), responsible for the production of national estimates; the Office of Research and Reports (ORR), responsible for doing basic research; and the Office of Current Intelligence (OCI), responsible for the production of daily current intelligence.

The bulk of the CIA's analysis thus fell to ORR, which concentrated on economic analysis throughout the 1950s. Aiding this effort was the recruitment of Max Millikan, an economist from the Massachusetts Institute of Technology, to head ORR. Millikan initiated an extensive recruitment program, hiring economists who formed the core group of CIA's economic analysts for the next decade. In addition, CIA reached a landmark agreement with the Department of State in 1951 that gave ORR responsibility for economic research and analysis on the Soviet Union and its East European satellites. ORR soon developed models of the Soviet economy that, with modifications over the ensuing decades, provided US policymakers with invaluable insights into the USSR's massive but cumbersome economy.

The 1950s and 1960s also saw a rapid expansion in the DI's production of finished intelligence on Soviet strategic capabilities. Contributing to this expansion was the development of modern overhead photographic reconnaissance, beginning with the U-2 aircraft and growing in sophistication with the CORONA satellite program and follow-on systems. These programs generated information in great quantities and caused a "collection revolution," creating a need for new analytical techniques. The small DI photo-analysis office established in 1952 eventually grew into the National Photographic Interpretation Center (NPIC) in 1961.[10]

Military analysis underwent a revolution as a result of the new imagery. Innovative approaches were undertaken within ORR under the auspices of the Office of National Estimates, and the increased data derived from expanded collection, as well as new analytical techniques, were instrumental in settling the "bomber" and "missile" gap debates in the 1950s and early 1960s. The Agency's performance in these and other issues raised the stature of its analysis of Soviet military intentions and capabilities. At the same time, the Office of Scientific Intelligence expanded to work on missile and other technical weapons issues as well as on atomic energy issues.

In the early 1960s, DCI John McCone recognized the new prominence of technological collection by forming the Directorate of Science and Technology (DS&T). It included both analytic elements and collection organizations, and the synergy between the two was noteworthy. Space and offensive weapons systems joined a new foreign missiles and space center that monitored Soviet missile developments. Defensive weapons systems, naval systems, and nuclear matters remained in OSI until 1973, when a new Office of Weapons Intelligence was formed that brought all the weapons-related issues together. In 1976, OWI and OSI were joined in a new Office of Scientific & Weapons Research, which in turn was moved to the DI, where its successors remain today.

Another element aiding CIA's analysis of the USSR in this period was the availability of information supplied by human sources such as Colonel Oleg Penkovsky. This information provided the Agency with unique insights into Soviet capabilities and planning, especially regarding Soviet strategic forces.[11]

The trend in functional specialization continued in the DI in the 1960s. In 1967, DCI Richard Helms created the Office of Strategic Research (OSR), which combined the units in ORR and OCI that engaged in military research. Thus, the military analysts at CIA, who were predominately concerned with the USSR, finally had an office of their own. Prior to this, most of the DI's military analyses were in the form of contributions to NIEs. Simultaneously, an Office of Economic Research (OER) was established. The workload of CIA's economists expanded considerably during the 1960s. Among the causes of this growth were

---

[10]NPIC remained in the DI until 1973, when it was transferred to the CIA's Directorate of Science and Technology. It became part of the National Imagery and Mapping Agency (NIMA) in 1996.
[11]William M. Leary, ed., *The Central Intelligence Agency* (Tuscaloosa, AL: University of Alabama Press, 1984), p. 70.

(1) the USSR's increasing use of foreign trade and assistance as instruments of its foreign policy, (2) concern in Washington that the Soviet Union would try to penetrate the emerging countries in the Third World economically, (3) the growing economic competitiveness of Japan and Western Europe, and (4) the gradual breakdown of the international monetary order that had been established at Bretton Woods in 1944.

The Office of Current Intelligence also took on a more prominent role in the 1960s when it created a new publication for President John F. Kennedy—the President's Intelligence Checklist—now called the President's Daily Brief. The President took an instant liking to the publication, significantly boosting OCI's prestige within the DI.[12]

OCI had in fact been the "political analysis" office in the DI since its inception in 1951, but a small group of political analysts in OCI had been freed from current intelligence duties in the wake of Stalin's death in 1953 to study high-level Soviet politics. The group grew into a Senior Research Staff (SRS) that was subordinated directly under the Deputy Director for Intelligence. It focused on lengthy, detailed studies of Soviet and Chinese affairs, Sino-Soviet relations, and international communism. During the 1950s and 1960s, the DI's analysis of Soviet political affairs was done by OCI, SRS, and the ONE staff.

In 1973, ONE (both its board and its staff) were abolished, as was SRS. A newly created group of National Intelligence Officers (organized by substantive expertise) took over the function of producing NIEs—the organization became the National Intelligence Council at the end of the 1970s. Most of ONE and SRS were combined into a new Office of Political Research (OPR), paralleling OSR and OER and coexisting with OCI. In 1976 a single Office of Regional and Political Analysis (later renamed Office of Political Analysis) replaced both OPR and OCI.

In 1981 the DI went through a large reorganization to pull together analysts from the political, economic , and military disciplines working on the same countries into regional offices. Thus, OSR, OER, and OPA were abolished and a series of geographic offices, including an Office of Soviet Analysis (SOVA) was created. The new SOVA was headed initially by the director of OSR, with the chief Soviet economist in OER as his deputy.

---

[12]The *President's Daily Brief* continues to be produced today as a premier product of CIA's Intelligence Directorate.

With this reorganization (which remains the basis of the Directorate's current structure), the DI's structure for analyzing the USSR returned to a model first pioneered by the OSS's Research and Analysis Branch in World War II. R&A had originally been organized like a college faculty, with separate offices for the various academic disciplines. In 1943, however, this structure was swept away and replaced with one designed to mirror the regional theaters of OSS global operations.[13]

The Document Selection Process

The body of DI documents on the Soviet Union published during the Cold War years, but not yet declassified, is far too large to have been reviewed for declassification and released for this conference. Therefore, the goal of the Agency was to assemble a collection of documents large enough and sufficiently diverse to ensure that (1) most, if not all, of the major developments and analytic issues that occurred during the period were represented, and (2) the tenor and substance of the DI's analysis was adequately captured.[14]

A threefold approach was taken in the document selection:

- First, reports reflecting in-depth or long-term research that generally contain analytic judgments, estimates, and forecasts were selected for review and release. A few memoranda or other special products, but virtually no current intelligence, were included.
- Second, using a listing of subject titles for reports published by the DI, the documents were selected for their substantive content. This selection was undertaken without regard to the quality of the analysis the documents provided. In no instance was any document excluded from the collection, nor was any information redacted to conceal analytic judgments that were subsequently proven wrong. No documents were withheld or redacted in a fashion to conceal differences between CIA's analysis and that of another US

---

[13]It was a traumatic experience for the economists in particular (who declared they would not serve with political scientists or historians), and a historian of the period stated that R&A chief William Langer (of Harvard University) "ought to have been decorated for his courage in assaulting the disciplinary fortifications..." Barry M. Katz, *Foreign Intelligence: Research and Analysis in the Office of Strategic Services, 1942-1945*, (Cambridge, MA: Harvard University Press, 1989), p.102. In 1981, there was less trauma, although the new office was promptly moved out of the CIA Headquarters compound for three years.
[14]The documents, as released, have been sent to the National Archives and Records Administration (NARA).

Government agency or any other organization, or because release might somehow embarrass the Agency.

- Third, the conference authors reviewed the documents chosen in the second step above to determine whether there were any substantive historical gaps in the collection. In some instances, National Intelligence Estimates were used to fill these gaps.

Concerted efforts were made to release as many documents as possible and to declassify as much information as possible in the documents that were included in the collection.

A number of complicating factors came into play in reviewing the documents. Some of the records could not be released in full without compromising still-sensitive intelligence sources and methods or harming current government-to-government relations. In these instances, we tried wherever possible to release the Summary, Conclusions, or Key Judgments of the paper, but the detailed supporting analysis was withheld. Some documents could not be released at all because they would have had to be so heavily redacted as to be meaningless or seriously distorted.

A Closer Look at the Newly Released Materials

About 860 DI finished intelligence documents, encompassing some 19,000 pages (see table), are being released for the first time in conjunction with this conference. About 50 percent of these documents analyze economic topics; more than 20 percent assess political issues; about 20 percent deal with military matters; and less than 10 percent are assessments of scientific and technical subjects.

The large proportion of economic documents, especially from the earlier period, is partially accounted for by the fact that the DI devoted the lion's share of its analytic resources to economic assessments during the 1950s. Moreover, much of CIA's military and technical analysis on the USSR ultimately appeared in print in the form of contributions to National Intelligence Estimates rather than as separate publications. In addition, scientific intelligence items are limited because many of the reports cite still-sensitive intelligence collection methods and specialized analytical techniques which, if divulged, could damage current security interests. Therefore, a significant amount of the work of the Office of Scientific Intelligence, the Office of Weapons Intelligence, and the Office of Scientific & Weapons Research was eliminated from review. As in the case of military analysis, moreover, CIA's scientific and technical analysis often found expression in National Intelligence Estimates.

The newly released documents are fairly evenly distributed over the time period. There are, however, a few more documents from the early years because the analysis produced in recent periods contains more still-sensitive information that cannot yet be declassified and released. The new release also includes 12 recently declassified NIEs on the Soviet Union to fill gaps in coverage when it was not possible to include DI finished intelligence reports that could be declassified.

A Large and Comprehensive Collection

Complementing the newly declassified DI documents released for the conference are several collections of DI intelligence documents previously released to the public:

1) In 1996, the Agency began to declassify DI analyses on the former Soviet Union. Since then, more than 1,600 reports containing approximately 51,350 pages of analysis on the former USSR produced by the Office of Research and Reports and successor entities between 1953 and 1991 have been released to the National Archives and Records Administration (NARA). This initiative was undertaken as part of the Agency's voluntary Historical Review Program as well as under the 25-year mandatory program.[15]
2) Approximately 475 DI documents on the former Soviet Union have been reviewed and released by the Agency under the Freedom of Information Act (FOIA) or as part of the mandatory review program under Executive Order 12958.
3) Finally, 40 documents, about 1,500 pages, originally distributed by the Agency as unclassified publications were made available to the conference as a convenience because most are now out-of-print.

Many National Intelligence Estimates on the former Soviet Union, the DCI's most authoritative written judgments, also have been previously declassified and released to NARA. The NIEs were produced by the National Intelligence Council (and its predecessor organizations) and reflect the views of the entire intelligence community. Their text generally reflects the Agency's

---

[15]A description of the CIA's voluntary historical review program and a listing of the documents released to NARA can be found on CIA's Electronic Document Release Center (also known as the FOIA) Web site at http://www.foia.ucia.gov.

analytic position on the issues, and, when it does not, the Agency's position is stated in a dissent. Since 1992, nearly 550 NIEs (of approximately 800) and other interagency intelligence issuances on the USSR, comprising over 13,000 pages, have been released to NARA.

In all, over 3,500 DI finished intelligence documents, National Intelligence Estimates, and miscellaneous DI documents on the USSR are now available for the conference, and for future scholarship. We believe this collection provides a representative and unbiased sample of the DI's economic, political, military, and scientific and technical analysis over the period in question. Many DI analytical products still remain classified, however, and thus there is much more still to be learned about the Agency's analysis of the former Soviet Union during the Cold War.

The Selection of Sample Documents for the Volume

The documents included in this volume were selected by five authors who wrote papers for the conference. Each author was given a list of the documents assembled for the conference. From that list, they selected the reports they wanted as research materials for their review and assessment of the DI's analytic record between 1947 and 1991.

In reviewing the documents to prepare their conference papers, the authors were asked to identify particularly noteworthy reports or key documents for publication in this volume. In most cases, only the redacted versions of the Summaries or Key Judgments are included because of space constraints. As noted earlier, however, the declassified documents in their entirety, as well as the documents declassified for the conference, will be available at NARA and on the CIA Electronic Document Release Center (or FOIA Web site) at http://www.foia.ucia.gov. In addition, compact discs containing the documents will be provided to conference participants.

Each section in the volume contains a brief explanation of the authors' reasons for including the summaries or key judgments of particular documents in the volume. The documents follow.

Gerald K. Haines, CIA Chief Historian
Robert E. Leggett, Office of Information Management, CIA

Declassified and Released DI and Intelligence Community Documents on the Soviet Union		
	Number of Documents	**Number of Pages**
Documents Produced by CIA's Directorate of Intelligence		
Newly Reviewed for the Princeton Conference	859	19,160
Previously released to NARA by CIA's Historical Review Program	1,152	36,720
Released to NARA by CIA's 25-Year Program*	481	14,629
FOIA and Mandatory Releases	473	9,300
Released Previously by CIA in Unclassified Form	40	1,505
TOTAL	**3,005**	**81,315**
National Intelligence Estimates		
Newly Reviewed for the Princeton Conference	12	285
Previously Released to NARA by CIA's Historical Review Program	546	13,710
TOTAL	**558**	**13,710**
GRAND TOTAL	**3,563**	**95,025**

*As mandated by E.O. 12958

Editors and Contributors to this Volume

Editors

Gerald K. Haines

Dr. Haines has an extensive background in US intelligence matters and on the Intelligence Community. He earned his doctorate in US diplomatic history at the University of Wisconsin-Madison in 1973. In the fall of 1974 he joined the National Archives as a foreign policy specialist. In 1981 he moved to the National Security Agency (NSA) as a staff historian. In 1989 he joined the CIA History Staff and became Deputy Chief in 1994. In 1995 he was asked to establish a new history office at the National Reconnaissance Office (NRO). In 1997 he returned to CIA's Center for the Study of Intelligence (CSI) to head the CIA History Staff and become the Agency's Chief Historian.

Robert E. Leggett

Dr. Leggett currently is a senior project manager in CIA's Office of Information Management (OIM), where among his other duties, he had overall responsibility for the declassification review and release of documents for this conference. He came to OIM with broad experience in the Intelligence Community. He previously served as the Chief of the Community Coordination Group in the Center for the Study of Intelligence (CSI) and before that in the National Intelligence Council (NIC) as Deputy National Intelligence Officer for Global and Multilateral Issues. Dr. Leggett served much of his career in CIA's Directorate of Intelligence with OSR, OER, and the Office of Soviet Analysis (SOVA) where he was a specialist on the Soviet economy. His academic work on the Soviet economy has appeared in scholarly journals, several books, and in Compendiums on the Soviet Economy published by the Joint Economic Committee of Congress. He also served on CIA's National Intelligence Daily Staff, Office of Congressional Affairs, as a Group Chief in the DCI Center for Security Evaluation, and in the Intelligence Community's Crime and Narcotics Center.

Contributors to this Volume

Donald Steury, a senior historian in the Center for the Study of Intelligence's CIA History Staff, is currently visiting professor at the University of Southern California.

Douglas Garthoff, a former senior CIA officer who served in the Directorate of Intelligence, is currently adjunct professorial lecturer at American University in Washington, DC.

Clarence Smith is a former Vice Chairman, Committee on Imagery Requirements and Exploitation, and a former Special Assistant to the Director of Central Intelligence. Smith is currently a senior industry executive with Space Applications Corporation and Emergent Information Technologies, Inc.

James Noren is a retired CIA economic analyst and the co-author of *Soviet Defense Spending: A History of CIA Estimates, 1950-1990* (College Station, Texas: Texas A&M University Press, 1998).

Raymond Garthoff, a prolific author on Soviet affairs and former US Ambassador to Bulgaria, is a guest scholar at the Brookings Institution in Washington, DC.

Origins of CIA's Analysis of the Soviet Union, 1947-1991

Origins of CIA's Analysis of the Soviet Union

Author's Comments: Donald Steury

Berlin, the political flashpoint of the early Cold War, was a catalyst for the development of a strategic analysis capability in CIA. The end of World War II found the Allies in an increasingly tenuous quadripartite occupation of the city, which was complicated by its position deep inside the Russian occupation zone. As the wartime alliance fragmented, the continued Western presence in Berlin assumed a growing importance to the stability of the Western alliance: first, as a concrete symbol of the American commitment to defend Western Europe; and, second, as a vital strategic intelligence base from which to monitor the growing Soviet military presence in Germany and Eastern Europe.

The continued division of the city offered no such advantage to the Soviet Bloc. Inevitably, the Kremlin came to regard the Western garrisons in Berlin as a more-or-less permanent challenge to the legitimacy of Soviet rule in Germany and Eastern Europe. Consequently, Soviet leader Joseph Stalin initiated a series of provocations and military demonstrations early in 1948 in an apparent effort to force the Western Allies out of Berlin. By March, the US Military Governor in Germany, General Lucius D. Clay, was sufficiently alarmed to warn Washington of "a subtle change in Soviet attitude which...gives me a feeling that (war) may come with dramatic suddenness."[1]

Clay apparently had intended only to warn the Joint Chiefs of Staff (JCS) of the need for caution in Central Europe, but the telegram caused considerable alarm in Washington. At the behest of JCS Chairman General Omar N. Bradley, the supervisory Intelligence Advisory Committee ordered CIA to chair an ad hoc committee to examine the likelihood of war.[2] The result was a series of three estimates (documents 1, 2, and 3) that examined and dismissed the possibility of a planned Soviet assault on Western Europe in 1948-1949, despite the escalating Soviet saber-rattling over Berlin. Although the estimates were brief, each reflected a relatively sophisticated and broadly-based understanding of Soviet national power. The analysis contained therein went beyond the military dimensions of the problem to analyze the political and economic implications of the issue. Together, the documents indicated a need for an independent analytical capability in Washington.

A fourth estimate, ORE 58-48 (document 4) provided a comprehensive assessment of the Soviet Union's potential to wage war. A highly controversial estimate at the time, this document nonetheless further validated ORE's role as a source of overarching analyses.

---

[1] William R. Harris, "The March Crisis of 1948, Act I," *Studies in Intelligence*, Vol. 10, No. 4, Fall 1966, p.7 (National Archives and Record Administration [NARA] Records Group 263).
[2] *Ibid.*, p.10.

The Berlin crisis sharply demonstrated the need for regular review of Moscow's war potential. With the reorganization of CIA in 1950-1951, this responsibility was formally given to the newly created Board of National Estimates (see SE-16, document 5).

Throughout much of the 1950s, CIA's analysis of the Soviet Union continued to be hampered by the lack of solid intelligence on Soviet military developments. Until the first remote sensors (such as the U-2 and the CORONA reconnaissance satellites) were deployed, CIA's analysis often was based on fragmentary sources at best. An essential component of the reorganization of CIA's analysis was the comprehensive review of the available intelligence on the Soviet Union completed in 1953 (document 6).

1.

ORE 22-48

TOP 

POSSIBILITY OF DIRECT SOVIET MILITARY ACTION DURING 1948

Report by a Joint Ad Hoc Committee *

THE PROBLEM

1. We have been directed to estimate the likelihood of a Soviet resort to direct military action during 1948.

DISCUSSION

2. Our conclusions are based on considerations discussed in the Enclosure.

CONCLUSIONS

3. The preponderance of available evidence and of considerations derived from the "logic of the situation" supports the conclusion that the USSR will not resort to direct military action during 1948.

4. However, in view of the combat readiness and disposition of the Soviet armed forces and the strategic advantage which the USSR might impute to the occupation of Western Europe and the Near East, the possibility must be recognized that the USSR might resort to direct military action in 1948, particularly if the Kremlin should interpret some US move, or series of moves, as indicating an intention to attack the USSR or its satellites.

* This estimate was prepared by a joint ad hoc committee representing CIA and the intelligence agencies of the Department of State, the Army, the Navy, and the Air Force. The date of the estimate is 30 March 1948.

2.

THE STRATEGIC VALUE TO THE USSR OF THE CONQUEST OF WESTERN EUROPE AND THE NEAR EAST (TO CAIRO) PRIOR TO 1950 *

Report by a Joint Ad Hoc Committee

STATEMENT OF THE PROBLEM

1. To analyze and evaluate the advantages and disadvantages that would accrue to the USSR if it should elect, prior to 1950, to overrun the European continent and the Near East (to Cairo), with a view to determining whether or not the strategic position thus acquired would be sufficiently strong *per se* to induce Soviet leaders to adopt such a course of action.

ASSUMPTIONS AND FACTS BEARING ON THE PROBLEM

2. The USSR has the military capability of overrunning Europe (excluding the UK) and the Near East to Cairo in a short period of time.

3. The Western Powers would undertake immediate counteraction, including maximum employment of US air power, using the atomic bomb at least against Soviet targets.

4. A substantial part of the merchant and naval ships belonging to the countries which were overrun would manage to avoid falling under Soviet control.

5. A large part of the Near Eastern oil facilities and installations would be seriously damaged or destroyed prior to evacuation by present operators.

6. The Western Powers, through naval blockade, would effectively cut off commerce between continental Europe on the one hand and the Western Hemisphere, Africa, and Southeast Asia on the other.

7. In addition to the assumptions enumerated above, the basic problem of analyzing the Soviet position following the occupation of the areas in question must be considered under two broad alternative assumptions:

a. That the USSR obtains a negotiated peace shortly after the occupation of these areas.

---

* This paper was prepared by a joint ad hoc committee representing CIA and the intelligence organizations of the Departments of State, the Army, the Navy, and the Air Force. It has been concurred in by the Directors of the intelligence organizations of the Departments of State, Army, and Navy. The dissent of the Director of Intelligence, Department of the Air Force, is appended as Enclosure B.

2

CONFIDENTIAL SECRET

TOP SECRET

b. That, after the occupation of Western Europe and the Near East as far as Cairo, the USSR is faced with a continuing global war with the US and its allies, involving ultimate US invasion of Soviet controlled territory.

(The first assumption is necessary because Soviet leaders might elect to exercise their current military capabilities in the belief that, after Soviet occupation of these areas, the US public would not support the continuation of a war to liberate the European continent, and because, under the assumption of a quick negotiated peace, the Soviet position would differ greatly from what it would be if the USSR were forced to sustain the weight of a continuing global war.)

8. The position of the UK following Soviet occupation of the European continent would obviously have an important bearing upon the basic problem, particularly under the assumption in 7 *b* above. If the UK were either occupied by the USSR or completely neutralized, US capabilities for counteraction, particularly through naval and air operations, would be reduced. If, on the other hand, bases for US Naval and air operations from the UK remain tenable, substantial continuing damage could be inflicted upon the Soviet war potential, and shipping along the European coast would be largely interdicted.

9. An effort has been made in this paper to develop the maximum number of factual data with reference to the basic problem. This has been possible to a considerable degree with respect to the economic, scientific, and military factors. In the final analysis, however, we are still to a large extent dependent upon "the logic of the situation" and upon deductions from the pattern of Soviet behavior for our conclusions as to the possibility of direct Soviet military action.

DISCUSSION

(See Enclosure A)

CONCLUSIONS

10. If the USSR could obtain a negotiated peace shortly after the occupation of Western Europe and the Middle East to Cairo, the potential economic, scientific, and military advantages to the USSR would appear to be very substantial, but the USSR would not begin to reap significant advantages for a period of from two to three years after the completion of the occupation.

11. The occupation of Western Europe and the Middle East, however, would involve the Soviet leaders in grave political risks.

12. We believe that, in spite of the prospect of substantial tangible economic, scientific, and military gains, the Soviet leaders would consider these political risks so serious a threat to their own positions of power and to their ultimate objective of a Communist world that they would be unlikely to undertake this operation—even under the assumption of a negotiated peace—unless they anticipated an attack or became involved in military action through accident or miscalculation.

3

13. An analysis of the economic and military position of the USSR under conditions of continuing global war against the US and its Allies prior to 1950, indicates clearly that the total realizable resources under Soviet control would be inadequate for the defense of the conquered areas.

14. We conclude, therefore, that neither the recognized military capability of over-running Western Europe and the Near East to Cairo, nor any strategic advantages to be gained thereby are of themselves likely to induce Soviet leaders to undertake this course of action prior to 1950.

15. It is emphasized that the foregoing conclusions are based on an effort to weigh objectively the various considerations with respect to the stated problem and do not reflect an over-all estimate of Soviet military intentions prior to 1950.

4

3.

ORE 22-48 (Addendum) ~~TOP SECRET~~

POSSIBILITY OF DIRECT SOVIET MILITARY ACTION DURING 1948-49

Report of Ad Hoc Committee[1] Reviewing the Conclusions on ORE 22-48

THE PROBLEM

1. We have been directed to estimate if the events of the past six months have increased or decreased the likelihood of a Soviet resort to military action during 1948-49.

BASIS FOR ESTIMATE[2]

2. Available intelligence bearing on the stated problem is too meager to support a conclusion that the USSR either will or will not resort to deliberate military action during 1948-49.

DISCUSSION

3. Our conclusions are based on considerations discussed in the Enclosure.

CONCLUSIONS

4. We do not believe that the events of the past six months have made deliberate Soviet military action a probability during 1948-49. They have, however, added some weight to the factors that might induce the USSR to resort to such action. It is considered, therefore, that the possibility of a resort to deliberate military action has been slightly increased.

5. However, the developments of the past six months which constitute setbacks to the Soviet international position have had the effect of adding to the pressure on the USSR. This pressure increases the possibility of the USSR resorting to diplomatic ventures which, while not constituting acts of war or even envisaging the likelihood of war, will involve an increased risk of miscalculations that could lead to war.

---

[1] This estimate was prepared by a joint ad hoc committee representing CIA and the intelligence agencies of the Departments of State, the Army, the Navy, and the Air Force. The date of the estimate is 27 August 1948.

[2] The Office of Naval Intelligence concurs generally in the discussion, as contained in the Enclosure.

However, ONI feels that the "Basis for Estimate" as stated is not valid. Evidence of Soviet intentions is meager, but such intelligence as is available does not indicate a resort to deliberate military action. If the position is taken that the intelligence available cannot support conclusions one way or the other, any conclusions drawn from such a basis of estimate are of doubtful value for U. S. planning.

Therefore, ONI feels that the conclusions stated in ORE 22-48, as modified by ONI comment, are still valid. ONI concurs, however, that the events of the past six months have increased slightly the possibility of military action through miscalculation as stated in paragraph 5 of subject report, and would include under miscalculation the possibility that minor military incidents might expand into uncontrolled conflict.

ENCLOSURE

DISCUSSION

1. Reference is made to ORE 22-48. In general, and except for such modifications as follow, it is considered that the discussion and conclusions thereof are still valid and are, particularly in respect to the economic and political factors involved, still generally applicable to the immediate future.

EVENTS WITHIN THE SOVIET ORBIT WHICH MIGHT INDUCE A USSR RESORT TO EARLY MILITARY ACTION

2. In the USSR itself, we find no reliable evidence of military, economic, or political developments of sufficient importance to warrant any revision of our previous conclusions.

3. In the Eastern European Satellites, signs of nationalist sentiment, of mass peasant antagonism to Communist agrarian policies, and of dissension in Communist ranks, have suggested the growth of wavering loyalties and resistance to central direction from USSR. The defection of Tito and the Yugoslav Communist Party is our most striking evidence for the existence of an unstable situation. There is no doubt that this situation has caused concern in the Kremlin. While the USSR might consider the use of force to correct this situation, and general war might result, we think such a decision unlikely unless the Soviet leaders believe that the issue has reached a point where it seriously threatens their control of the Soviet orbit. At such a time the risk of war might seem preferable to the risk of losing control. There is no reliable evidence, however, that this point has been reached.

EVENTS IN WESTERN EUROPE WHICH MIGHT INDUCE A USSR RESORT TO EARLY MILITARY ACTION

4. The following events in Western Europe may have brought about some change in Soviet strategic thinking:

a. The positive effort of the US to recreate economic and political stability through the European Recovery Program (ERP).

b. The increasing firmness of the Western Powers toward Soviet-Communist expansion, with the growth of military solidarity among Western European nations.

c. The initial steps to establish a Western German Government.

d. The failure of Communist tactics in Western Europe.

5. In ORE 22-48, we stated that "the opportunities for further Soviet gains through the exploitation of economic, political and social instability, while recently diminished, are by no means exhausted." These opportunities probably appear to Soviet analysts to be still further limited in Western Europe. While it can be argued that an increasing reduction of opportunity may be an inducement to early Soviet military action, it is

possible that the events noted above have added to the strain on the Communist political control of Eastern Europe and therefore contributed to the weaknesses discussed in paras. 2-3 above. It is considered that the USSR, although confronted with resistance to Communist expansion in Europe, is still capable of exploiting existing political and economic instability, and is therefore more likely to continue to employ these means than to accept the risk of direct military action in the immediate future. Although Europe will remain the major objective, strategic areas elsewhere are also available for profitable exploitation.

EVENTS IN THE UNITED STATES WHICH MIGHT INDUCE A USSR RESORT TO EARLY MILITARY ACTION

6. Since Soviet leaders view, and Communist Parties are indoctrinated to regard the US as the chief bulwark of capitalism, and hence the major antagonist of the USSR, the strategy and tactics of the Kremlin are probably strongly influenced by an analysis of US capabilities and intentions.

7. Until recently, it has been supposed that Soviet planners were assuming a severe economic crisis in the US by the end of 1948, and that from this would follow a progressive weakening of US power potential. In turn, the political and economic recovery of Western Europe would be inhibited. It now appears possible that this assumption is being revised, and that Soviet planners now assume that US economy will continue productive and prosperous so long as it enjoys the export markets provided by the European Recovery Program.

8. It appears probable that Soviet leaders will be forced to admit a miscalculation of factors in US domestic politics which they earlier considered favorable. Neither the isolationists, the pacifists, nor the Wallace "Progressives" have seriously undermined popular support of a firm US diplomatic line or of adequate US defense proposals. Opinion with respect to US foreign policy has not been fundamentally split along partisan lines. Never before, in peacetime, has US opinion been so uniform on a question of foreign policy.

9. In ORE 22-48, we stated that "Soviet leaders may have become convinced that the US actually has intentions of military aggression in the near future." Recent events may have somewhat strengthened Soviet conviction in this respect. The passage of a peacetime Draft Act, the continued development of atomic weapons, the general acceptance of increased military appropriations, the establishment of US bases within range of targets in the USSR, the activities of US naval forces in the Mediterranean, and the movement to Europe of US strategic airforce units are instances in point. We think it unlikely, however, that these events have actually led Soviet leaders to the conclusion that positive US aggression must be soon expected. It is considered that they are more probably taken to mean that the ultimate conflict with the capitalist system will be resolved by force rather than by the methods of "cold war." While the danger of an early Soviet military move, made in calculated anticipation of this ultimate conflict may be slightly increased by these circumstances, we do not estimate that such a move has become a probability.

10. Soviet analysts, examining these evidences of US intentions, might conclude that they can no longer assume the early disintegration of the capitalist world, and that US military potential, now low, will steadily improve and will ultimately be accompanied by an improvement in the military potential of Western Europe. This might, in turn, suggest looking to military action for the achievement of their aims. However, since the usefulness of non-military methods has not yet been exhausted in Europe, and since there are other regions open to significant exploitation, we do not estimate that a USSR resort to deliberate military action has become a probability.

11. Several recent events—especially the Soviet blockade of Berlin—have served to increase the tension between the USSR and the US. With this heightened tension has come a corresponding increase in the possibility of a miscalculation which might result in general conflict.

ORE 46-49 ~~TOP SECRET~~

THE POSSIBILITY OF DIRECT SOVIET MILITARY ACTION DURING 1949

Report of a Joint Ad Hoc Committee *

THE PROBLEM

1. We have been directed to estimate the likelihood of a Soviet resort to direct military action during 1949.

DISCUSSION

2. Our conclusions are based on considerations discussed in the Enclosure.

CONCLUSIONS

3. The USSR has an overwhelming preponderance of immediately available military power on the Eurasian continent and a consequent capability of resorting to direct military action at any time. The principal deterrent to such action is the superior war-making potential of the United States.

4. There is no conclusive factual evidence of Soviet preparation for direct military aggression during 1949.

5. A deliberate Soviet resort to direct military action against the West during 1949 is improbable. Moreover, the USSR is likely to exercise some care to avoid an unintended outbreak of hostilities with the United States.

6. As part of its efforts to counteract the Atlantic Pact and US military aid program, however, the USSR will seek to intensify and exploit the universal fear of a new war. In this it will pay special attention to Scandinavia, Yugoslavia, and Iran. It is unlikely, however, to resort to even localized direct military action.

7. The fact remains that international tension has increased during 1948. It will probably increase further during 1949. In these circumstances, the danger of an unintended outbreak of hostilities through miscalculation on either side must be considered to have increased.**

* This estimate was prepared by a Joint Ad Hoc Committee composed of designated representatives of the CIA and of the intelligence organizations of the Departments of State, the Army, the Navy, and the Air Force. It has been concurred in by the Directors of those agencies, except as indicated in the footnote below. The date of the estimate is 21 April 1949.

** The Director of Intelligence, Department of the Army, believes that the last sentence of paragraph 7 implies a greater possibility of war in 1949 than, in fact, exists; and that it should read "In these circumstances, the small but continuing danger of an unintended outbreak of hostilities through miscalculation on either side must be considered."

ENCLOSURE

1. As of 30 March 1948, we estimated that the preponderance of available evidence and of considerations derived from the "logic of the situation" supported the conclusion that the USSR would not resort to direct military action during 1948. Our present task is to prepare a corresponding estimate with respect to the possibility of Soviet military action during 1949.

2. The USSR continues to enjoy an overwhelming preponderance of immediately available military power on the Eurasian continent. During the past year it has maintained, and possibly accelerated, its efforts to enhance its military capabilities through both the intensive development of basic war industries and the qualitative improvement of its military forces. There has recently been a significant increase in Soviet troop strength in Germany through the arrival of recruits from the 1928 class. It is not yet apparent whether this increase is temporary or permanent. In general, however, Soviet military preparations appear to be precautionary or long-term. There is no factual evidence of Soviet preparation for aggressive military action during 1949.

3. In the absence of conclusive factual evidence, our estimate must depend on our appreciation of the fundamental objectives and strategy of the USSR. This appreciation, set forth in ORE 60-48, ORE 41-49, and elsewhere, need not be repeated here at length. The pertinent conclusion is that the USSR would be unlikely to resort to direct military action unless convinced that a military attack by the West on the USSR was in active preparation and impossible to forestall by non-military means.

4. Our estimate of 30 March 1948 (ORE 22-48) has been borne out by the event. We may be permitted, then, to assume that the situation as it existed a year ago was not such as would cause the USSR to resort to direct military action. Consequently we limit our present consideration to developments since that date which might cause the USSR to resort to such action. These developments are:

a. An increasingly evident US determination to resist further Soviet encroachment in Europe, the Mediterranean, and the Near East, and to encourage, organize, and support local resistance in those areas. In the context of Soviet thought, this development must appear to be essentially hostile and preparatory to eventual US aggression, though not indicative of immediate attack. The USSR is particularly sensitive to the extension of US influence from Western Europe and the Mediterranean into Scandinavia on the one hand, the Balkans and Iran on the other.

b. A gradual increase in the will and ability of Western Europe to resist Soviet political aggression, and a corresponding decline in Communist political and revolutionary capabilities in that area.

c. Increasing rigidity in the partition of Germany and the development of an extremely taut situation at Berlin; in particular, the success of the airlift in defeating the blockade as a means of coercion with respect to Berlin, progress toward the establishment of Western Germany as a political and economic entity within the Western European community, and deterioration of the Soviet position in Eastern Germany and in Germany as a whole.

d. The persistence of individualism and nationalism in Eastern Europe, despit further forcible consolidation of the Soviet position in that area (excepting Yugoslavia)

e. Tito's successful defiance of the Kremlin, a matter of greatest significance in the development of international Communism and Soviet hegemony.

f. Failure of the situation in the Near and Middle East to develop as advantageously, from the Soviet point of view, as might have been expected, and the current trend toward adjustment and stabilization in the internal conflicts within that region

Communist successes in China and prospects in Southeast Asia are matters manifestly unlikely to cause the USSR to resort to direct military action.

5. The rulers of the USSR are presumably realistic enough to perceive that these developments do not constitute a danger of immediate attack. They will appreciate, however, that the opportunity for Soviet expansion westward by non-military means has ended for the time being, and they will be apprehensive lest a continuation of the present trend result eventually in a corresponding stabilization of the situation in the Near East, a further deterioration of the Soviet position in Eastern Europe, and an ultimate danger of US attack upon the USSR. In these circumstances the USSR must give serious consideration to the advisability of resort to preventive war while it still enjoys a preponderance of immediately available military power on the Eurasian continent.

6. The deterrents to such a decision are the realization that it would precipitate an immediate decisive conflict with the United States, a present lack of adequate defense against atomic attack and of means for a decisive military attack on the United States, respect for the present general superiority of US war industrial potential in terms of a long struggle, and reasonable hope of improving the position of the USSR in these respects with the passage of time. Philosophically prepared to take the long view in the absence of an immediate threat and confident that future crises of capitalism will produce new opportunities for Soviet aggrandizement by non-military means, the Kremlin would have reason to avoid a premature showdown while assiduously developing its capabilities for eventual defense or aggression.

7. On balance we conclude that the USSR is unlikely to resort to preventive war during 1949 at least. Its most probable course of action will be to continue its preparations for eventual war while seeking to arrest or retard the indicated adverse trend of developments (para. 4) by political and psychological counterefforts in forms currently familiar. In following this course the USSR will seek to intensify and exploit the universal fear of a new war. It will pay special attention to Scandinavia, Yugoslavia, and Iran. It is unlikely, however, to resort to even localized direct military action, except possibly with respect to Finland and Yugoslavia. In any such action taken, it will probably exercise care to avoid direct collision with the United States.

8. US and Soviet forces are in actual contact only in Germany and Austria. The fact that in the course of a year of acute tension the USSR has carefully avoided any action there calculated to precipitate armed hostilities establishes a presumption that the USSR would not resort to direct military action merely to break the deadlock at Berlin or to secure a satisfactory solution of the German problem. On the contrary, present indications are that the USSR may soon discard coercion, as repre-

sented by the blockade of Berlin, for the time being, in order to seek a more satisfactory situation through political negotiation.

9. The vulnerability of Finland to Soviet pressure and the gravity with which the USSR views Norwegian adherence to the Atlantic Pact requires specific consideration of that case. Threatening gestures toward Finland and Scandinavia might be expected to discourage any possible Finnish hope of rescue from the West, to confirm Swedish adherence to neutrality, and to inhibit Norwegian implementation of the Pact. A Soviet military occupation of Finland, however, might have exactly the opposite effect, driving Sweden into the arms of the West and stimulating Norwegian demands for direct military support. For these reasons, increasing intimidation is to be expected, but direct military action is unlikely.

10. Similarly, threatening Soviet gestures might be more effective ~~that~~ than direct action in inhibiting Yugoslav rapprochement with the West. Basically, however, the continuing existence of the Tito regime is intolerable from the Soviet point of view and real efforts to liquidate it must be expected. Any attempt to do so by force of arms would probably take the form of insurrection within Yugoslavia with covert Satellite support, as in the case of Greece. Direct Soviet military intervention would be unlikely unless it became the only means of preventing the military alignment of Yugoslavia with the West. Even in that case, Soviet intervention would not be intended to precipitate a general war and could do so only if the West chose to take armed counteraction.

11. Soviet sensitivity with respect to Iran requires specific consideration of that situation also. In terms of the internal factors involved, the situation in Iran is more stable than it was a year ago. There has been, however, an intensification of Soviet pressure upon Iran and there remain opportunities for indirect Soviet intervention through indigenous "liberation" movements, as with respect to Azerbaijan and the Kurdish tribes. The immediate Soviet purpose appears to be to prevent Iranian adherence to a Near Eastern pact analogous to the Atlantic Pact and acceptance of substantial US military aid. Although the USSR has been at some pains to build up a legalistic basis for direct intervention with reference to the Treaty of 1921, this appears to be part of the war of nerves. Direct Soviet military action in Iran during 1949 is considered unlikely.

12. Accepting our estimate of Soviet intentions, the fact remains that international tension has increased during 1948 and will probably increase further during 1949. Both sides are actively preparing for eventual war. In these circumstances there is increasing danger of an undesired outbreak of hostilities through miscalculation by either side. Such miscalculation could occur in underestimating the determination of the opposing side or in exaggerating its aggressive intentions. Both miscalculations would be present in a situation in which one side took a position from which it could not withdraw in the face of an unexpectedly alarmed and forceful reaction on the part of the other.

5.

~~TOP SECRET~~

THE STRENGTH AND CAPABILITIES OF SOVIET BLOC FORCES TO CONDUCT MILITARY OPERATIONS AGAINST NATO

THE PROBLEM

To analyze the strength and capabilities of Soviet Bloc forces to conduct military operations against NATO during the period 1951-1954, including the capacity of the Soviet Bloc to maintain and increase these forces after the outbreak of war.

ANALYSIS

See the Enclosure.

CONCLUSIONS

1. The USSR has at present and will probably have through mid-1954 military strength of such magnitude as to pose a constant and serious threat to the security of the NATO powers, especially in view of the aggressive nature of Soviet objectives and policies.

2. Politically, economically, and militarily the Soviet Bloc is capable of undertaking a major war. Its over-all strength and war potential should increase considerably by mid-1954.

a. Despite continued political tensions within the Soviet Bloc, both the Soviet population and the European Satellites are under firm Kremlin control. In the event of war various internal tensions will tend to become more acute, but they probably will not become serious enough to pose a major obstacle to Soviet ability to sustain a major war effort until

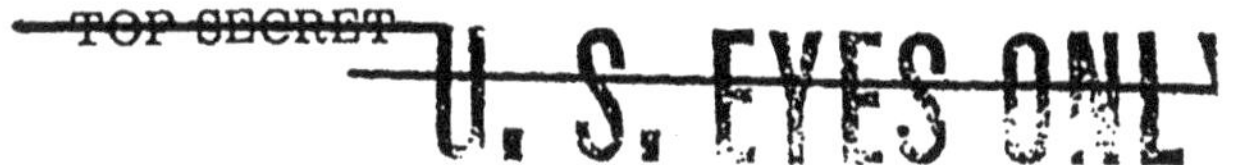

~~TOP SECRET~~

the latent disruptive elements within the Soviet Bloc acquire a reasonable expectation and hope of the ultimate victory of the anti-Soviet forces. The potential of such disruptive elements will probably increase substantially and at an accelerated pace if and as the Soviet Bloc suffers damaging internal reverses.

b. The Soviet economy is already at a high state of war-readiness and its productive capacity is such as to enable the USSR to undertake a major war effort. In the event of war, the Soviet economy, unless crippled by a strategic air offensive, could support a substantial increase in war production.

c. The over-all conventional military strength in being of the Soviet orbit is the greatest in the world today. While the personnel strength of the Soviet Bloc forces should increase only moderately through mid-1954, the completion of current programs should materially improve their mobilization potential and combat effectiveness. Soviet atomic capabilities, already substantial, should also materially increase.

3. In view of the high state of war-readiness of the Soviet economy and armed forces, the USSR is at present capable of initiating hostilities against the NATO powers with little or no warning. It now has the capability of simultaneously conducting a series of land campaigns against Western Europe and the Middle East, as well as air and submarine attacks against the UK, the US and Canada, and NATO sea communications. By mid-1954, growing Soviet military and economic strength, particularly in atomic weapons, should materially enhance Soviet ability to conduct these operations.

- 2 -

~~TOP SECRET~~

6.

~~TOP SECRET~~

NSC
7 Wiseman
3/31/53

INTELLIGENCE ON THE SOVIET BLOC

The adequacy of intelligence on the Soviet bloc varies from firm and accurate in some categories to inadequate and practically nonexistent in others. We have no reliable inside intelligence on thinking in the Kremlin. Our estimates of Soviet long range plans and intentions are speculations drawn from inadequate evidence. At the other extreme, evidence confirming the existence of major surface vessels in the bloc naval forces is firm and accurate. Operational intelligence in support of current military operations in Korea is generally excellent. Other phases of Soviet bloc activities fall into intervening degrees of intelligence coverage.

~~TOP SECRET~~

Approved For Release 1999/09/08 : CIA-RDP80R01443R000100120001-8

SCIENTIFIC AND TECHNICAL INTELLIGENCE

In the field of atomic energy, our estimates of future Soviet stockpiles of fission weapons are reasonably adequate. The margin of error is such that the actual stockpile may be from 1/3 less to twice the estimate. However, gaps exist regarding production of U-235, and more important, their thermonuclear program.

Intelligence on Soviet biological and chemical warfare programs is extremely limited. On the other hand, we have a fairly good picture of Soviet capabilities in contributing scientific fields.

Knowledge of Soviet electronics has improved significantly in the last eighteen months. Intelligence on Soviet electromagnetic warfare capabilities is now very good. While our knowledge of the electronics aspects of Soviet air defense has improved, there are still serious gaps.

Knowledge of current Soviet guided missiles programs is poor, although certain projects based on German developments are fairly well known.

Technical intelligence on conventional military weapons and equipment is reasonably good as far as standardized items are concerned. However, there is little knowledge of important improvements in such fields as underwater and aerial ^[tank – T/54] warfare.

With respect to basic scientific research, present estimates of long-range developments are very weak, but our estimates of the current status are believed to be more nearly adequate.

Sci manpower ± 10% –

6. (continued)

ECONOMIC INTELLIGENCE

The adequacy of economic intelligence on the Soviet Bloc varies widely from one industry to another and from one country to another. The best intelligence is on the USSR.

Our intelligence is believed best on output of basic industries in the USSR -- the primary metals, fuels and power, transportation, and some machinery and chemical industries. This intelligence is based in part on official Soviet announcements. Although contrary to what is usually regarded as Kremlin practice and not in keeping with Soviet character, such announcements have been shown to be reliable. The validity of official Soviet statistics has been confirmed by several independent studies based on intelligence materials. We believe, therefore, that official releases are not distributed for propaganda purposes. Nevertheless, there may be a margin of error due to faulty statistical practices and to falsification by the lower echelon. Thus our evidence on most major industries is probably within ten per cent of accuracy and, in the case of critical items such as steel, oil and electric power, within five per cent.

For other industries and for agriculture output estimates are built up from fragmentary intelligence. The techniques used include

25X1B4d [redacted] plant studies based on reports of prisoners of war, defectors, and returned scientists and technicians who were employed in the bloc in the post-war period; and crop-weather correlation analyses to estimate biological yields. Improvement in such estimates will depend in the future

6. (continued)

upon refinement of research techniques and upon improved collection of raw intelligence materials. To date, these techniques have given output estimates for all major agricultural commodities, and for several branches of industry which range from within ten per cent to within twenty-five per cent of accuracy.

There are still a large number of industries about which little is known. These include producers of certain machinery and equipment items and a few of the rare minerals.

By combining all available output statistics, annual growth rates for industry, agriculture, and gross national product are derived. We believe that they are probably within one percentage point of accuracy, that is, an estimated annual growth rate of six per cent for Soviet gross national product is probably no higher than seven per cent and no lower than five per cent.

Information for East Germany is the most complete, for Czechoslovakia and Poland it is fairly good, while that for China is the least adequate.

At present, intelligence is too fragmentary to permit estimates on strategic stockpiles and working inventories in all Bloc countries.

6. (continued)

ARMED FORCES INTELLIGENCE

Military intelligence concerning the Soviet Bloc is considered from two points of view, tactical and strategic.

Tactical

Intelligence on the activities of the Soviet Bloc armed forces varies with the geographical area under consideration. Intelligence needed in support of ground military operations in Korea is generally excellent. Intelligence on the installations and on developments in Manchuria, such as the movement and activities of the Chinese Communist forces and North Korean units, is inadequate.

Order of battle and equipment intelligence on the USSR, Communist China and - to a lesser degree - the European Satellites, is partial and inadequate. Intelligence on the Communist Bloc units and equipment in most areas with which the US or nations friendly to the US are in contact is more nearly complete and reliable.

Intelligence concerning the strength of the Soviet Bloc and Satellite ground forces is believed to be of a fairly high order of reliability. Intelligence on the navies of the Soviet Bloc is, ~~however~~ moreover, in general, satisfactory and adequate because of the greater accessibility of naval forces to observation.

Air

Estimates of Soviet air strength are derived from intelligence which is considered of acceptable reliability, but collection coverage is incomplete. Estimates of over-all size and composition of Soviet Air Forces are derived from identification of individual units and from estimated Table of Organization and Equipment strengths authorized for the various types of air regiments. Current estimates of jet fighter and medium bomber strength are considered reasonably valid.

Strategic

Reliable intelligence of the enemy's long-range plans and intentions is practically non-existent. Little improvement in these deficiencies can be expected in the near future despite our efforts.

Warning of Attack

The period of warning which the Western Powers might expect to receive if they were attacked by the Soviet Union vary according to the circumstances of the attack. There is no guarantee that intelligence will be able to give adequate warning of attack prior to actual detection of hostile formations. Opportunity for detection of indications of Soviet or Satellite attack varies from fair in the border areas of Germany and Korea to extremely poor in the Transcaucasus and Southeast Asia.

6. (continued)

~~TOP SECRET~~

In the event of a surprise attack we could not hope to obtain any detailed information of the Soviet military intentions. There would be no detectable redeployment of forces. We could therefore expect at most a few hours warning of air attack and hostile action might well take place in Germany or other territories bordering the Soviet Orbit before any warning at all had been received.

In the event of Soviet strength being fully mobilised for war, we could expect from overt sources at least a month's warning, with confirmation of Soviet hostile intentions building up continuously thereafter.

The period of warning in the event of partial Soviet mobilization for war would vary from the few hours of the surprise attack to something less than the warning to be expected when the attack was delayed until the full strength of the Soviet forces had been mobilized.

~~TOP SECRET~~

Analyzing Soviet Politics and Foreign Policy

TASS/SOVFOTO

Analyzing Soviet Politics and Foreign Policy
Author's Comments: Douglas Garthoff

The documents in this section were selected to reflect different kinds of products, including analytic memoranda as well as research studies, assessments, and estimates. Unfortunately absent is any product by analysts at the Foreign Broadcast Information Service, who produced some of the finest analysis on Soviet politics and policies.

In the wake of Stalin's death in 1953, CIA sought to understand Nikita Khrushchev's rise to power and the USSR's less rigid policies. NIE 11-4-54, the first of the comprehensive annual Soviet estimates supporting the regularized NSC policy process of the Eisenhower era, was safely wary: the USSR was being conciliatory "for the time being" but remained expansionist. In 1956, a Senior Research Staff on International Communism report found much to discuss regarding the startling 20th congress of the ruling Communist Party. In late 1961, Board of National Estimates chairman Sherman Kent covered the highlights of CIA's views on Soviet matters—including the critical issue of Sino-Soviet differences—in an analytic memorandum prepared for a new Director of Central Intelligence, John McCone.

The next two documents are broad estimates of Soviet policy that captured CIA's view of the period of Brezhnev's ascendancy as East-West "détente" began to flower. NIE 11-69 was done as President Richard Nixon was taking office, and NIE 11-72 as he was about to depart for his summit meeting in Moscow at which the initial SALT accords were signed.

As America began to view détente more skeptically by the mid-1970s, CIA expended much analytic effort trying to divine Soviet intentions. One CIA study of Soviet perceptions from this period depicted a more confident and powerful USSR conflicted between simultaneous desires for stability and for change. Another political analysis written in 1978 looked at the problems that the election of a Polish pope might cause for the USSR.

With new and disturbing Soviet actions in Afghanistan and elsewhere influencing American thinking, and with the advent of the Reagan administration, a different tone entered CIA's analysis of Soviet policy. One estimate selected from the early 1980s took up concerns about Soviet support for international terrorism (a particular concern of new Director of Central Intelligence William Casey). The last two documents of CIA political analyses in this volume were efforts to interpret what Mikhail Gorbachev and his policies meant for the United States. The first was an estimate done just before President Reagan's meeting in Reykjavik with the Soviet leader, and the other tried to foresee how Gorbachev's policy initiatives would affect the Soviet system and Soviet foreign policy. They demonstrate a timeless theme of CIA's analysis of the USSR: the struggle to understand and depict change in a country whose leaders could not themselves foresee the consequences of their decisions.

7.

Document ID:> 269322:269322

15 SEP 54 NIE 11-4-54

~~TOP SECRET~~

CONCLUSIONS

SOVIET CAPABILITIES AND PROBABLE COURSES OF ACTION THROUGH MID-1959

THE PROBLEM

To estimate Soviet capabilities and probable courses of action through mid-1959.

CONCLUSIONS

General

1. We believe that the stability and authority of the Soviet regime will not be significantly affected during the period of this estimate by conflicts for power or differences respecting policy within the ruling group. Any internal conflicts arising out of such developments would probably be resolved within the confines of the ruling group and the higher echelons of the Communist Party and would not lead to civil wars or disturbances of major proportions.

2. The appearance of new leadership in Moscow has had no apparent effect on the character of relations between the USSR and its Satellite states in Eastern Europe. We believe that Soviet authority over the Satellite regimes will remain intact during the period of this estimate.

3. Communist China is more an ally than a Satellite of the USSR. It possesses some capability for independent action, possibly even for action which the USSR might disapprove but which it would find difficult to repudiate. We believe that despite potential sources of friction between the two powers arising from occasional conflicts of national interests, the cohesive forces in the relationship will be far greater than the divisive forces throughout the period of this estimate.

Economic

4. The *rate* of growth of the Soviet economy has declined in the past five years from the very high rate of the immediate postwar period. We estimate that during the next two years Soviet gross national product (GNP) will increase by about 6 or 7 percent, and in 1956–1959 by about 5 or 6 percent, per year. If US GNP should increase during the period of this estimate at its long-range annual average of 3 percent, Soviet GNP would at the end of the period be about two-fifths of US, as compared with about one-third in 1953.

5. The pattern of resource allocation in the Soviet economy in 1953 showed about 14 percent devoted to defense, 28 percent to investment, and 56 percent to consumption. Current economic programs indicate that for at least the next two years the amount of expenditure on defense, instead of continuing the rapid increase that prevailed in 1950–1952, will

~~TOP SECRET~~

remain about the same, while expenditure on investment and consumption will increase. We believe the chances are better than even that the Kremlin will continue its policies along these lines throughout the period of this estimate. The chief emphasis will almost certainly continue to be on further development of heavy industry.

6. The chief weakness of the Soviet economy as a whole has been in agricultural production, which has remained since 1950 at approximately the prewar level, though the population is now about 10 percent greater than in 1940, Soviet leaders appear to have recognized that continuation of the serious lag in agriculture would ultimately make it difficult to meet the food requirements of the growing urban population, the raw material requirements of the expanding industrial economy, and the export requirements of Soviet foreign trade, in which agriculture plays a major role. To remedy the situation the regime has embarked on a vigorous program, with the aim of achieving by 1956 a 50 percent increase in agricultural production over 1950. We believe that this goal will not be met, and that even in 1959 agricultural production will be no more than 15 to 20 percent higher than in 1950. Even this increase, however, would be sufficient to achieve a moderate increase in the per capita availability of foodstuffs and textiles.

Military

7. We believe that, generally speaking, the size of Soviet armed forces-in-being will remain approximately constant during the period of this estimate. However, the over-all effectiveness of these forces will increase, mainly because of the following factors:

a. A great increase in numbers of nuclear weapons, and in the range of yields derived from these weapons;

b. An increase in the number of all-weather fighters and jet medium bombers, and the introduction of jet heavy bombers in 1957;

c. A great increase in the number of long-range submarines;

d. An increase in combat effectiveness of Soviet ground forces, primarily due to improved weapons, equipment and organization, and to changes in doctrine and tactics designed to increase their capabilities for nuclear warfare.

8. The principal limitations of Bloc armed forces during the period of this estimate will be: deficiencies in experience, training, and equipment for long-range air operations and air defense; lack of capability to conduct long-range amphibious and naval operations; and the logistic problems, especially for operations in the Far East, arising from the size of Bloc territory and the relatively inadequate road and rail network and merchant fleet. The questionable political reliability of the Satellite armies places a significant limitation upon their military usefulness.

Probable Courses of Action

9. We believe that during the period of this estimate the Kremlin will try to avoid courses of action, and to deter Communist China from courses of action, which in its judgment would clearly in-

volve substantial risk of general war.[1] However, the USSR or one of the Bloc countries might take action creating a situation in which the US or its allies, rather than yield an important position, would decide to take counteraction involving substantial risk of general war with the USSR. We believe, moreover, that the Kremlin would not be deterred by the risk of general war from taking counteraction against a Western action which it considered an imminent threat to Soviet security. Thus general war might occur during the period of this estimate as the climax of a series of actions and counteractions, initiated by either side, which neither side originally intended to lead to general war.

10. The progress being made by the USSR in the development of nuclear weapons, and the increasing Soviet capability to deliver these weapons, are changing the world power situation in important respects. Soviet leaders almost certainly believe that as Soviet nuclear capabilities increase, the unwillingness of the US, and particularly of its allies, to risk general war will correspondingly increase, and that the Kremlin will therefore have greater freedom of action to promote its objectives without running substantial risk of general war. In any case, the USSR will probably be increasingly ready to apply heavy pressure on the non-Communist world upon any signs of major dissension or weakness among the US and its allies. Nevertheless, we believe that the Kremlin will be extremely reluctant to precipitate a contest in which the USSR would expect to be subjected to nuclear attack. The extent to which the Kremlin uses its increasing freedom of action will depend primarily on the determination, strength, and cohesiveness of the non-Communist world.

11. We believe that the USSR will continue to pursue its expansionist objectives and to seek and exploit opportunities for enlarging the area of Communist control. It will be unswerving in its determination to retain the initiative in international affairs and to capitalize on successes in order to keep the Free World on the defensive. For the near term, however, the Kremlin will almost certainly continue to direct its external policies towards the immediate objectives of weakening and disrupting the mutual defense arrangements of non-Communist states, preventing or retarding the rearmament of Germany and Japan, undermining the economic and political stability of non-Communist states, and isolating the US from its allies and associates in Europe and Asia. At the same time it will continue to expand the industrial strength of the Bloc, and to maintain large modern

[1] The Assistant Chief of Staff, G-2, and the Director of Intelligence, USAF, believe that the following should be substituted for the first sentence of paragraph 9: "Although the Kremlin will probably try to avoid courses of action and to deter Communist China from courses of action that entail substantial risk of involving the USSR in general war, it may be more willing to support courses of action that would involve risk of a localized war between the US and Communist China. The support given such courses of action would depend largely on Soviet judgment as to the probable outcome of the war. If the Soviet leaders believed that it would result in a severe defeat to Communism, or the full-scale participation of the USSR in general war, they would probably exert pressure on the Chinese to avoid courses of action which would precipitate hostilities. On the other hand, if they estimated that the conflict could be limited to war localized in the Far East, and that it would result in greater relative damage to US strengths than to Communist strengths, they probably would support more adventurous courses of action on the part of the Chinese Communists."

forces-in-being as a guarantee of the integrity of the Bloc and as an instrument of intimidation in support of its policies abroad.

12. The Communists will vary the methods used to accomplish the foregoing aims and will time their actions so as to exploit situations that in their judgment offer the most favorable opportunities. For the time being, the Kremlin seems to feel that its foreign objectives will be best served by a generally conciliatory pose in foreign relations, by gestures of "peaceful co-existence" and proposals for mutual security pacts, by tempting proffers of trade, and by playing on the themes of peace and disarmament. The purpose of these tactics is to allay fear in some parts of the non-Communist world, to create the impression that there has been a basic change in Soviet policy, and thereby to destroy the incentive for Western defense and to undermine US polices. At the same time, however, the Communists continue to support and encourage nationalist and anticolonial movements, and to maintain their efforts to subvert governments outside the Bloc. We believe that the Kremlin will revert to more aggressive and threatening conduct whenever it feels that such conduct will bring increased returns. By such varieties and combinations of tactics the Soviet leaders almost certainly consider that they can improve the chances for further Communist strategic advances. We do not believe that such tactics indicate any change in basic Communist objectives, or that they will involve any substantial concessions on the part of the Kremlin.

13. We believe that Southeast Asia offers, in the Communist view, the most favorable opportunities for expansion in the near future. The Communists will attempt to extend their gains in Indochina, and will expand their efforts to intimidate and subvert neighboring countries by political infiltration and covert support of local insurrections. We do not believe that the Communists will attempt to secure their objectives in Southeast Asia by the commitment of identifiable combat units of Chinese Communist armed forces, at least during the early period of this estimate. However, we find the situation in this area so fluid that we are unable to estimate beyond this early period.

DISCUSSION

I. BASIC COMMUNIST OBJECTIVES AND BELIEFS

14. The Communist leaders now in power in the USSR, or any that are likely to succeed them, almost certainly will continue to consider their basic objective to be the consolidation and expansion of their own power, internally and externally. In pursuing this policy most Soviet leaders probably envisage ultimately: (a) the elimination of every world power center capable of competing with the USSR; (b) the spread of Communism to all parts of the world; and (c) Soviet domination over all other Communist regimes.

15. Soviet leaders probably are also committed to the following propositions concerning the expansion of the power of the USSR:

a. The struggle between the Communist and the non-Communist world is irreconcilable;

b. This struggle may go on for a long time, with periods of strategic retreat possibly intervening before the final Communist triumph;

8.

THE 20th CPSU CONGRESS IN RETROSPECT:
ITS PRINCIPAL ISSUES AND POSSIBLE EFFECTS
ON INTERNATIONAL COMMUNISM

Pertinent Background Factors

1. The CPSU is the leading Communist Party in the world. Its ideological leadership has been acknowledged even by the Chinese Communist Party. Being in control of the Soviet state, it controls the political, military and economic power of the USSR, the stronghold of World Communism. Thus its pronouncements on doctrine, strategy, and tactics are of decisive importance to International Communism. Communist courses of action are determined primarily in Moscow; the Chinese "People's Republic", for all its potential strength, is still dependent upon Soviet guidance and assistance. The USSR remains the base of world Communism, and there is no indication that this situation is about to change. If now, at the fountain of Communist wisdom, a new course is set which appears to deviate considerably from that of the Stalin era, repercussions are likely to occur which may be of great moment for both the Communist and the non-Communist world, if not immediately, at least in the foreseeable future.

2. The reasons for the announced changes must be sought far back in the Stalin regime. Long before his death, the men around Stalin must have recognized that he paid only lip service to the doctrine of flexibility. After World War II, when the USSR had become a great power, the rigidity

-1-

of Stalinist thought and action produced a stalemate in Europe, fear of Soviet interference in non-committed nations, and a widening gap between the Party and the Soviet people. It is probable that designs for altering the basis of the regime were pondered - and perhaps to some extent discussed - in the dictator's entourage. When it became obvious that Stalin's days were numbered, immediate plans for a reorganization of government and Party were made, and these were put into action upon his death. The successors to Stalin must have realized that the reorganization and economic incentives, initiated by Malenkov's "new course", could not, by themselves, create the desired political climate at home and abroad. Even the liquidation of Beriya and the sharp limitation of police power were not sufficient to demonstrate that Soviet Communism had embarked on a new, less violent, more gradualistic approach toward its objectives. Only an official break with the symbol of past policies, Stalin, could really impress the Soviet people and the world. The underlying purpose of the leadership was to promote political security and socio-economic incentives internally, to develop the concept of "competitive coexistence" externally, and to achieve global Communist "respectability". These objectives were defined during the three years following Stalin's death; they were confirmed and explained by the 20th CPSU Congress and made explicit through the denigration of Stalin. It is against this background that the 20th Congress must be understood.

The Main Issues of the Congress

3. The institution of Communist Party Congresses cannot be likened

to democratic conventions. Primarily, these Congresses are used as sounding boards for the justification of past policies and the outlining of new ones. The 20th Congress served these traditional purposes, even though it differed from previous Congresses in both tone and substance. The results did not indicate that Communist fundamentals are to be sacrificed. On the contrary, the Congress emphasized that Communism is, and remains the wave of the future. But it did point out that the successes of International Communism have given the "Socialist camp" a more solid status in world politics and have thereby rendered Stalinist tactics obsolete. The revolution has not been called off, the Congress admitted; revolutionary techniques, however, are being changed. Revolution can become more gradual and respectable. In other words, the policies set forth by the 20th Congress are designed to make the anticipated eventual victory of Communism more easily acceptable and to eliminate at least the more dangerous tensions which have troubled the world throughout the cold war. To put this new approach on a firm ideological basis, some doctrinal "modifications" were announced, primarily with a view to rationalizing the type of successor regime, discarding some of the more obnoxious Stalinist principles, and advertising the so-called "return to Leninism".

4. However, a change from violence to "diplomacy" and from tension to relaxation, no matter how well explained, cannot but have a deep psychological impact on the people inside the Communist orbit and on the Communist parties outside. Even if such "mellowing" process is only superficial, it may set in motion forces extending far beyond the contemplation of the present

8. (continued)

collective leaders of the CPSU. These leaders must be mindful that the Bolshevik regime is a unique historic phenomenon. It has been able to maintain itself in power for almost four decades after its original objective, the victory of the Bolshevik revolution, was achieved. It has achieved this extraordinary feat by what might be called "permanent revolution from above". Tensions had to be kept high in order to prevent a peaceful post-revolutionary development. Totalitarian dictatorship had to be justified by alleging the necessity for an unending struggle against the "class enemy" within and "capitalist imperialism" without, according to Lenin's concept of the "inevitable death struggle between the socialist and capitalist camps". Stalin merely extended and exacerbated this struggle, and, since the significance of nuclear weapons apparently escaped him, he continued it without letup after World War II. Since the new Soviet-Communist platform calls for a general relaxation of tensions, the question naturally arises whether the leaders of the CPSU and other parties can dispense with permanent tension without at the same time undermining their monolithic dictatorship. The 20th Congress refrained from exhorting the people to continue the "relentless struggle against the class enemy"; the bugaboo of internal danger was, for the time being, played down. However, it maintained the theory of hostile camps, albeit in a much milder form. The Party has modified its strategy against the capitalist camp enough to tone down the "struggle against foreign enemies of socialism", thereby weakening the argument that socialist vigilance requires the continuation of the dictatorship of the proletariat. It is unlikely that the shrewd managers

-4-

of the USSR have not recognized these problems. The fact that they nonetheless decided to launch their new approach, suggests that their reasons must have been weighty indeed, and their confidence great.

Internal Aspects

5. Stalin's successors, generally speaking, have heavily emphasized inducements rather than force. There is apparently less of arbitrary police cruelty; slave labor camps are allegedly being dismantled. Labor laws have been liberalized, and - with few exceptions - economic inducements, first introduced by Malenkov, have been continued by Khrushchev though with changed emphasis. But while Malenkov, still very much under Stalin's spell, counted on the support of the governmental bureaucracy against the Party whose influence had been waning, Party leader Khrushchev re-established Party predominance and turned dictatorial power back to it. At the same time, Khrushchev sought to improve relations between the Party and the people, which in the Stalin era had seriously deteriorated. This method is likely to strengthen Party dictatorship in a time of diminishing tensions. The Soviet leaders are as unwilling now as they have ever been - and will be in the foreseeable future - to democratize their system and to permit public discussion of political problems. This was demonstrated by the lack of discussion during the 20th Congress, as well as by PRAVDA's recent warning not to extend criticism to include the Party and the system.

6. It is clear, therefore, that the "return to Leninism" does not mean the return to "Party democracy". Nor is the substitution of Party dictatorship for one-man rule necessarily an improvement from the viewpoint of US security.

5

8. (continued)

There is no reason to assume that the modified "Neo"-Leninism, now so heavily propagandized, is more than formally different from the Soviet system as we have known it. It may be recalled that the practice of "Party democracy", or "democratic centralism", was severely limited by Lenin, who warned against "fractionalization" as early as 1921, after the Kronstadt revolt. At the 10th CPSU Congress in the same year, Lenin justified his position by referring to the danger of hostile class interests using the instrument of debate for their own counter-revolutionary purposes. Nevertheless, there still occurred occasional intra-Party discussions, cautiously airing opposing views. So strong was this habit that Stalin, having succeeded Lenin, could not completely eliminate its remnants until 1928 when his position was firmly consolidated. During the remainder of Stalin's regime "party democracy" disappeared under the secret police terror. The collective leaders of the USSR now claim that they are re-instating this principle. However, the mere fact that Khrushchev has called for more frequent plenary meetings of the Central Committee is no proof that genuine "democratic centralism" has been restored. He may permit perfunctory discussions so long as they do not show any deviationist tendency. Generally, however, such meetings probably can and will be used as a means of maintaining better control of this body and of coaxing - or pressuring - it into rubberstamping the edicts of the collective leaders without resort to the overt threat of police action. In truth, the heavily advertised "return to Leninism" consists primarily of a change in methods. The leaders of the CPSU have given up the Byzantine trimmings of the Stalin "cult of personality" without relinquishing any of their powers.

7. The return to Leninism, we are told, means the return to "collective leadership". There were, indeed, traces of this principle under Lenin, which Stalin managed to eliminate by 1928, prior to forced collectivization. Its highly vaunted renovation does not mean that power will now be distributed with checks and balances; it merely indicates a different method of using power. At best, "collective leadership" might develop into an oligarchy with quasi-"democratic" trappings. It might transform the present despotism into a form of "enlightened absolutism". Collective leadership at present is a euphemism for the Presidium of the Central Committee of the CPSU. Within this Presidium, predominant power is exercised by the half-dozen active "old Bolsheviks", of whom Khrushchev seems to be primus inter pares. In contrast to Stalin, Khrushchev and his colleagues appear to be willing to listen to arguments and consult with experts. They may be demanding and receiving more objective intelligence reports. As they develop a more realistic attitude toward the facts of international life, they may be able to look beyond the narrow confines of their ideology and formulate more realistic and subtle policies to achieve their goal peacefully. The result of this change can already be seen. The Soviet leaders have recognized both the destructive consequences of war and its futility in the nuclear age. They have therefore resorted to such peaceful methods as economic competition in lieu of military pressure. They are trying to stabilize their own economy by stimulating productivity; and they have introduced measures improving the lot of their own underdogs while at the same time whittling down the incomes of the nouveaux riches.

8. In order to carry out these policies, the break with Stalin had to be complete. The break itself was not a surprise. Surprising, only, was the violence of Khrushchev's attack against Stalin in his "secret" speech of 25 February. This action may have been designed to perform psychological surgery onthe Party. But it was also conceived as a warning to the Communists throughout the world that flexibility had been restored to Soviet policy, which could now employ tactics adequate to cope with the fact that the nature of revolution had changed. The reversal of more than 25 years of Stalinist indoctrination unquestionably will force many communists throughout the world to make difficult adjustments. But such adjustments have been made before and have not impaired the continuing vigor of the International Communist movement. The Soviet leaders must have known that the 20th Congress would produce a period of confusion, particularly among the parties outside the orbit. But they probably calculated that eventually adjustments could and would be made. In any case, the interests of the USSR both as a nation and as the base of world Communism had to take precedence. We suggest that the Soviet leaders earnestly pondered these problems for many months and, having come to their conclusion, felt no hesitation to consummate the break with Stalin. If this assumption is correct, it would appear that they had not been forced to make the violent attack against Stalin on 25 February because of internal or external pressures.

External Aspects

9. It was stated above that the CPSU leaders left the "class enemy"

within unmentioned. The same cannot be said of the "capitalist imperialists". even though the noise of sabre rattling sounded rather muffled. The Soviet leaders have continued to emphasize the differences between the socialist and imperialist camps; by implication they have retained the thesis of basic irreconcilability. Nevertheless, they did transform their once rude and vitriolic aggressiveness into a politer version of Communist verbiage, which was made more tolerable, if not actually conciliatory, by diplomatic flourishes and by some actual "concessions" such as the withdrawal from Austria. The development of nuclear weapons and jet propulsion, together with the growing belief, especially since the Summit Meeting, that the West does not now harbor aggressive designs, probably contributed decisively to Communist confidence in the future and led to the reinvigoration of what had long been known as "peaceful coexistence". Stalin had used this term in the Twenties but never gave it practical meaning. Malenkov reintroduced the concept, and Khrushchev, applying "creative interpretation", transformed it into "competitive coexistence". This new doctrine harmonizes admirably with the de-emphasis of armed power. At the same time the Soviet leaders may believe that it will stimulate the domestic Soviet economy while at the same time weakening the Western economic system. This, in turn, would stimulate the "contradictions among capitalist states fighting for world markets". Moreover, by inferring that the USSR is no longer isolated but has become the center of a world-wide system of socialist states, the Soviet and Communist leaders have admitted implicitly that at least some of the former "colonial and semi-colonial countries" have become politically independent. Their policy of creating a non-committed "peace bloc", of keeping it at least neutral, and perhaps winning it over to the socialist camp, may have led to revisions of their classic colonial doctrine.

10. The break with Stalin signifies that the leaders of the CPSU will no longer insist that they have a monopoly on the "correct" way to "socialism". During Stalin's lifetime the only ex-post-facto blessing of a deviation from this Soviet doctrine was that which he had reluctantly given to Mao. A Canossa trip to Belgrade would have been unthinkable. The Leninist formula that various ways can lead to Socialism - with the end of the road always the conquest by Communist revolution - was not used by Stalin. The reaffirmation of this formula by the 20th Congress has probably quelled some misgivings on the part of the less sophisticated neutrals. It is likely to create increasing demands from the satellites to follow their own path to "socialism". If Moscow denies them this right, it will have proved its insincerity before the world and may lose, thereby, much of the good will it now possesses in some non-committed countries. Nor will it, in the long run, be able to maintain the appearance of respectability, particularly vis-a-vis potential United Front partners. Much less will it be able to impress non-Communist democracies with its claim that it will attempt to gain power legally by parliamentary means, and not by violent overthrow of governments.

11. It should be restated here, and it cannot be emphasized too strongly that recognition by the Soviet leaders of the significance of nuclear weapons is the underlying cause for their policy shift. For the present, at least, atom and jet are the basic deterrents to general war, and probably also

to local wars. Despite repeated pronouncements that a nuclear war would destroy only Capitalism, the Communists have no real ideological "guide to action" in this field; they surely must realize that the atom knows no ideological preferences. Stalin probably tried hard but in vain to come to grips with this problem since the day of Hiroshima. His successors appear to have found a temporary solution by shifting from dangerous military pressures to less dangerous economic blandishments. Nevertheless, although their policies are designed to avoid war and to let capitalism die "peacefully", there is no prohibition for Communists to divide the capitalist camp and render it harmless. Meanwhile, the "socialist" camp will continue to solicit allies among the imperialists, be they states, groups, or individuals. 20th century changes in capitalist economy are minimized or ridiculed. The Leninist view of the inevitable downfall of capitalism at its highest stage, imperialism, has remained intact. Evolutionary tendencies, which goaded Lenin into writing vitriolic pamphlets, are still outlawed in spite of United Front overtures to socialist "opportunists".

The Meaning of the Congress for International Communism

12. The basic structure of Marxist-Leninist Communism has remained untouched. There is no indication that the present Soviet leaders have renounced the goal of world domination. However, they no longer insist that this conquest can and must come to pass under exclusive Soviet leadership. Nor is there any hint that a Communist world would have to be dominated by the USSR. This means the acceptance of a gradualist approach

-11-

to Communist objectives which not only is considered feasible in view of the strength of the Sino-Soviet bloc and the growth of the uncommitted neutralist "peace camp", but also is made necessary by the destructiveness of nuclear weapons and by the great jeopardy to Communism's continued existence in the event of war. The post-Stalinist concept of Communist victory is the achievement of "socialism" in individual countries in a manner suited to national conditions, followed by the joining of such countries in a loose community of "socialist" states. At first, these states would retain their national identities but as time goes by they would gradually merge into a World-Communist community which would rule itself according to ideologically motivated universal laws, having discarded national governments as we know them today. Apparently the Soviet leaders anticipate the completion of the first step, the end of capitalism in individual nations, by the end of the century. It is conceivable that they think in terms of a classless society emerging only in the 21st century, inasmuch as the establishment of such a society is hardly possible so long as politically inimical camps continue to exist.

13. If this view of the Soviet leaders' estimate is correct, it would follow that they can give considerably more leeway to the satellite parties. From the Soviet point of view, the military and economic integration of these countries with the USSR is sufficiently strong to permit a modicum of what Stalinists used to call "nationalist deviation". Communism in the Far East has to be adapted to conditions prevailing in that area, as was already recognized in the Soviet acceptance of Maoism. While there is, and

probably will continue for some time to be, confusion among the Party rank and file, resulting from the break with the Stalin idol, this confusion is unlikely to provoke many defections. Outside the USSR, it will be easier to achieve socialism by the "national" road than under the Soviet yoke. Soviet control and influence will be maintained, but in a subtler manner. Resistance against Communism will thus be overcome by a process of attrition rather than revolution.

14. The confusion resulting from the break with Stalin will last longer and probably have deeper consequences in the parties outside the Communist orbit. Their doubts will be shared by leaders of international Front organizations. This period of efforts to adjust policies and methods to the new Soviet approach could be lengthened, and confusion could be widened if Western political warfare adequately exploits this unique opportunity. Nevertheless, the climate of political relaxation in non-Communist governments and the prospect of broader interpretation of the Communist objectives will enable the leaders of these parties and fronts to maneuver overtly with a minimum degree of obnoxiousness, while covertly strengthening their cadres for the tasks ahead.

15. It is suggested that the long-range result of the 20th CPSU Congress will turn out to be beneficial from the Communist point of view - provided the lack of tension does not soften the movement's hard core vanguard. The Soviet approach is realistic and ingenious. It takes into account military facts of life. It explores the increased stature of the Communist part of the world and the nationalistic sensitivities of the former "colonial

and semi-colonial" countries. It feels strong enough to engage the US in an economic popularity contest. It tries hard, and not altogether unsuccessfully, to raise the level of Communist respectability. On the other hand, it does not hesitate to stir up trouble in areas of political vacuum, such as the Middle East, if it can thereby advance its influence to hitherto closed parts of the world. Unless it is stopped, it will do the same in Latin America and Africa. Altogether, Moscow, under Stalin, has learned its lesson. It now uses psychology, taking initiatives designed to put the West on the defense. With this strategy, and appropriate tactics, it appears hopeful of a bloodless victory over a system which, in the Communist belief, is doomed to collapse sooner or later - probably sooner.

16. The question arises whether the new Soviet-Communist line will require more of an organization than is presently at its disposal. Not enough is known about the intricacies of Communist international communications to come to definite conclusions. Overtly at least, the Soviet missions abroad avoid contact with national Party and Front leaders. Covert connections exist to provide personnel guidance, policy directives, and financial assistance. This machinery, however, is expensive, cumbersome, haphazard, and dangerous. Thus the problem may arise how to give comprehensive guidance to the apparatus in different countries whose political, social and economic developments vary. Better means of overall coordination may have to be developed. It is therefore possible that sometime in the future a new device may be put into operation which would take care of

-14-

Communist communication in a more systematic way. This would probably not be an organization as such. Rather, it might be an international Party "conference", possibly under an "innocent" cover, and conceivably with participation of non-Communist Marxists, set up to transmit policy directives and solve operational problems. Such a "conference" would be particularly necessary if the Communist leaders came to the conclusion that the relaxation of tensions had produced a slackening of Party discipline and a deterioration of Communist resourcefulness. This possibility raises certain fundamental questions: Can Communism withstand the changes resulting from the 20th Party Congress without losing its revolutionary zeal? Is there in preparation a "mellowing process" which in time will bring about a metamorphosis of Communism? Or, is the present line merely a gigantic shift of tactics, imposed by the development of nuclear weapons and their jet-propelled delivery and made possible by both the greater strength of the Communist bloc and the emerging independence of former colonial nations?

17. We cannot but assume that the Communist leaders would reject a "mellowing" process. They will try to do all in their power to prevent it from developing. Their only concept of Communist metamorphosis is linked to the shift from socialism to Communism, i. e. from the dictatorship of the proletariat to a classless society. They are likely to seek a period of some years of relaxation during which they can extend their influence with the help of overt respectability while building up and toughening their covert organizations and, what is more important, strengthen-

15

8. (continued)

ing the overall potential of the USSR. At the same time, they might also consider the usefulness of permitting the Satellites a greater show of independence. As national states, remaining under veiled Soviet control, they would testify to Moscow's good faith. They might assist in the development of relations with Western Europe, possibly through their own liberated socialists who might be put in touch with Free World socialist parties. This would greatly advance the United Front tactic on an international scale. But all these measures would be designed only to further basic Communist objectives. Since violence has characterized Communist actions in the past, subtler methods could be mistaken, even by Party members, as an indication of "mellowing". Nothing would be farther from Soviet-Communist intentions.

18. There is, however, an outside chance that Khrushchev's newer course, deviating as it were from the irreconcilable, aggressive precepts of Lenin and Stalin, may carry the germs of revolutionary paralysis within itself. It is conceivable that a psychological transformation could vitiate the Marxist doctrine of historical materialism. Once freed from the confines of permanent tensions, mental attitudes may develop which could become stronger than Communist faith and discipline. Such a transformation would be slow, at first hardly noticeable, but it might work itself up persistently from the grass roots to the "leading circles". It is impossible to estimate how long such a process would need to become apparent, nor is it possible to foresee its ultimate outcome. Much would depend upon the character of future Soviet leadership.

19. The premise for a successful Communist holding operation is the continuation in power of the CPSU's Presidium as presently constituted. The shrewd "old Bolsheviks" will ruthlessly (and noiselessly) suppress any evidence of "mellowing". Nor can it be expected that the middle and higher ranks of functionaries and officers have any intention of jeopardizing their position by crowding the present leaders. It is futile to speculate on the character of the regime which will succeed today's collective leaders, but it is possible that the present constellation may last 5-10 years, provided "peaceful coexistence" continues. If antibiotics of transformation have penetrated the Communist body politic, their effect, if any, probably will not show during this period. If transformation is permitted to come to the surface later, it will do so very slowly, almost unnoticeably. It may be a generation or two before tangible changes become apparent. Moreover, any major disruptive event, such as internal upheavals or local wars, would be likely to interrupt the healing process. Thus it cannot be expected that a "mellowing process" could become effective during the next decade. Nor is it overly pessimistic to predict that a healthy transformation of Communism into a movement of constructive social endeavors cannot be expected in the foreseeable future. Meanwhile we shall be compelled to continue warding off a diabolically clever opponent whose ingenuity and resourcefulness, unfortunately, is growing.

* * *

9.

MORI DocID: 220326 UNCLASSIFIED

11

CENTRAL INTELLIGENCE AGENCY
OFFICE OF NATIONAL ESTIMATES

21 December 1961

MEMORANDUM FOR THE DIRECTOR

SUBJECT: An Appraisal of Soviet Intentions

1. In pursuing their struggle against the West, the Soviet leaders follow a strategy which they call "peaceful coexistence." By this they declare their intention to wage a persistent and aggressive campaign by a variety of means — propaganda and political pressure, military threat, economic and scientific competition, subversion and internal war — aimed at the victory of their cause on a world scale. The new aspect in Khrushchev's formulation of Soviet foreign policy is the explicit proposition that general war is an unacceptable means of prosecuting this struggle. Unlike Stalin, he has founded Soviet policy on the belief that the "imperialists" can be forced into final submission by a steady undermining of their world position and that, during this process, Soviet military power will deter them from a resort to arms.

SECRET

2. This is but one of a series of innovations which Khrushchev has sponsored in the total range of Communist internal and foreign policies. His revisions of doctrine and practice have frequently been radical in Communist terms, and they have not gone unopposed within the Soviet party and the international movement. The XXII Congress was the scene of a great effort by Khrushchev, using the most dramatic means available to him, to make these policies binding, both at home and abroad. This effort embraced domestic, Bloc, and foreign problems, and while the main lines of the peaceful coexistence strategy have been firmly reasserted, crucial questions have been raised concerning the Soviet Party's commanding role in world communism. The cource of political controversy within the Soviet Party, and more importantly, of the mounting tensions in Soviet relations with China will obviously have a significant bearing on the conduct of Soviet relations with the non-Communist world.

-2-

SECRET

Internal Problems

3. We believe that Khrushchev has not had to fear for his position since his victory over the so-called antiparty group in 1957. Despite this victory, however, and despite the cult which subsequently developed around his own personality, he has continually met with difficulties within the party, and on two counts. In the first place, in the past year or two other high level leaders appear to have succeeded in limiting the revisions which he wished to make in economic priorities (greater benefits for the consumer) and military policy (downgrading conventional forces and traditional doctrine). In the second place, Khrushchev has found the party apparatus which he inherited a far from satisfactory instrument for carrying out his numerous reforms. The great majority of party officials were trained in the Stalinist period to execute mechanically orders from above and to regard the population as recalcitrant and untrustworthy subjects. They have tended to become bewildered, resentful, and concerned for their careers as Khrushchev demands of them that they display initiative, elicit it from others, and draw the masses into a positive identification with the regime and active support of its policies.

-3-

6442382 #19

4. The savage attack upon Stalin was meant, in the domestic context, to break the emotional attachment to Stalin's person and methods which still exists in the Soviet Party. It was also meant to discredit certain Stalinist dogmas, such as the proposition that heavy industry must at all times grow faster than light industry, which had become imbedded in Soviet ideology and stood in the way of Khrushchev's reforms. The concurrent blackening of the antiparty group served to dramatize the penalties of resisting Khrushchev's demands for a new style of work and to destroy any luster which the unrepentant and still argumentative Molotov retains as a "conservative" spokesman among the middle and lower reaches of the apparatus.

5. The full internal consequences of the Congress will be a long time in working themselves out. Certainly Khrushchev has succeeded in putting his stamp upon the present era and establishing a direct succession to Lenin. The present compromise formulations of economic and defense policy, however, indicate that his programs remain subject to some sort of consensus among the top leaders, who share his general outlook but cannot be equated to the terrorized yesmen around Stalin. Remaking the entire party apparatus in Khrushchev's own image will, we believe,

-4-

continue to be a long and difficult process. And among critically-minded elements of Soviet society — the youth, the cultural intelligentsia, perhaps even younger party members — virtually the whole of Soviet history has been brought into question, and along with it the activities of present party leaders during that period. We doubt that the attack on Stalin and the cult of Khrushchev will strengthen belief in the party's claim to wisdom and the right of absolute leadership. These factors are more likely to work in the long run toward a weakening of the propositions on which party rule is based, and to complicate the problems which Khrushchev's successors must face.

Bloc Politics

6. The consequences of the Congress for Bloc relations are much more immediate and far-reaching. With his surprise attack upon the proxy target of Albania, Khrushchev made his third attempt (the Bucharest meeting in June 1960, the Moscow Conference later in the year) to repulse the Chinese Communist challenge to Soviet leadership. In doing so, he chose a time of great Chinese weakness. He also gave his attack the greatest possible force, short of an explicit challenge, by coupling it

-5-

9. (continued)

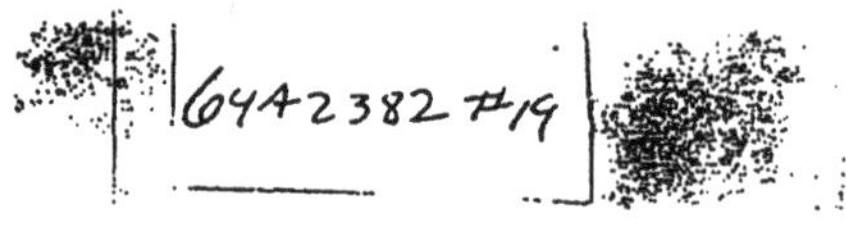

SECRET

with the condemnation of Stalinist principles and practices in the sharpest form. He intended by this to force the Chinese to choose between submitting and being openly condemned as deviationist. Yet in the ensuing two months Peiping, while withholding an equally dramatic response, has made clear its determination to hold to its positions. It appears that a showdown of historic proportions may be imminent.

7. For Soviet policy, this is but the latest in a long series of problems arising from the Soviet leaders' inability to reconcile the contradiction between the force of nationalism and their own insistence upon Soviet hegemony over world communism. For the Sino-Soviet conflict is at bottom a clash of national interests. While each professes devotion to Communist unity, each seeks to mobilize the entire world Communist movement in the service of its own aims. The ideological element, far from providing a basis for reconciliation, imparts a special bitterness and intensity to this rivalry.

8. As the lines are now drawn, it seems unlikely that the dispute can be papered over by a compromise along the lines of last December's 81-party conference. Economic relations have

-6-

SECRET

been substantially reduced, and military cooperation, never very high, is minimal. The entire Communist world has been made aware of the deep differences between the two, and each is vigorously using all the weapons of pressure and persuasion to hold and enlarge its retinue of supporters. At the least, it appears certain that full harmony cannot be restored. Yet the question of whether the two powers, poised now on the brink of an overt break in party relations, take this final step remains an important one. So long as they do not, the way remains open for a return to tolerable cooperation and a surface appearance of unity, and the strains on other parties can be kept within manageable proportions. If they do, the resulting hostility would be more profound and probably longer lasting than that which divided the Yugoslavs from the Communist camp after 1948, and few Communist regimes or parties would escape its effects.

9. From their present behavior, it appears that both parties are able to contemplate this possibility. Each still hopes that the other will in the last analysis make the concessions necessary to avoid a final split, but neither seems prepared to retreat on the fundamental issue of the locus of authority over world

-7-

communism. At this moment, a trial of strength is occurring in the Soviet campaign to bring down the Albanian leaders; success here would deal a major blow to Chinese pretensions and to any inclinations in other parties to escape Soviet domination. We believe that the odds are against Moscow in this campaign, but even if it succeeds, the present Chinese leadership would almost certainly return to the lists.

10. In appraising Sino-Soviet relations, we have regularly stressed the great benefits of a close alliance to the national interests of both partners and, conversely, the great losses which each would suffer from a true rupture. Yet the record of the past 18 months shows a consistent refusal, on the part of the Soviets, to limit their authority in matters of general Communist policy. Over the same period, the Chinese have persistently proven unwilling to remain content with the role which the Soviets would assign them in the movement. Barring a radical change in Chinese outlook or leadership, we now believe that the chances of a full break in party relations between the two during the next year or so have increased very substantially.

-8-

6442382 #19

SECRET

11. Should such a break occur, the logic of ideological conflict and the history of Communist parties everywhere make it likely that the result would be an acrimonious and protracted struggle. Each side would be impelled to proclaim itself the repository of doctrinal truth and to call for the overthrow of the competing leadership. Communists everywhere would be pressed to declare themselves; purges and splits would probably occur in many parties; some, especially those in Asia, might eventually align themselves with the Chinese.

12. In these circumstances, the military alliance between the USSR and Communist China would in effect become inoperative. The Chinese probably already consider it of dubious value; they probably do not feel able any longer to count on full Soviet support in the event that they become embroiled in military hostilities with the US.

13. The Soviet and Chinese leaders may still find some way to get past the current tensions. Even if they do, we believe that the result will be an uneasy and distrustful truce, marked by cooperation at various times and places and by competition at

-9-

SECRET

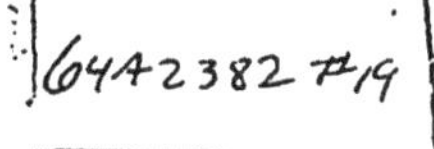

others. In short, we believe that the Sino-Soviet relationship rests upon an unstable foundation, and that a breach, if it is avoided for the present, will remain in the foreground as a continuing possibility.

Foreign Policy

14. A central problem in Sino-Soviet contention has been policy toward the non-Communist world. This has involved a great deal of misrepresentation on both sides. Thus Khrushchev's allegation that the Chinese regard general war as either inevitable or desirable, while a telling argument insofar as he can make it convincing, is not true. Similarly, Chinese charges that Khrushchev's strategy of peaceful coexistence is a denial of revolutionary aims are a gross exaggeration, although the zeal with which Molotov's parallel criticisms were attacked at the Congress suggests that this indictment finds considerable resonance in the Soviet and other parties.

15. The peaceful coexistence line, far from being an abandonment of Soviet expansionist goals, is a tactical prescription considerbly more effective than the compound of heavy-handedness and isolationism which was Stalin's foreign policy.

-10-

UNCLASSIFIED

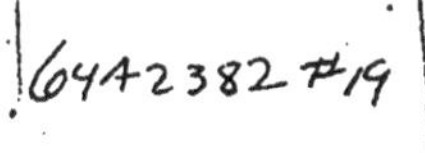

SECRET

It is informed by an appreciation of the manifold opportunities presented by all the great strains and disharmonies of the non-Communist world — national rivalry, colonialism, the desire for economic development, the yearning for peace and disarmament. Peaceful coexistence seeks to capture these sentiments and turn them against the "imperialist" states, using all the weapons of political struggle, economic assistance, and subversion, and underlining its points with demonstrations of Soviet military, scientific, and economic prowess.

16. At the same time, this policy also embraces the proposition that general nuclear war would bring intolerable damage upon the USSR itself and should therefore be avoided. The Soviets are continuing to develop their already formidable defense establishment. But the programs presently underway do not reflect a belief that it is possible to achieve a decisive advantage over the West, one which would permit them to launch general war with assurance of success at some acceptable cost. Rather, what we know of these programs, and of Soviet strategic thinking as well, suggests that the Soviet leaders are aiming in

-11-

SECRET

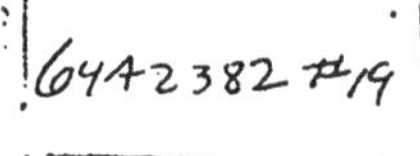

the first instance at a capability large enough to deter a Western resort to general war.

17. The Soviets apparently believe that they have already in large measure achieved this end. But they recognize that the forward policies which they wish to pursue involve some element of risk, and that they may not always be able to control these risks. In building their forces, they are probably seeking an offensive nuclear capability large enough, not only to deter their opponent, but also to bring under attack those elements of Western striking power and national strength which can be effectively attacked by ICBMs and other long-range delivery systems. On the defensive side, in addition to improving their defenses against manned bombers and cruise-type missiles, they are exerting major efforts to develop and deploy an effective anti-ballistic missile system. At the same time, they also intend to retain large and modernized ground and naval forces. In all these programs, the Soviets will be seeking a combination of forces which would permit them to undertake a pre-emptive attack on the US, should they conclude that a US attack was imminent, and to prosecute general war effectively if deterrence should fail.

-12-

18. The Soviet leaders are alert to search out areas where their military power can be brought into play to shield Communist efforts to advance by safer means, such as internal war in Southeast Asia or political blackmail in Berlin. We believe, however, that the USSR will wish to avoid involvement of its own forces in limited combat on the Bloc periphery and, if such conflict should occur, to minimize the chances of escalation to general war. Consequently, it would not in most circumstances take the initiative to expand the scope of such a conflict. The degree of Soviet commitment and the actual circumstances of the conflict would of course determine this decision. But we believe that, in general, the Soviet leaders would expand the scope of the conflict, even at greater risk of escalating to general war, only if a prospective defeat would, in their view, have grave political repercussions within the Bloc itself or constitute a major setback to the Soviet world position.

19. Within the limits set by these appraisals, the Soviet leaders have purposefully displayed both militancy and conciliation, at various times and in various proportions as seemed most profitable to them. Over the past year or so, however, the

-13-

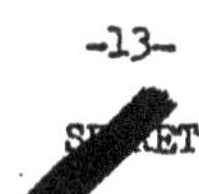

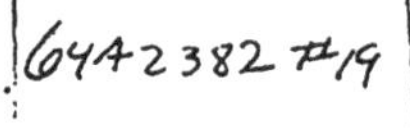

pressure of the Chinese challenge has been one factor helping to keep the "hard" line in the foreground. The thrust of the XXII Congress in this respect was to reassert the USSR's insistence upon full tactical flexibility. Thus the USSR has not only continued its attacks on Chinese positions but has made some conciliatory moves, such as removal of the Berlin deadline, agreement on a disarmament forum, and publication of Adzhubey's interview with the President.

20. These measures have accompanied, not replaced, the harsher tactics which comprise the militant side of peaceful coexistence. At the same time Finland has been bullied; atomic tests have been resumed; Soviet military strength has been stressed; the Soviet position on Berlin remains highly demanding. The Congress attacks on the opponents of peaceful coexistence were meant only to make room for a full range of maneuver, not to seek a genuine accommodation with the West.

21. Currently, however, Soviet foreign policy is by no means completely freed of the pressures for more militancy which stem from the Chinese challenge. Should an open break occur, Moscow's initial reaction would probably be to emphasize "hard"

-14-

tactics in order to justify tighter controls in Eastern Europe and to demonstrate that it was as vigorously anti-imperialist as its Chinese competitor. Over the long run, the consequences might be quite different; a protracted break might give important support to that tendency in Soviet foreign policy which seeks to put relations with the West on a more stable footing. It is conceivable that, faced with an actively hostile China whose strength was growing, the USSR might in time come to accept, at least tacitly, some mutual delimitation of aims with the West and thus some curb upon its expansionist impulse.

22. For the present, nevertheless, we conclude that the XXII Congress has initiated no marked departures in the foreign policies which have emerged under Khrushchev's leadership of the last five years. On Berlin, the USSR is presently in an interim phase, marking time in order to determine whether its earlier pressures will bring the West to the negotiating table with at least some concessions, or whether another round of threats, and perhaps even unilateral action, is required. Even a Sino-Soviet rupture would not be likely to alter the basic Soviet

-15-

position on Berlin and Germany, since a major element in that position is the desire to stabilize the Soviet-controlled regime in East Germany and, by extension, those of Eastern Europe.

23. In the disarmament field, we perceive in recent Soviet moves no appreciable desire for agreements on terms which the West could regard as acceptable. Instead, the USSR continues to regard this as an arena for political struggle and, via maneuverings over parity and the composition of a forum, for enhancing Soviet stature and cultivating neutralist opinion. In addition to the theme of general and complete disarmament, the Soviets will probably also agitate such limited measures as regional schemes, agreements to limit the spread of nuclear weapons, and other proposals which might inhibit Western defense programs.

24. Sino-Soviet strains raise considerable uncertainties regarding prospective Soviet tactics in Southeast Asia. The USSR will probably continue to press cautiously its advantages in Laos and South Vietnam, seeking simultaneously to advance Communist prospects there, to avoid a major US intervention, and

-16-

to keep Chinese influence from becoming predominant. A further radical worsening of relations between Moscow and Peiping, however, could lead to a breakdown of Bloc cooperation in these ventures. In this event, Moscow would probably try to retain as much control as possible through the North Vietnamese regime, which, at least initially, would seek to preserve the Soviet connection as a counterweight to China.

25. In recent years the USSR has consistently looked upon the underdeveloped countries of Asia, Africa, and Latin America as the prime targets for its tactics of peaceful coexistence. Beginning in about 1960, however, Soviet pronouncements have betrayed a sense of disappointment at the failure of some of the "older" neutrals, such as Nehru and Nasser, to move from the achievement of independence into a full association with Soviet policies and thence along the path toward Communist control. Nevertheless, the Soviet appraisal of its prospects in these areas remains highly optimistic. The USSR continues to believe that, by harnessing anti-Western and anticolonial sentiment, extending judicious offers of military and economic assistance, and sponsoring the political ambitions of new governments, it can make important gains in weakening Western positions and

-17-

preparing the ground for further advances. The Soviets will not abandon those states which they have unsuccessfully sought to draw into a client relationship. But they will probably increasingly focus their main energies upon Africa and Latin America and, within these continents, upon the radical nationalist leaders who are most easily set against Western ties. Soviet activity in these areas will continue to conflict with, and normally to take priority over, any desire to adopt a conciliatory line toward the major Western powers.

FOR THE BOARD OF NATIONAL ESTIMATES:

Sherman Kent

SHERMAN KENT
Chairman

-18-

10.

BASIC FACTORS AND MAIN TENDENCIES IN CURRENT SOVIET POLICY

NOTE

This paper considers in broad perspective the principal factors which underlie the USSR's external policies at present and its aims and intentions with respect to certain key areas and issues. As such, while it suggests the limits within which Soviet policies are likely to operate, it does not estimate likely Soviet conduct and positions in detail. In view of the intimate interaction between Soviet and American policies, this could not be done in any case without specific assumptions about American policy and actions.

PRINCIPAL OBSERVATIONS

A. Ideology in the Soviet Union is in a certain sense dead, yet it still plays a vital role. This paradox explains much about the nature of Soviet society and the USSR as a world power today. While the regime's doctrines now inhibit rather than promote needed change in the system, the leaders continue to guard them as an essential support to their rule. They also view developments at home and abroad mainly within the conceptual framework of the traditional ideology. This fact will continue to limit the possibilities of Soviet-American dialogue.

B. Changes in the system and the society have probably made collective leadership of the Party Politburo less vulnerable to new attempts to establish a personal dictatorship. This seems particularly true so long as the men who now comprise the leadership remain. Nevertheless, a crisis within the present leadership, accompanied by high domestic tensions and greater unpredictability of external policy, could occur at any time without warning. If stability of the leadership continues, a relatively deliberate, bureaucratically compromised manner of decisionmaking will also continue.

C. The Soviet leaders face severe problems at home. A decline in the rate of economic growth is tightening the perennial squeeze on resource allocation. Dissidence and alienation in the professional classes is of growing concern to the Soviet leaders. Generally speaking, however, they are not at this time constrained by domestic problems from continuing the general line of foreign policy they have followed in recent years.

D. The leadership believes that the USSR's net power position in the world, as affected by both military and political factors, has improved in the years since the Cuban missile crisis. But this is qualified by instability in its main security sphere in Eastern Europe and by increased strains in the Soviet economy and society. This appraisal by the Soviet leaders probably argues for continuing an external policy of cautious opportunism and limited pressures, perhaps with some increased watchfulness against the development of uncontrolled risks.

E. There is a tendency in Soviet foreign policy to give increased weight to geopolitical considerations as against the traditional conception Moscow has had of itself as the directing center of a world revolutionary movement. This is evident in the concentration of diplomatic and aid efforts in recent years on countries around the southern periphery of particular strategic interest to the USSR. It is seen also in the guidance given to most Communist parties to pursue moderate tactics, which are now more compatible with Soviet foreign policy interests.

F. Soviet aims to bring about a European settlement which would secure the USSR's hegemony in Eastern Europe, obtain the withdrawal of US forces, and isolate West Germany have suffered a severe setback because of the action taken to suppress Czechoslovakia's attempt to follow an independent course. For the present, the Soviets are unlikely to be responsive to any new Western initiatives to promote a European settlement, unless the West seems willing to contemplate recognition of the Soviet sphere in Eastern Europe and of the division of Germany.

G. The Soviets have a double concern in the Middle East at present: to keep their risks under control and to do this in such a manner as to avoid diminishing the influence they have won with the Arab

States. Should renewed hostilities occur, the USSR might be drawn into assisting the defense of the Arabs, but it would not want to run the political and military risks of joining in attacks on Israel or actually threatening its survival. At that stage, the Soviets would probably collaborate tacitly with the US to control the situation.

H. Beginning as an attempt to move into the vacuum left by the end of Western colonialism, Soviet policy in Asia in recent years has been geared increasingly to the containment of China. Nevertheless, the Soviets still act in particular situations, including Vietnam, basically on the premise that the Soviet-American relationship in Asia is competitive. The major risks which may eventually arise from the growth of Chinese power, however, may persuade them to move toward some tacit collaboration.

I. Though the inducements to reach a strategic arms limitation agreement with the US are probably stronger at this time than ever before, Moscow's policy-bureaucratic argument over this issue is not resolved. The Soviets probably hope that talks themselves, even if no agreement is reached, will ease the pressures of the arms race by slowing US decisions on new programs.

J. Even though the Soviet system appears ripe for change because it is now poorly suited to managing a complex industrial society, its rulers remain tenacious in defending their monopoly of power and acutely fearful of adaptive change. The wider involvement of the USSR in world affairs and possible shifts in world power relations may eventually generate stronger pressures for change. Short of this, the outlook is for chronic tensions in Soviet-American relations, perhaps caused more frequently by events over which neither side has much control.

11.

SOVIET FOREIGN POLICIES AND THE OUTLOOK FOR SOVIET-AMERICAN RELATIONS

SUMMARY

The USSR's View of Its World Position

A. Developments of recent years have given the USSR increased confidence in its security and strategic posture, in its capacity to engage its adversaries on favorable terms, and in the prospects for the long-term growth of its international influence. The Soviets have thus begun to pursue a more vigorous foreign policy and to accept deeper involvement in many world areas.

B. The attainment of rough parity in strategic weapons with the US has contributed more than anything else to the USSR's self-confidence. The Soviets have also been encouraged to see the US suffering a loss of influence in certain areas, facing economic difficulties at home and abroad, and coming under domestic pressure to curtail its world role. Largely on the basis of these considerations, Moscow believes that the US no longer enjoys a clear international predominance. It does not appear to have concluded, however, that US power has begun a precipitate or permanent decline; US economic, military, and technological capabilities continue to impress the Soviets. Thus, while they may be tempted to conclude that the US will no longer be the competitor it once was and may therefore be inclined as opportunities

occur to use their greater strength and flexibility more venturesomely, they can still see themselves getting into serious difficulties with the US if they press too hard.

C. The China problem is another factor which limits Soviet confidence. It has become increasingly clear to the Russians that China is capable of seriously undermining their international positions, keeping them off balance ideologically, and in the longer term, constituting a serious strategic threat. It unquestionably concerns the Soviets that China's ability to challenge them in all these ways would be all the greater in circumstances of Sino-American rapprochement.

Domestic Political and Economic Factors

D. The present Soviet leadership has been notable for its stability, and this has resulted in continuity in the decision-making process during most of the seven years since Khrushchev's overthrow. Brezhnev has clearly emerged as the principal figure in the regime and has been taking a vigorous lead in the area of foreign policy; he now has a personal stake in the USSR's current policy of selective détente. Decision-making, however, remains a collective process. Indeed, there are occasional signs of stress over the content and implementation of foreign policy. And maintaining a consensus behind a more active Soviet foreign policy, in circumstances of greater international complexity, may become increasingly difficult over time.

E. The USSR has been able to achieve rates of economic growth which are high by international standards and to maintain a military effort roughly equal to that of the US. But the Soviet economy is still backward in some sectors and it faces serious problems stemming from low productivity, the declining effectiveness of investment, and technological lag. Economic constraints do not *oblige* the Soviets to reduce military spending, however. While an agreement on strategic arms control would relieve somewhat the heavy demands which military programs impose on high quality human and material resources, agreements of the sort now contemplated would not enable the Soviets to increase the rate of economic growth appreciably.

The Strategic Weapons Relationship with the United States

F. We believe that the USSR has concluded that the attainment of clear superiority in strategic weapons—i.e., a superiority so evident

SECRET

that the Soviets could be assured of success in a confrontation and even "win" should they press the issue to nuclear war, say, by a first strike—is not now feasible. Nevertheless, there are no doubt those in Moscow who believe that it may still be possible to obtain a meaningful margin of advantage in strategic weapons which would give the USSR increased political-psychological leverage. The Soviet leaders must, at the same time, reckon with the possibility that any attempt to gain such an advantage would look to the US much the same as an attempt to move toward clear superiority and would produce the same counteraction. The course they have chosen, at least for the immediate future, is to attempt to stabilize some aspects of the strategic relationship with the US through negotiations, and they appear to believe that a formal antiballistic missile agreement and an interim freeze on some strategic offensive systems, on terms they can accept, are within reach.[1]

G. Assuming such an agreement is reached, the Soviets would continue serious negotiations on more comprehensive limitations. But the Soviet leaders are probably not clear in their own minds as to where these negotiations should lead. They may fear that too comprehensive an agreement might involve disadvantages they could not anticipate or foreclose developments which might eventually improve their relative position. And the more complex the agreement being considered, the greater the difficulties the Soviet leaders would face in working out a bureaucratic consensus. Thus, their approach to further negotiations would almost insure that these would be protracted.

The Sino-Soviet Conflict

H. The Soviets understand that their difficulties with China are in many ways more urgent and more intractable than their difficulties with the US and that, as Chinese military power grows, the conflict may become more dangerous. Moscow no doubt expects that the approach to normalization in US-Chinese relations will strengthen Peking's international position and will make China even more un-

[1] For separate statements of the views of Lt. Gen. Jammie M. Philpott, Acting Director, Defense Intelligence Agency; Vice Adm. Noel Gayler, Director, National Security Agency; Rear Adm. Earl F. Rectanus, Director of Naval Intelligence, Department of the Navy; and Maj. Gen. George J. Keegan, Jr., Assistant Chief of Staff, Intelligence, USAF, see their footnotes to paragraph 28, page 16.

SECRET

SECRET

willing than before to consider concessions to the USSR. It has also occurred to the Soviets that the US may gain some increased freedom of maneuver against them and that Washington and Peking will in some situations follow parallel policies to Moscow's detriment. The new US-Chinese relationship could, in addition, make a military solution to the Sino-Soviet conflict seem to the Soviets an even less attractive alternative than before.

I. Sino-Soviet relations will not necessarily remain as bad as they are now. At some point, the two sides might arrive at a *modus vivendi* which would permit them to "coexist" more or less normally. But to obtain any deep and lasting accommodation the Russians would have to pay a price they would consider unacceptably high, including a lifting of military pressures, some territorial concessions, disavowal of Moscow's pretensions as the paramount authority among Communists, and acknowledgement of a Chinese sphere of influence in Asia.

J. The Russians are likely to want to establish a wider role in Asia in the next few years. Consolidation of the Soviet position in South Asia, with the focus on India, will be one feature of this effort. The Russians will also continue to work to prevent an increase in Chinese influence in North Korea and North Vietnam. In the case of the latter, this will mean that Moscow will remain staunch in its support of Hanoi's effort to obtain a favorable settlement of the Vietnam war. The Soviets will, as a further objective of their policy in Asia, try to increase their influence in Japan, and an improvement in relations has already begun. Soviet prospects in this regard are, however, probably limited by Tokyo's greater concern for its relations with the US and China.

Soviet Policy in Eastern and Western Europe

K. Although Moscow has made progress in restoring order in Eastern Europe, it has not come to grips with the root causes which have in recent years produced unrest or even defiance of Soviet authority there—in Romania, Czechoslovakia, and Poland. Many East European leaders still hope for greater national autonomy and wider political and economic intercourse with the West. The USSR's task of reconciling its efforts to consolidate its hegemony in Eastern Europe

with an active policy of détente in Western Europe can therefore only be complicated and delicate. If it came to a choice between erosion of their position in Eastern Europe and détente in Europe as a whole, the Soviets would choose to let the latter suffer.

L. The USSR's security concerns in Eastern Europe, its own economic weaknesses, and growing preoccupation with the Chinese have turned it away from a policy of crisis and confrontation in Europe. At the same time, the changing pattern of US-West European relationships and trends within Western Europe itself have evidently convinced Moscow that its long-standing European aims—including a reduction of the US role and influence there—have become more realizable than ever before. A conference on European security represents for Moscow one way of encouraging the favorable trends in Western Europe and slowing the adverse ones. The Soviets also hope that a conference would open the way to a definitive and formal acknowledgement of the status quo in Germany and Eastern Europe. Rejection of the West German-Soviet treaty by the West German Bundestag would deal a setback to Soviet confidence in the viability of its German policy and possibly of its wider European policy. We believe, however, that in these circumstances Moscow's inclination would still be, perhaps after an interval of threatening talk, to try to salvage as much as possible of these policies rather than to reverse course completely.

M. The USSR's position on force reductions in Europe appears to stem mainly from its overall European tactics rather than from economic pressures or from military requirements related to the Sino-Soviet border. Moscow has doubts about the desirability of reducing its forces because of its concerns about Eastern Europe and about its military position vis-à-vis NATO. We believe, nevertheless, that Moscow is coming to accept that, assuming continuation of present trends in East-West relations in Europe, it could safely withdraw some of its forces from Eastern Europe, particularly from the large contingent in East Germany. This does not mean the Soviets have decided on any reduction or soon will. But, if they should decide to move beyond their present position, they will presumably see advantage in thoroughly exploring the possibilities of a negotiated agreement rather than acting unilaterally. On the other hand, if they should

conclude that such negotiations are unpromising, they might make limited withdrawals on their own, mainly because they would judge that this would lead to more significant US withdrawals.

The USSR's Position in the Middle East

N. In order to protect their close political and military ties with Egypt, the Soviets have been willing to increase their direct involvement and to accept larger risks in the context of the Arab-Israeli conflict. A full-scale renewal of the Arab-Israeli war would, however, be unwelcome to the Russians and the present situation causes them some anxiety. There is thus some chance that Moscow will come to see the desirability of urging the Arabs to accept a limited, interim agreement which would diminish the dangers of renewed hostilities, while still allowing the Soviets to enjoy the fruits of continued Arab-Israeli animosity. The Soviets are, however, unlikely to be amenable to an explicit understanding with the US limiting the flow of arms to the Middle East, though they might see advantage in some tacit restraints.

O. The Russians are probably generally optimistic about their long-term prospects in the Middle East, believing that radical, anti-Western forces there will assure them a continuing role of influence and eventually an even larger one. But the Soviets are uncomfortable because their present position is tied so closely to the exigencies of the Arab-Israeli conflict. They have also seen that radical nationalism can occasionally take a violently anti-Russian turn and with increasing involvement they will probably encounter greater difficulty in following a coherent and even-handed policy among the diverse and quarrelsome states of the area. In order to put their position in the Middle East on a firmer foundation for the future, they are likely to try both to forge stronger political ties with the "progressive" Arab parties and to develop their diplomatic relations with the moderate Arab states.

The Third World

P. The USSR's policies in the Third World are greatly affected by its urge to claim a wider world role for itself and by the need to protect its revolutionary credentials, especially against the Chinese challenge. In addition to its strong position in the Middle East, the USSR

has over the years won for itself a pivotal role in South Asia. It has also gained wider influence in Latin America. In Africa, the Soviet record is considerably more mixed and Soviet activities there now have a relatively low priority. In the Third World as a whole, partly because of some serious setbacks in the past, the Soviets are now inclined to view their prospects somewhat more soberly than they once did. Their approach is in general characterized by opportunism and a regard for regional differentiation. Nevertheless, by virtue of its acquisition in recent years of a greater capability to use its military forces in distant areas—a capability which is likely to continue to grow—Moscow may now believe its options in the Third World are expanding.

Future Soviet-American Relations

Q. The USSR has compelling reasons for wanting to keep its relations with the US in reasonably good repair, if only in order to control the risks arising from the rivalry and tensions which Moscow assumes will continue. It realizes that the larger world role it seeks is unrealizable except at the expense of the US. Whether the USSR will in particular circumstances lean toward sharper competition or broader cooperation with the US will naturally depend on the interaction of many variables. Crucial among these will be Moscow's appraisal of US intentions and its assessment of developments in the triangular relationship involving the US, China, and itself.

R. Progress in talks on strategic arms limitations might, by buttressing the USSR's sense of security, help to wear away some of its suspicion of US intentions. But problems in other areas where the political interests of the two countries are deeply engaged may prove to be of a more intractable sort. The conflict of interests in the Middle East seems likely to be prolonged. This may be true also in Europe where the Russians have an interest in the kinds of agreements which contribute to the security of the Soviet sphere but not in a genuine European settlement.

S. Whether the future will bring a more meaningful modification of the Soviet international outlook seems likely to depend ultimately on the USSR's internal evolution. And here the crucial question may be how the Soviet leaders deal with the problem of adaptive change in

Soviet society, including the problem of economic modernization: by minimal measures or by serious reform. The entrenched bureaucratic oligarchy now in charge is resistant to change. Among the younger men in the Politburo who now seem most likely to take over from the aging top leadership there may be some who harbor reformist views. But such tendencies, if they exist, are not now in evidence.

T. Thus, for the foreseeable future at any rate, Soviet policy, for reasons deeply rooted in the ideology of the regime and the world power ambitions of its leaders, will remain antagonistic to the West, and especially to the US. The gains the Soviets have made in relative military power, together with the heightened confidence these gains have inspired, will lead them to press their challenge to Western interests with increasing vigor and may in some situations lead them to assume greater risks than they have previously. At the same time, their policies will remain flexible, since they realize that in some areas their aims may be better advanced by policies of détente than by policies of pressure. They will remain conscious of the great and sometimes uncontrollable risks which their global aims could generate unless their policies are modulated by a certain prudence in particular situations.

CHANGING SOVIET PERCEPTIONS

SECRET

SYNOPSIS

A new note of Soviet self-confidence in international affairs, seen in Moscow as validating the concept of a progressive historical march, is emerging in the 1970s. Other major powers are not viewed as having changed their basically hostile attitudes toward the USSR, but the Soviets feel greater assurance about their capacity to deal with them and less exaggerated concern for their effects on Soviet security. Since insecurity has been a major factor motivating Soviet policies in the past it is not surprising that new directions in Soviet foreign policy have accompanied the new psychological mood. Moscow perceives a new need today for normalized relations with major states, especially the US, and has learned from experience that working within the existing international system is more likely to serve Soviet interests than frontal challenges to other great powers or to the system itself. Largely for this reason the Soviet leaders have developed an increased stake in international stability and have come to accept the prospect of an indefinite period of coexistence with the West.

Moscow still expects and seeks international change. But the USSR cannot, in a period of detente, be the direct agent for much of the change its leaders still hope will occur. And while a residual belief in the eventual attainment of ultimate Soviet aims in the basic world struggle still exists in the USSR, the Soviets have increasingly adjusted their sights, conceptually and operationally, to short-run and intermediate-range goals. Achievement of even these, the Soviets realize, depends on success in working with forces that often act independently of Soviet sway and in overcoming simultaneous countervailing trends.

Sources of Soviet Perceptions

Soviet ideology supplies the basic conceptual framework used by Soviet observers in analyzing international affairs. The interpretation of world events this ideology provides is dynamic: it posits a fundamental struggle on a global scale, presupposes constant change, and gives impetus to an activist foreign policy. Yet while Marxism-Leninism attunes Soviet observers to the key role that events *within* states play in affecting international behavior, it explains little beyond the general and abstract about relations *among* states. And although the Soviet outlook could be called utopian in terms of its stated goals, most Soviet leaders from 1917 onwards have consciously stressed realism and

2

SECRET

caution in practical policy matters and warned of the dangers of adventurism in the long-term international competition between the emerging new order and the declining old. In this regard, Brezhnev follows the examples of Lenin and Stalin rather than Khrushchev.

The wider Soviet involvement in recent years in world affairs and a belief that internal progress, especially toward economic goals, is increasingly dependent on international relationships have led Soviet leaders to seek a more accurate picture of the world. They have tried to enhance the capabilities of their channels of information about foreign events and, of particular note, to obtain more and better analysis of that information. A larger role has been assigned to the academic institutes in Moscow, especially the Institute of US and Canadian Studies and the Institute of the World Economy and International Relations, which are involved in providing policy-makers with estimative judgments about international affairs.

How deeply rooted the newer Soviet perceptions have become cannot be told with certainty. The current leaders lived through the Stalin era, with its articulate and heavily propagandized set of ideas stressing the hostility of the international environment, Soviet insecurity, and the necessity of avoiding foreign contact. This era has left deep and widespread Soviet doubts about the wisdom and orthodoxy of enmeshing the USSR in dealings with the capitalist powers and making compromises with the West. Yet despite the persisting influence of ingrained views, perceptions do not remain static. Doctrinally pure positions are possible only when events are viewed at a distance. Involvement with events requires that dogma make room for pragmatism, lest unrealism drive the Soviet state into an isolationist position. The post-Stalin generation of Soviet leaders has already changed its outlook in significant ways because of international experience, the influence of personal and institutional roles and interests, and newly perceived needs. A new generation of post-Brezhnev leaders could also develop new perceptions of international problems and new ideas of what Soviet national interests require in terms of international behavior.

The New International Situation

The measuring standard and key determinant of the USSR's progress in the worldwide political struggle postulated by the Soviets is the international "correlation of forces." In weighing the strengths of the two sides, the Soviets attach great importance to the power of the principal states, especially their economic and military capabilities and potential. But less tangible social and political factors are also

considered to be important, hence the continual Soviet assessing of US domestic cohesion and willpower.

In the Soviet view the world since 1917 has been in gradual transition from a purely capitalist system to a socialist one, the most dramatic single advance being the Sovietization of East Europe after World War II. But the 1970s, the Soviets argue, have brought a further significant, even radical favorable change in the international balance. Some Soviet commentary seems to imply a tipping of the balance past a notional midway point, as though "socialism" now possessed more than half of a world power pie. The factor mainly responsible for the new correlation of forces, in Moscow's view, is Soviet strategic nuclear strength, built up over the last ten years to a level roughly equivalent to that of the US. Also contributing to Soviet optimism is the combination of economic, social, and political problems currently plaguing the West, which Moscow views as unprecedented. In Soviet eyes these problems have made the present phase of capitalism's "general crisis" unusually deep and persistent and have thrown the West into its most serious disarray since World War II.

The Soviets are unsure about what developments will flow from this "crisis," however, and realize that any relative advantages they now enjoy rest on an uncertain foundation. More pronounced leftward trends in West European politics (especially Communist participation in coalition governments in France and Italy) seem likely to them, but they also see in the present-day Western condition the seeds of possible civil wars and the specter of revived fascism. The Soviets apparently believe that capitalism cannot escape suffering permanent disabilities as a conseqence of its problems and that it is already in a qualitatively new stage of its decline. But at the same time they have respect for the capacity of the capitalist system to devise effective methods for coping with even such serious problems as the oil issue and to bounce back because of the overall size and resiliency of the Western economic system.

The Soviets have also had difficulties in determining the meaning of the Western disarray for their own foreign policy. Some Party elements reportedly feel that not enough is being done to take advantage of the new international situation, and West European Communist parties are receiving conflicting signals from Moscow on just how best to improve their individual political positions. So far, however, in line with the Soviet propensity in the 1970s increasingly to dissociate the world revolutionary struggle from the ordinary conduct of interstate relations and place emphasis on the latter, the most authoritative Soviet expositions of the Western "crisis" have been more

4

in the nature of efforts to steer the detente policy over the shoals of this unanticipated situation than justifications for revising course.

In no case has this been more clearly true than for Soviet relations with the US, which remain the key factor affecting the overall Soviet international role. In the 1970s the US moved toward detente with the USSR and accommodated itself to the growth of Soviet strategic forces and a Soviet role in resolving major world problems. Whether this "realistic" US attitude will be sustained is the chief question for Soviet policy-makers. The Soviets believe that the US altered its foreign outlook in the early 1970s largely for pragmatic reasons: the old policy was simply becoming less effective and too expensive. But the new US policy, the Soviets believe, rests on an unconsolidated domestic base; the consensus supporting earlier US policies has broken down, but no agreement has yet been reached on what should take its place. The Soviet reading of the situation in the US throughout the 1975 "pause" in detente has been that the pro-detente forces are still more powerful than their enemies, but that the latter remain strong, still tapping a reservoir of anti-Soviet feelings not yet completely dissipated from the Cold War.

The newfound Soviet confidence is not free from counterbalancing factors, and Moscow does not see the shifts in the international "correlation of forces" wholly one-sidedly. For one thing, the favorable changes that have occurred in the 1970s are not irrevocable. In this critical regard they differ from postwar Soviet gains in East Europe, which are judged to be "irreversible." Even the lengthy and expensive Soviet nuclear missile buildup does not guarantee future strategic stability or even parity.

Moscow is also clearly aware of the storm clouds on its international horizon. Chief among them is China, whose "loss" greatly damaged the USSR's image as the nucleus of an ever-increasing international political movement and whose deep-seated hostility threatens to outlive Mao. But Europe too, the recent collective security agreement notwithstanding, contains a self-assured West Germany and has shown little susceptibility to increases in Soviet influence despite spells of political turmoil and lessened fears of the Soviet military threat. The emergence of several secondary power centers in the world is welcomed by Moscow as representing a decline in US authority among its chief partners, but the Soviets are uneasy about what direction these newly independent political forces will take. While the Soviet perception of the world as enemy is changing, it has not been replaced by one of the world as oyster, ripe with opportunities to be exploited.

5

The Soviet International Role

Soviet policy today is informed by a sense of "having arrived" internationally. By successfully weathering critical trials over the years, the Soviets believe that the USSR has demonstrated a capacity to sustain itself and grow in a dangerous and unpredictable international environment. There is also considerable national pride connected with the Soviet international role that is important to a people whose sense of inferiority *vis-à-vis* other great powers and cultures has been great and to a regime in need of evidence of its own competence and legitimacy. The Soviets feel that their international prestige is more solidly based today than was the case under Khrushchev, whose incautious political moves aroused rather than impressed adversaries and bought little influence in other countries. A stronger and more secure USSR does not guárantee success in all foreign undertakings, but it does mean a more active and influential Soviet international presence.

Current Soviet perceptions of world affairs, however, imply a degree of instability for Soviet policy. Although political changes such as those in southern Europe, from Turkey to Portugal, tempt Moscow to see and act on opportunities for Soviet advantage, the Soviet leaders are aware that greater militancy would damage their relations with the West without assuring any expansion of Soviet influence. While the Soviets are prepared to intervene abroad in areas and on occasions when they think the political and military risks are justified—as seems to be the case in Angola—they must continuously reassess the costs involved. In the rest of the 1970s and beyond the USSR may find itself even more subject to the strains inherent in its contradictory international roles: how effectively can it continue to represent itself as revolutionary, progressive, and the patron of the have-nots of this world while seeking expanded friendship with the US, recognition as a rich and advanced country, and stability in certain regimes and regions? There will probably continue to be a strong Soviet attitude in favor of keeping relations with the US and other major powers on a reasonably even keel, despite inevitable ups and downs. But mutuality of interest and viewpoint between East and West has long been anathema in the USSR, and reaching genuine compromises with the West will never be an easy or a natural process for Soviet leaders.

13.

~~CONFIDENTIAL~~

2261 7

CENTRAL INTELLIGENCE AGENCY
National Foreign Assessment Center
19 October 1978

MEMORANDUM

SUBJECT: The Impact of a Polish Pope on the USSR

Key Judgement

The elevation of the Archbishop of Poland's former royal capital and ancient cultural center--Krakow--to the Papacy will undoubtedly prove extremely worrisome to Moscow, if only because of the responsiveness his papacy is likely to evoke in East European communist societies. The selection of a Polish Pope, which reflects the uniquely vital Polish church, will make even more difficult Moscow's traditional attempts to bind culturally Western Poland more closely to the East, to integrate the Poles more closely into a Soviet-dominated bilateral and multilateral system of alliances, and to foster greater social and political discipline in Poland by consolidating the power of the Polish communist party. Because of the impact of John Paul II, particularly his impact on Polish nationalism, the Soviets will now find it even more difficult to check and to counter Poland's instinctive, cultural, and political gravitation to the West.

When the USSR faces its so-called empire in East Europe, it confronts a seriously unstable area where problems of nationalism have caused major rifts with the Soviet Union (Yugoslavia in 1948 and Albania in 1961), significant policy deviations with the Romanians, and differences among Warsaw Pact states over such disputed areas as Macedonia, Bessarabia, and Transylvania. The Soviets have never been able to cope successfully with the legacy of Polish nationalism, particularly Polish opposition to foreign occupiers and alien political systems. The origin of the state itself is linked to the

---

This memorandum was prepared in the Office of Regional and Political Analysis. Comments on it are welcome and may be addressed to

RPM 78-10395

②

~~CONFIDENTIAL~~

papacy when--more than a millenium ago--the king of Poland converted to Roman Catholicism and turned his back on Kieyan Rus. The election of Cardinal Wojtyla as Pope will give a tremendous boost to this formidable national pride and thereby make it more difficult for the regime to ignore the church's wishes.

A Polish pope will in particular have a long-term impact on a variety of internal issues between church and state that will ultimately demand Moscow's attention. Polish Catholics have been treated as second-class citizens by the party and have always looked to the church as a political alternative. Now the church can be expected to stiffen its position on such issues as establishing the legal status of the Roman Catholic church, permitting greater access to the media for church officials and religous services, and allowing an uncensored church press. The Pope's support for human rights issues as well as the emphasis by the Polish Catholic church on the country's cultural heritage could increase problems for Edward Gierek as well as the potential for mass discontent. Gierek's reaction to these problems will be watched closely in every Warsaw Pact cpaital, but none so closely as Moscow.

The elevation of the Cardinal to the papacy also marks an irreversible setback for Moscow's efforts since the end of WWII to weaken the various connections between the East European branches of the Catholic Church and Rome, and to create in their place docile national churches. A Polish pope not only buttresses the position of the Polish church as an alternate source of power but lends verisimilitude to the Polish view that only the church genuinely represents Polish national interests. Soviet actions in the past have already implicitly acknowledged that the neutrality of the church is essential to rule Poland, and Soviet leaders presumably must realize that the bargaining position of the church on a variety of issues has now been enhanced. The inability of the Poles to collectivize agriculture, for example, is in part a reflection of the power of the church's support for an independent peasantry.

The Soviets have in recent years been well aware of the need for caution imposed on their dealings with Warsaw due to Poland's intractable domestic economic and foreign trade problems and to the fact that Poland has a higher level of social tension than that of any other East European country. In fact, Moscow's careful response to the worker riots in Poland in 1970 and 1976 revealed that its ultimate concern was to ensure that political stability reigned in Poland. As long as Poland's nationalistic feelings do not give vent to overtly anti-Soviet actions, Moscow is likely to continue

2

to show caution in response to any disruptive effects of Poland's societal and intellectual tensions. If this occurs, Gierek will probably have increased bargaining leverage in getting Soviet cooperation in responding to issues between the party and the church.

Both the Church and the Kremlin, moreover, presumably share the popular Polish view that there is no viable alternative to what have thus far been Gierek's cautious tactics in handling Poland's domestic and social problems. In 1976, for example, the Soviets supported his careful response to the riots against the regime; last year, the church supported his efforts to maintain social peace in the country. In the near term, therefore, there should be no crisis in Soviet-Polish relations as a result of Wojtyla's elevation to the papacy.

Over the long run, however, the election of a Polish pope will contribute to an increase in nationalism in East Europe and will raise the consciousness of Orthodox churches and churchmen in the area. East European perceptions of Moscow's handling of any domestic crisis that results will be significant. Intellectual dissent in Poland and Czechoslovakia is already increasing and dissident groups will press the outer limits of permitted expression if the Soviets are perceived as too conciliatory. Hungary's quiet and careful experimentation in economic reform would also be enhanced by any signs of Soviet willingness to allow additional church freedom in Poland. A revival of the Protestant church in East Germany is already underway.

Indeed, the ripple effect on all of the East European countries as a result of any increase of Polish nationalism will cause the Soviet leadership to pay close attention to each sign of responsiveness to a Polish papacy in communist societies. The selection of a pope from Poland, moreover, adds to the problems of an aged and tired leadership in the Kremlin that is already facing its own pre-succession problems. Finally, the Soviets will be especially alert to any fallout from the Pope's election because the current Chinese leadership is particularly anxious to exploit any signs of a revival in East European nationalism and any signs of Soviet vacillation in responding to the challenge of such a revival.

The potential spillover effect of East European nationalism to the USSR is also considerable, particularly in the Ukraine where the Uniate Church has many adherents, in Byelorussia which contains former Polish territories that were once heavily Catholic, and in the Baltic countries where there are several million Catholics. The Soviets have always

3

CONFIDENTIAL

been more hostile toward Catholicism than toward officially recognized and relatively subservient churches, such as the Russian Orthodox, because of the Western orientation of the Catholics and their susceptibility on Soviet borders to outside influence. A Polish pope will reinvigorate the Catholic faith in these areas and may embolden Catholic dissidents to engage in more vigorous protest activities. These issues were presumably discussed in a meeting between Ukrainian First Secretary Shcherbitsky and the Polish Ambassador to the USSR in a meeting in Kiev on 17 October, only one day after the Pope's election.

If nothing else, a Polish papacy provides resonance to the activities of the Lithuanian Catholic dissidents, whose samizdat publication--<u>The Chronicle of the Lithuanian Catholic Church</u>--is already one of the most vital underground journals in the USSR. Dissent in Lithuania is largely a product of religious-national sentiment, and the two most important external influences on Lithuania are the Catholic church and Poland. For several centuries Poland and Lithuania were united in a single state and the Lithuanian capital still contains a sizable Polish minority.

The impact of a Polish papacy on the Ukraine will depend largely on the position of the new pope toward the Uniate church. Unlike the Catholic church in Lithuania, which has a precarious legal status, the Uniate church was formally outlawed after the war. As a condition for better Soviet-Vatican relations, Moscow has unsuccessfully insisted on Rome's recognition of the liquidation of the Uniate church. Such recognition would be a particularly difficult decision for a Polish pope.

On balance, it will take a long period of time for these problems to sort themselves out, but the Soviet leadership is probably already anxious about how to cope with the ultimate impact of a Polish papacy on East European nationalism as well as such derivative issues as Eurocommunism and Soviet dissidence. Having successfully coexisted with a Communist regime in Poland, the new Pope will have more than symbolic impact on those communist parties in such heavily Catholic countries as Italy, France, and Spain. The communists in these countries may now feel more free to stress their independence from Moscow. Conversely, it will be more difficult for such parties as the Christian Democrats in Italy to use the influence of the Church against these communist parties. The long-range problems are thus far different from those that have faced previous Soviet regimes and once led Stalin to rhetorically but derisively dismiss the impact of the Vatican by asking "how many divisions has the Pope?"

14.

SOVIET SUPPORT FOR INT'L TERRORISM

TOP SECRET
NOFORN/NOCONTRACT/ORCON

KEY JUDGMENTS

- The Soviets are deeply engaged in support of revolutionary violence worldwide. Such involvement is a basic tenet of Soviet policy, pursued in the interests of weakening unfriendly societies, destabilizing hostile régimes, and advancing Soviet interests.
- The USSR pursues different policies toward different types of revolutionary groups that conduct terrorist activities (that is, hijackings, assassinations, kidnapings, bombings, and the victimization of innocent civilians).
- Whether terrorist tactics are used in the course of revolutionary violence is largely a matter of indifference to the Soviets, who have no scruples against them. The Soviet attitude is determined by whether those tactics advance or harm Soviet interests in the particular circumstances. Revolutionary groups that employ terrorist tactics are simply one among the many instruments of Soviet foreign policy.
- There is conclusive evidence that the USSR directly or indirectly supports a large number of national insurgencies [1] and some separatist-irredentist [2] groups. Many of these entities, of both types, carry out terrorist activities as part of their larger programs of revolutionary violence. A notable example of Soviet involvement is the case of El Salvador, where the Soviets have coordinated and directly participated in the delivery of arms to revolutionary groups that use terrorism as a basic tactic.
- Some revolutionary groups that employ terrorism do accept a measure of Soviet control and direction, but many do not.
- The International Department of the Central Committee of the Soviet Communist Party has primary responsibility for managing contacts with movements in opposition to established govern-

[1] *National insurgencies* are broad-based movements which seek to transform the fundamental political orientation of a society by armed revolutionary means. Examples of such groups which the USSR supports or has supported are SWAPO (in Namibia) and ZAPU (in the former Rhodesia).

[2] *Separatist-irredentist movements* believe that they constitute nations without states and seek to assert their national autonomy or independence. Examples of such movements which the USSR supports or has supported are several of the Palestinian groups.

1

TOP SECRET

14. (continued)

TOP SECRET
NOFORN/NOCONTRACT/ORCON

ments. The KGB, the GRU, and the 10th Directorate of the Soviet General Staff provide a broad range of military and paramilitary training to members of revolutionary groups, in various camps in the USSR and elsewhere, and provide arms and other assistance to a wide spectrum of revolutionary groups in the world, particularly Palestinians, Africans, and Latin Americans.[3] Much of this support is readily utilizable in terrorist activities.

- The Soviets support certain allied or friendly governments and entities—notably Libya, certain Palestinian groups, East European states, South Yemen, and Cuba—which in turn directly or indirectly support the terrorist activities of a broad spectrum of violent revolutionaries, including certain of the world's nihilistic terrorist groups.[4]

- The USSR accepts these support actions of its allies and friends. It does so on occasion because these actions also serve Soviet interests and on other occasions because they are part of the price to be paid for maintaining and increasing its influence with allies and friends. The USSR has not made its backing for them contingent on their desisting from aiding nihilistic terrorists or other violent revolutionaries. In this sense, Moscow is wittingly providing support, albeit indirectly, to international terrorism.

- With respect to Soviet policy toward nihilistic, purely terrorist groups, available evidence remains thin and in some respects contradictory, even though the human intelligence collection programs of the United States and its friends have been giving this problem close scrutiny for some years.

- The activities of some of the nihilistic terrorist groups are carried out by individuals trained by Soviet friends and allies that provide them with weapons; such terrorists have sometimes transited Soviet Bloc nations. Yet the terrorist activities of these groups are not coordinated by the Soviets.[5]

---

[3] See annexes A and B for details.

[4] *Nihilists* are small groups, with little public support, which rely almost exclusively on terrorist acts to destroy existing institutions to make way for new ones. Leading examples are the Baader-Meinhof group in Germany, the Japanese Red Army, and the Red Brigades in Italy, which profess the view that Western institutions are their major antagonists.

[5] *Following is an alternative view of the Director, Defense Intelligence Agency; the Assistant Chief of Staff for Intelligence, Department of the Army; the Director of Intelligence, Headquarters, Marine Corps; and the Assistant Chief of Staff, Intelligence, Department of the Air Force. They believe that the Soviets do provide some coordination to nihilistic terrorists either directly through the contacts of Soviet advisers with these terrorists in training camps in Middle Eastern countries, or elsewhere, or indirectly through East European countries, Cubans, Palestinians, or other entities through which the Soviets work.*

2

SECRET

14. (continued)

- The Soviets have on occasion privately characterized certain nihilistic terrorism as "criminal," and have urged other revolutionary groups to cease and desist from terrorist acts the Soviets considered "self-defeating."[4]
- Public protestations by the Soviets that they do not back terrorism are compromised by the indirect Soviet support received by certain nihilistic terrorists, as well as by the direct support the Soviets afford to national insurrections and separatist-irredentist movements which conduct terrorist acts.
- The Soviet policy of differentiated support of various kinds of revolutionary violence benefits Soviet overall interests at low risk or cost, and without significant damage to Soviet prestige. It is therefore likely to continue.
- There is no basis for supposing that the Soviets could be persuaded to join the West in genuine opposition to international terrorism as a whole.
- The broader phenomenon of revolutionary violence is a more significant and complex issue for the United States than is its terrorist component per se. The severe instabilities that exist in many settings in the Third World are chronic, will not soon be overcome, and in many instances would continue to exist regardless of the USSR.
- There is no simple or single solution to these problems because of the variety and complexity of circumstances leading to revolutionary violence and terrorism. In every case, the indicated measures include a mixture of three approaches: reduction or elimination of external support, police and/or military action to combat violence, and the opening of channels for peaceful change.

---

[4] *Following is an alternative view of the Director, Defense Intelligence Agency; the Director of Intelligence, Headquarters, Marine Corps; and the Assistant Chief of Staff, Intelligence, Department of the Air Force. They believe that this judgment is misleading. Moscow has not supported terroristic activities which it considers counterproductive. The holders of this view note, however, that, as stated in the fourth Key Judgment (page 1), on other occasions "the Soviets have coordinated and directly participated in the delivery of arms to revolutionary groups that use terrorism as a basic tactic."*

15.

Secret

Soviet Society in the 1980s: Problems and Prospects

Key Judgments

Information available as of 30 November 1982 was used in this report.

Both Western observers and Soviet officials recognize that the Soviet Union now faces a wide array of social, economic, and political ills including a general social malaise, ethnic tensions, consumer frustrations, and political dissent. Precisely how these internal problems will ultimately challenge and affect the regime, however, is open to debate and considerable uncertainty. Some observers believe that the regime will have little trouble coping with the negative mood among the populace. Others believe that economic mismanagement will aggravate internal problems and ultimately erode the regime's credibility, increasing the long-term prospects for fundamental political change

Whatever the ultimate prognosis, these problems will pose a challenge for the new Soviet leadership. The Politburo's approach probably will be based on its assessment of the threat posed and the degree to which these issues can be addressed by policy shifts. Three broad categories of problems—the quality of life, ethnic tensions, and dissent—are surveyed in this paper. Of these, popular discontent over a perceived decline in the quality of life represents, in our judgment, the most serious and immediate challenge for the Politburo. According to [ ] sources, the Soviet people are no longer confident that their standard of living will continue to improve. Popular dissatisfaction and cynicism seem to be growing. This popular mood has a negative impact on economic productivity and could gradually undermine the regime's credibility. Such discontent has already led to some isolated strikes and demonstrations, developments that immediately get the leadership's attention. Other manifestations of discontent—crime, corruption, and alcoholism—are evident as well but pose no direct challenge to the regime. Such ills, nonetheless, have a detrimental effect on Soviet economic goals, are harmful to the social climate in general, and in turn are made worse by the slow rate of economic growth.

Ethnic discontent—rooted in cultural, demographic, and economic problems as well as political suppression—remains primarily a latent but potentially serious vulnerability. Currently, there is no widespread, politically disruptive protest or dissent among the Soviet nationalities. The regime's policies—granting to national minorities some linguistic, territorial, cultural, and administrative autonomy; raising the standard of living; expanding the educational base; and using overwhelming police power when needed—have been largely successful so far. Although the potential for political unrest and sporadic violence in the Baltic republics remains high because of economic, demographic, and cultural grievances, Baltic concerns have little impact elsewhere in the USSR and can be suppressed if necessary. With more time (perhaps decades), however, similar problems could become much more consequential in Muslim Central Asia, requiring the regime to manage this problem more adroitly.

Finally, the range of political, religious, and cultural discontent that is expressed in the Soviet dissident movement does not, at present, seriously challenge the regime's political control, but the regime deals with it as if it does. Soviet dissidents cause concern because they have an international audience and their activities embarrass the regime. Moreover, the leadership remains psychologically insecure and is unwilling to allow any hint of challenge to its authority, apparently because it fears such dissidents could appeal to a wider audience by articulating more widely held discontent over food shortages and the like. For these reasons, the regime, particularly of late, has used widespread arrests and imprisonment of dissident leaders, confinement in psychiatric hospitals, and exile to crush the movement. The movement, however, is not likely to die and in the long run could grow if it can capitalize on increasing discontent, cynicism, and alienation among the populace.

The sharp slowdown in economic growth since the mid-1970s is the underlying problem that ties all these issues together and makes them potentially more troublesome for the regime. Unless this trend is reversed, increasing alienation and cynicism, especially among young people, are likely; and other social ills—crime, corruption, alcoholism—could get worse. The regime, to be sure, has impressive resources for trying to deal with particular economic problems—especially in its centralized control over priorities and resources, but a return to the more favorable economic conditions of the 1960s and early 1970s, when there were substantial improvements in the standard of living, is highly unlikely. The pervasive police powers at the Politburo's disposal, when coupled with the Soviet populace's traditional passivity toward deprivation and respect for authority, should, however, continue to provide the regime with the necessary strength to contain and suppress open dissent.

15. (continued)

Secret

Difficult decisions regarding resource allocation and new management approaches, nevertheless, will probably be needed to deal with the Politburo's economic problems and to reverse the malaise that has set in. How the new leadership will handle these issues over the long run is uncertain. Its policy options range from undertaking major "reforms" and reallocating resources away from defense to greater reliance on administrative controls and repression. Some mix of policies involving both directions might be attempted. No solutions it is likely to attempt, however, offer any certain cure for its growth problem and the malaise related to it. This situation will likely require the leadership to fall back even more on traditional orthodox methods to control dissent and suppress challenges to its authority while continuing efforts to avoid an overall decline in a "quality of life" that has become the regime's real basis for legitimacy.

v

Secret

16.

MORI DocID: 265004 UNCLASSIFIED

~~CONFIDENTIAL~~

Gorbachev's Domestic Challenge: The Looming Problems (U)

Key Judgments

Information available as of 2 February 1987 was used in this report.

General Secretary Mikhail Gorbachev is off to a strong start. He has consolidated power with unprecedented speed, put in place an ambitious program for economic revitalization that has already achieved some results, set higher standards of accountability for the bureaucracy, and improved the image of the Soviet leadership at home and abroad.

But Gorbachev's greatest challenge lies ahead. He has staked his leadership on radically improving the functioning of the Soviet system while keeping up with the United States abroad. The cautious changes he has sanctioned so far are, in our view, insufficient to achieve these goals. Over the next few years, he is likely to face tough choices between accepting results that will fall well short of his goals--and a resultant erosion of his power--or pushing the Soviet leadership toward far more difficult--and politically controversial--policy measures.

Revitalizing the Economy. Gorbachev has made economic revitalization his priority issue, arguing that Soviet national security and influence abroad are dependent on a sharp economic improvement. So far, despite the urgency of his rhetoric, he has relied on traditional methods--discipline, organizational streamlining, new people, refocusing investment to machine building--and some modest reforms to achieve his goals. While these steps are improving things somewhat--and from the Soviet perspective are impressive and significant--they appear likely to fall well short of achieving both the growth and technological progress Gorbachev is seeking over the next five years.

To achieve his goals for improved economic performance, he will have to consider more politically risky and economically disruptive reforms. Moreover, progress on the economy is inextricably linked to developments on a host of other controversial political and social issues. Gorbachev is already facing strong opposition from those who see their jobs, status, and sinecures threatened by his efforts to turn the Soviet economy and society around. His cadre policy--to replace government and party bureaucrats to increase efficiency, imagination, and commitment--is at the focal point of the struggle.

~~CONFIDENTIAL~~

Page 1

Mastering the Bureaucracy. To implement successfully even the changes he has announced so far, Gorbachev will have to transform a bureaucracy renowned for its ability to resist leadership direction into a more responsive and efficient instrument of change. Despite his political success to date, he has only begun to accomplish this task. His words and deeds clearly show determination to tame the party and state bureaucracies, but resistance to his initiatives is fierce

unrelenting pressure to get his agenda implemented is already creating a large pool of disgruntled apparatchiki intent on blocking his program, and he may well have to consider even more forceful measures.

Managing the Politburo. From Gorbachev's perspective, the need to address these interrelated problems will seriously complicate his greatest challenge--maintaining a consensus within the Politburo. The independent-minded officials who make up Gorbachev's Politburo appear to agree that there is a need for new policy directions and personnel to carry them out, but they appear to differ over specific approaches. The convergence of the institutional, economic, social, and defense issues Gorbachev must face will make consensus decisionmaking even tougher to accomplish than it has been so far.

Limiting the Defense Burden. Without restricting the defense burden, Gorbachev will find it increasingly difficult to generate the significant increase in resources he needs to devote to civilian industrial investment, particularly machine building. Unless there is a sharp upturn in economic performance--which we think is unlikely--or major reductions in defense spending--which would be very controversial without a significant reduction in the perceived threat--by the end of the decade, demands for investment in the civilian sector will come increasingly into conflict with demands for more investment in the defense industries. The prospect of such a choice has already led Gorbachev to pursue a bold strategy for managing the US relationship that probably is controversial within the Soviet elite and could, in conjunction with economic considerations, eventually lead him to confront fundamental obstacles inhibiting economic progress.

Managing Societal Pressures. Gorbachev may find that the Soviet populace, long accustomed to a paternalistic state that provides job security and basic necessities at low prices, is a major obstacle to achieving the social-economic transformation he wants. The regime has already pressed workers to be more productive while refusing to devote a greater share of resources to consumption in order to provide incentives. Many Soviet reformers believe further changes in social policy—reduced subsidies for necessities, a less egalitarian wage structure, and a more tolerant attitude toward unemployment—will be required to produce sustained improvements in economic performance. Although societal problems are unlikely to reach crisis proportions over the next five years, Gorbachev will need to manage popular concerns effectively to improve morale and productivity as well as to prevent increased discontent.

The Soviet leader has considerable advantages and assets for pushing his agenda. Nevertheless, as these problems converge over the next five years, we believe he will face an increasingly clear choice between settling for half measures that fall well short of his demands and perhaps his needs, or forcing the Politburo to make some difficult and divisive decisions. Failure to take on this challenge probably would not cost him his job but would open his administration to charges of Brezhnev-style immobilism that he seems determined to prevent. The leadership style Gorbachev has demonstrated so far, as well as his rhetoric, suggests that he will turn to more radical policy alternatives rather than accept that fate. He will find some advisers eager to push for a harsher neo-Stalinist path as well as those arguing for more radical policy or systemic reforms. We do not know what mix of these options he might choose or even how hard he will push. But the complexities of the issues and absence of easy alternatives guarantee that the struggle will be protracted and the outcome uncertain both for him and the Soviet Union.

CIA's Analysis of Soviet Science and Technology

CIA's Analysis of Soviet Science and Technology
Author's Comments: Clarence Smith

By the 1950s it was clear that the USSR possessed both nuclear weapons and long-range delivery methods. But key questions remained for US policymakers. How advanced and how effective were these capabilities? Could they be used against the continental United States and its Allies on the USSR's periphery? The answers were fundamental to the US strategic deterrent position.

Technical intelligence was the primary tool used to address these questions because the USSR, Eastern Europe, and China were "denied areas" that presented difficult challenges to traditional human and military reconnaissance collection. These countries were repressive police states that severely restricted internal movement and foreign contacts; they also had effective air defenses. This meant traditional espionage and reconnaissance methods were too limited to provide the access or the information needed by the West to monitor Soviet Bloc weapons and remote test sites. To counter this, the CIA and the Intelligence Community (IC) invented innovative collection approaches using remote sensors. A lack of "hard" intelligence was the key driver in developing US satellite imaging and signals intelligence collection systems. In addition to the actual technical collection, it was necessary to develop ways of deriving analytical results from the raw products of these new collection sources. The IC's challenge was not only to create new collection methods but to derive useful information from the data.

The CIA's Office of Scientific Intelligence, and later the Directorate of Science & Technology (DS&T), led technical intelligence collection and analysis activities. Those who had been involved in analyzing activities such as the Berlin Tunnel taps of Soviet military headquarters in East Germany, formed the original nucleus. Also included were analytical components dealing with science, technology, and weapons. These analysts had to answer key questions about Soviet strategic weapons: How many weapons did the USSR have? What were their capabilities? Where were they located?

The intelligence reports and estimates selected for this volume from the early 1950s through the mid-1980s reflect the impact of advancements in technical collection and analysis. NIE 11-5-59, "Soviet Capabilities in Guided Missiles and Space Vehicles," reflects a basic agreement within the Intelligence Community on Soviet capabilities. By October 1964 (NIE 11-8-64), however, there were debates within the IC about Soviet ICBM capabilities and the number of deployed sites. These disagreements were primarily the result of the fact that, while the United States now had more data, there were now more opportunities for different interpretations of the information. Similarly, in the defensive missile area, IC analysts disagreed over Soviet ABM capabilities. NIE 11-3-65 addresses the beginning of the SAM upgrade issue. These strategic offensive and defensive missile concerns stayed in the forefront of the challenges facing IC analysts well into the 1970s. The selected documents reflect these issues.

17.

CENTRAL INTELLIGENCE AGENCY

30133

Copy # 11

12 October 1949

INTELLIGENCE MEMORANDUM NO. 237

SUBJECT: Capabilities of the USSR in Air-to-Air Guided Missiles and Related Proximity Fuses

Part I. 1 May 1950

It is just possible that reproductions of German air-to-air missiles might be ready in limited quantities (less than one hundred) for operational use by the Soviets in 1950. These missiles would be relatively ineffective against a heavily armed bomber of the B-36 type. It is also possible that a relatively crude proximity fuse might be used since such a fuse need not utilize miniature or ruggedized vacuum tubes. See Appendix A for a summary of intelligence data.

Part II. 1 May 1953 and 1 May 1956

Assuming that Soviet scientists engaged in the development of an air-to-air guided missile are the equal of scientists in America and assuming further that they have the benefit of espionage directed against U.S. efforts, it is believed that a Soviet-developed, supersonic, air-to-air guided missile might be ready by 1955. See Appendix A.

-1-

APPENDIX A

Substance of Intelligence on Air-to-Air Guided Missiles and Proximity Fuses for Them

Except for the comments of one moderately well-placed source, we have no data on Soviet development of air-to-air guided missiles. This source does not know whether or not any of the German projects are being followed up, but he thinks it more than likely, since the Soviets have always been interested in rockets for air-to-air combat.

Two air-to-air missiles were under development by the Germans at the end of World War II. One of these, the X-4, was to be carried aloft and launched from the FW 190 and Me262 aircraft. Development tests of this missile appeared successful, but the missile was never used operationally because of the inherent danger in the liquid-fuel propellant system. A power rocket unit was under development for a safer and more practical propulsion system.

The X-4 had an approximate maximum speed of 820 feet/second and a maximum Mach number of 0.795. The missile was remotely controlled by electrical impulses transmitted along a pair of fine insulated wires connecting it with the parent aircraft. The sense of the signals transmitted and hence the direction the missile travelled was determined by the motion of a joystick operated by the pilot of the parent aircraft. The maximum distance at which the missil- could be operated was approximately 3-3/4 miles.

Information on stability and position of the missile in flight was obtained visually by means of a reflector-type aiming device. The operator was assisted in his guidance by means of candle flares carried

[redacted]

on the missile. During the period of guidance, it is believed that the launching aircraft would be very susceptible to fighter attack. Harassing tactics by opposing aircraft would be sufficient to disturb the aim of the pilot.

The other air-to-air missile under development was the Hs-298, which was designed for use against enemy bombers. It was carried underneath the wing and fuselage of fast bombers or fighters equipped with special launching rails. The German government placed high priority on the development of the Hs-298. By early 1945 it was being mass produced. Production was discontinued in February of the same year, however, probably because of the discovery of the vulnerability of the parent planes to attacks by fighters. Test flights were carried out with three missiles. Two missiles were successfully launched, but one exploded prematurely and the other nose-dived and crashed. The third stuck on the launching rail. We have no data on completely successful flights. The missile was never used operationally. It was anticipated that the missile could attack a target flying without evasive action at a slant range of 5,000 yards. The missile was to be capable of attacking a target 1,000 yards above the point of release. Targets always had to be attacked visually within a limited field. The approximate maximum speed of the Hs-298 was 790 feet/second, and it had a maximum Mach number of 0.72. Its maximum range was about 5,000 yards.

The guidance system was to be similar to that of the X-4 except that at first a radio link instead of a wire link was planned. Since such a radio link was susceptible to jamming, a wire link was developed. We do not believe any flights were made using this method of control.

Two crew members of the parent aircraft were required to operate the

2.

TO[redacted]

17. (continued)

aiming system. One sighted on the target with an aiming device, and the other guided the missile by looking through a telescope and operating a joystick. The pilot had to maneuver the parent aircraft so as to keep the target ahead and to starboard, since the aiming device was mounted on the starboard side.

It was planned to use proximity fuses with both the X-4 and Hs-298 but none was available by the end of the war.

CONFIDENTIAL

3.

Approved For Release : CIA-RDP78-01617A000700280001-0

18.

FUTURE SOVIET EARTH SATELLITE CAPABILITIES

PROBLEM

To define near future Soviet earth satellite Space Vehicle capabilities.

CONCLUSIONS

It is concluded that Sputnik III, by the use of a combination of propulsion stages, could be one of the following types:

1. A 160-300 lb scientific earth satellite.

2. A large satellite up to 5,000 lbs containing an animal passenger with the intention of returning the animal to earth.

3. The orbiting of a preliminary (1000 - 5000 lbs) reconnaissance satellite.

4. Impacting a payload (100 - 400 lbs) on the moon.

In view of the extremely high priority placed on the effects of outer space on mammals and high interest in manned space flight it is considered most probable that Sputnik III will contain an animal suitable for space studies.

DISCUSSION

The Soviet Union announced that Sputnik I, orbited on 4 October 1957, had a weight of about 185 lbs. and Sputnik II, orbited on 3 November 1957 had a weight of about 1120 lbs. Sputnik III could probably be launched at any time and, according to Soviet statements, additional satellites will probably be launched at about one month intervals throughout the remainder of the IGY.

We believe that the Soviet ICBM and the Soviet earth satellite vehicles probably utilized the same first and second stage propulsion system. The Soviet ICBM is estimated to have a gross weight of about 300,000 lbs. with a propulsion system consisting of paired nominal 100 metric ton thrust engines or an equivalent single engine in the first state and a nominal 35 metric ton engine in the second stage.

- 1 -

Additionally, although no evidence exists, we believe the Soviets are probably capable of adding a third propulsion stage to this system. The capability of such a staged propulsion system to orbit satellites or propel payloads to the moon are approximately:

	STAGES	CONFIGURATION	SATELLITE WT. ORBITED	MOON IMPACT WEIGHT
1.	2	paired 100 mt engines plus a 35 mt engine	200 lbs	----
2.	2	paired 120 mt engines plus a 35 mt engine	1200 lbs	----
3.	3	paired 100 mt engines plus a 35 mt engine plus 12 mt engine	3000 lbs	100
4.	3	paired 120 mt engines plus a 35 mt engine plus 12 mt engine	5000 lbs	400

The use of super fuels in large quantities would allow greatly increased payload weights, but would also introduce hazardous handling problems for personnel, and cause equipment and site contamination problems. Major thrust unit component redesign would also be necessary, requiring additional R & D flight tests. None of these problems are insurmountable but do take time to solve. Small quantities of super fuels (up to about 10%), however, could be added to conventional fuels without particular difficulty thereby increasing the specific impulse and allow payload weights to be increased to some degree. There have been contradictory statements by knowledgeable Soviet officials about whether a super fuel was used in the Sputnik II launchings, and firm knowledge on this point is lacking.

We believe that the present Soviet capability for Sputnik III probably includes the orbiting of up to about 5000 lbs. of satellite. We believe that Sputnik III will be in one of the categories, which are discussed in the following:

1. The orbiting of a 160-300 lb. scientific earth satellite.

2. The orbiting of a large satellite (up to 5000 lbs.) containing an animal passenger with intention of returning the animal to earth.

- 2 -

18. (continued)

3. The orbiting of a preliminary (1000-5000 lbs) reconnaissance satellite.

4. Impacting a payload on the moon (100-400 lbs).

If Sputnik III is devoted to purely scientific aspects of upper atmosphere research, it will most probably carry instrumentation for the study of cosmic rays, x-rays, ultraviolet radiation, the earth magnetic field, temperature, pressure, meteors and ionospheric phenomena. A 300 lb. satellite could carry the necessary equipment and power for about two-three weeks of transmissions providing satelli transmissions were not continuous. Satellite to ground command data readout would have to be fairly frequent due to limited data storage facilities in a satellite of this size.

The biological experiment in Sputnik II could have allowed determination of a dog's major physiological reactions during launching and at high altitude with a single major exception of cosmic radiation effects. Recovery and study of the animal is essential to this radiation effects determination. The effort involved in returning a mammal to earth includes the provision of an additional propulsion stage to remove the satellite from orbit and provision of escape or deceleration apparatus to allow safe re-entry conditions. It is possible that the first satellite intended to return an animal to earth will have a low orbit, short life and more predictable recovery location.

While Soviet interest in a reconnaissance satellite is probably not as high as that of the US, the capability to orbit at least 1200 lb. satellite (by two stage rocket system) is high and includes the possibility of the payload being optical or electronic reconnaissance equipment and the transmission of such information to Soviet recording stations. There is no reason to believe that the USSR would not be able to provide this equipment.

The fact that a longer interval of time has been required to launch Sputnik III may be indicative of a more complex launching device, such as a three stage vehicle orbiting a large satellite or a lunar flight.

Implicit in the Soviet orbiting of a mammal in their second satelli attempt is the extremely high priority placed on the effects of outer sp on mammals and high interest in manned space flight.

- 3 -

19.

DOCID: 124245 UNCLASSIFIED

GEOPHYSICAL AND ASTROPHYSICAL INSTRUMENTATION OF SOVIET SPUTNIKS I, II, AND III

SUMMARY

The recent development of Soviet artificial earth satellites as carriers of instruments in sustained flight above the shielding effects of the earth's atmosphere represents a major technical advance potentially of great importance in the geophysical and astrophysical sciences and to the successful achievement of manned space flight. All three Soviet sputniks placed in orbit to date are important in contributing knowledge of the physical environment and communication conditions for subsequent astronautical efforts of the USSR.

The Soviet Union has obtained an advantage over the United States in geophysical and astrophysical research because it has placed in orbit much larger satellites capable of carrying more varied and heavier instrument payloads. With the exception that Soviet satellites have not penetrated as far into space as U.S. satellites, the near-polar orbits of the Soviet satellites offer more advantages than the near-equatorial orbits of the U.S. satellites.

Although Sputniks I and II were not outstanding in their geophysical and astrophysical instrumentation, Sputnik III represents a scientific achievement of considerable magnitude because of the large number of significant observations that are conducted simultaneously. The equipment for detecting primary gamma rays is apparently unique and, if successful, would provide data of considerable scientific significance. The numerous cosmic ray and auroral particle experiments are of special value because Sputnik III traverses the auroral zones. Instruments included in Sputnik III, not duplicated in the U.S. satellite program, for the IGY, are magnetic and ionization manometers, mass spectrometers, flux meters, and ion traps. Sputnik III apparently is similar to advanced U.S. satellites in that it employs solar as well as chemical batteries and has telemetering systems that probably store data for release at a later time when the satellite is interrogated * as it passes over a receiving station. Sputnik III also may contain equipment that has not been described by the Soviets. On the other hand, Sputnik III apparently lacks a means of orientation control; therefore, it probably contains no elaborate earth-scanning device, such as a television camera. The Soviet instrumentation generally is heavier and less refined than similar U.S. equipment; but some miniaturization has been noted, and much of the equipment in Sputnik III appears to be transistorized. There are indications that the Soviets have copied some U.S. instruments.

Soviet ground equipment for optical and radio tracking of satellites appears to be adequate but less elaborate than U.S. equipment. The Soviets are steadily expanding and improving their capabilities for precision tracking and are placing considerable emphasis on this phase of their observations.

* In response to a radio signal from the ground, the satellite transmits stored data.

20.

TOP SECRET

SOVIET CAPABILITIES IN GUIDED MISSILES AND SPACE VEHICLES

FOREWORD

This advance portion of the forthcoming national intelligence estimate on all Soviet missile development programs has been prepared to meet the immediate needs of intelligence consumers and to facilitate work by the intelligence community on certain parallel estimates and projects. It will be incorporated into the final version of NIE 11–5–59 (due in October 1959), subject to any further modification or revision which may be required by additional evidence or reanalysis in the interim. This text supersedes those portions of NIE 11–5–58 relating to the missiles discussed herein.

THE PROBLEM

To estimate Soviet capabilities and probable programs for the development of 700 nautical mile and 1,100 nautical mile ballistic missiles, intercontinental ballistic missiles, and fleet ballistic missiles, including their major performance characteristics and dates of operational availability.

THE ESTIMATE

SURFACE-TO-SURFACE BALLISTIC MISSILE SYSTEMS

1. The USSR has developed a family of surface-to-surface ballistic missiles through an intensive and well conceived program conducted at high priority since shortly after World War II. Missiles known to have been developed or to be under development at present include those with maximum ranges of about 75 nautical miles (n.m.), 200 n.m., 350 n.m., 700 n.m., 1,100 n.m., and intercontinental ballistic missiles (ICBM).[1] We have more extensive information on the ballistic missile program than on any other Soviet missile program. We therefore estimate this program with considerable assurance, although our confidence in the details varies.

[1] As a rule of thumb, a ballistic missile can be considered capable of firing to about one-third of maximum operational range without serious degradation in accuracy, and to even shorter ranges with degraded accuracy.

2. A substantial body of evidence supports our belief that the Soviet ballistic missile development program has for a number of years been well coordinated, extensively supported, and conducted by qualified personnel with access to excellent facilities. It has resulted in the development of operational missiles whose reliability, accuracy and other performance characteristics meet high standards.

3. We believe that in the development of longer range systems, maximum use has been made of proven components. On the basis of indirect evidence and the logic of a coordinated development program, we consider it reasonable to conclude that the two active Soviet ballistic missile test ranges (Kapustin Yar for missiles up to 1,100 n.m. range, Tyura Tam for ICBMs and space vehicles) have been mutually supporting with respect to component testing and shared experience.

4. The type of warhead employed with Soviet ballistic missiles will vary with the specific mission of the missile. In general, however, we believe that for missiles with maximum ranges of less than 700 n.m. high explosive (HE), nuclear, or chemical warfare (CW) warheads will be employed in accordance with Soviet military doctrine, depending upon nuclear stockpiles, missile accuracy, character of the target, and results desired. We estimate that for missiles with ranges of 700 n.m. and over, only nuclear warheads will be employed, although we do not exclude the possibility of CW use in 700 n.m. missiles for certain limited purposes. We believe that the USSR is capable of developing techniques for missile dissemination of biological warfare (BW) agents, although we have no specific evidence relating BW and missile research and development. In view of operational considerations we consider BW use in ballistic missiles unlikely, although possible for certain special purposes.

5. Mobility appears to be a basic consideration in Soviet ballistic missile design and we have good evidence of road mobility on some systems with ranges of 700 n.m. and less. The size and weight of the 1,100 n.m. missile may be such as to limit its road mobility to selected first class road nets; in view of this limitation, we believe it may be road and/or rail mobile. In the case of road mobile systems, it is probable that missile carriers and support vehicles are readily adaptable for rail transport. Mobility as it applies to an ICBM system is discussed below in paragraphs 27–29.

700 Nautical Mile Ballistic Missile System (SS–4)

6. There is considerable evidence[ ]that a missile which would meet the Soviet requirement for a 700 n.m. range weapon has been under test at Kapustin Yar for many years. We believe that test firings began in about 1953; an average of about two per month have occurred since mid-1955. We estimate that this system has been available for operational use since about 1956, although no operational sites or units have been identified.

7. Until recently we were unable to determine whether the largest missile in the 7 November 1957 Moscow Parade (nicknamed SHYSTER for recognition purposes) was the 700 n.m. missile or the 350 n.m. missile. [ ] evidence[ ] together with statements and photographs released by the USSR, has provided sufficient data to permit the determination that SHYSTER is probably the 700 n.m. missile. Analysis of this evidence has caused us to change our previous estimate of maximum warhead weight from 5,000–6,000 pounds to approximately 3,000 pounds.

8. We continue to estimate that prior to 1958 this missile utilized radio/inertial guidance and that commencing in 1958–1960 an all inertial system would become available. There are some indications[ ]that inertial components were being tested in late 1958. Missiles already produced and equipped with the radio/inertial system will not necessarily undergo retrofit to the all inertial system.

9.[ ] We do not believe a second generation missile of this range is yet being developed. There are indications that the 700 n.m. missile has contributed to the development of other missiles, but the exact nature of this contribution cannot be determined.

10. We estimate that this missile system is operational and in production in the USSR, and that it probably has the following characteristics: [2]

US Designation	SHYSTER—SS-4
IOC Date[3]	1956
Maximum Range	700 n.m.
Length	68 feet
Diameter	Approximately 5 feet
Propulsion	Single thrust chamber, jet vane controlled (no verniers), approximately 90,000 lbs. thrust, liquid oxygen/kerosene, two step thrust cutoff.
Configuration/Structure	Single stage ballistic, integral tankage.
Guidance	1956–1958 radio/inertial, 1958–1960, all inertial (retrofit optional).
Accuracy	1–2 n.m. CEP at 700 n.m. under average operational conditions.
Maximum Warhead Weight	Approximately 3,000 lbs., in a separating nosecone.
Ground Environment	Road Mobile

1,100 Nautical Mile Ballistic Missile System (SS–5)

11.[ ] a missile of about 1,100 n.m. maximum range has been under test at Kapustin Yar for over two years; since mid-1957 more than 40 such missiles have been test fired. There have been periods of high firing rate as well as periods of inactivity, the latter including one as long as nine months.[ ]the 1,100 n.m. missile could have become operational in late 1958 or early 1959, although no operational sites or units have been identified.

[2] For estimates of reliability and reaction times under various conditions for this and other systems discussed herein, see Annexes A and B.

[3] Date at which one or more missiles could have been placed in the hands of trained personnel in one operational unit.

12.[ ] There are indications of inertial components, of engine burning time, and of four combustion chambers in the engine. Like the V–2 and the 700 n.m. missile, this engine shuts down in two steps. Jet vanes are probably used for missile stabilization and control. We no longer believe that the 1,100 n.m. missile is essentially a modified 700 n.m. missile, although it would be in keeping with Soviet practice for this system to make maximum usage of proven components and designs from other programs.

13. On the basis of all available evidence, we estimate that the 1,100 n.m. system is operational and in production in the USSR, and that it probably has the following characteristics:

US Designation	SS-5
IOC Date	Late 1958 or early 1959
Maximum Range	1,100 n.m.
Propulsion	Four combustion chambers, liquid oxygen/kerosene, two step thrust cutoff, jet vane stabilization and control.
Configuration	Single stage ballistic
Guidance	Radio/inertial or all inertial
Accuracy	2 n.m. CEP at 1,100 n.m. under average operational conditions.
Maximum Warhead Weight	Approximately 3,000 lbs., in a separating nosecone.
Ground Environment	Road and/or rail mobile.

Intermediate Missile Systems of Longer Range

14. Assuming deployment within Soviet territory, 700 n.m. and 1,100 n.m. missiles are capable of reaching a large majority of critical targets in Eurasia and its periphery. It is possible that the USSR intends at a later date to develop a ballistic missile system with maximum range of about 1,500 to 2,500 n.m. to supplement existing target coverage and to permit deployment in more secure areas. In 1949, fairly early in the USSR's ballistic missile program, the Soviets instructed German missile specialists to make design studies on missiles with ranges as great as 1,600 n.m. We know of no further developmental work

on such missiles, and we do not believe there have been any test firings or preparations for firings to intermediate ranges of greater than 1,100 n.m. We conclude that an intermediate missile of longer range has had a fairly low priority. In any case, the initiation of test firings would probably precede first operational capability by 18 months to two years.

Intercontinental Ballistic Missile System (SS–6)

15. In our most recent estimate on Soviet development of ICBMs (NIE 11–4–58, paragraphs 125 and 126), we considered it probable that the USSR would achieve an initial operational capability with 10 prototype ICBMs at some time during the year 1959. We also held it to be possible, although unlikely, that a limited capability with comparatively unproven ICBMs might have been established in 1958. These conclusions rested on a variety of factors, including the estimated very high priority the USSR placed on achieving an ICBM capability for both political and military purposes, the estimated willingness of Soviet planners to accept considerable risks in initiating ICBM production and deployment, and the available evidence on Soviet test firings and capabilities in ballistic missile development.

16. We now have considerable additional knowledge of the ICBM test firing program, [ ] This evidence shows that during 1959 the test program has proceeded in an orderly manner which we believe is effectively testing a complete ICBM system. There is good evidence that from the beginning of the test firing program in 1957 until the present there have been well over a dozen ICBM test firings, a high percentage of which have been successful in traveling from the Tyura Tam rangehead over a distance of approximately 3,500 n.m. to the terminal end of the range in the Kamchatka Peninsula area. In the test program, since its inception in August 1957, we have observed periods of launching activity and inactivity, but the evidence is not sufficient to determine whether this was due to a setback in the program. Reanalysis of test firing patterns for both ICBM and shorter range missile systems leads us to believe that this periodicity of test firing activity is the Soviet method of conducting an orderly program. In any event, both the rate and number of ICBM test firings are lower than we had expected by this time.

17. *Operational Capability Dates.* Considering all the evidence, we believe it is now well established that the USSR is not engaged in a "crash" program for ICBM development. We therefore believe it extremely unlikely that an initial operational capability (IOC) was established early in the program with prototype missiles or with missiles of very doubtful performance characteristics.

18. On the other hand, we still consider it a logical course of action for the USSR to acquire a substantial ICBM capability at the earliest reasonable date. (The IOC for the ICBM marks the beginning of the planned buildup in operational capabilities and represents the date when the weapon system could be counted on to accomplish limited tasks in the event of war.) The hard evidence at hand does not establish whether or not series production of ICBMs has actually begun, nor does it confirm the existence of operational launching facilities. However, Khrushchev's statements of the winter of 1958–1959 regarding the establishment of ICBM series production are consistent with a logical decision to tool up for series production and to begin preparation of operational units and facilities before all technical aspects of the system had been fully demonstrated. Considering that production lead times are probably on the order of 12–18 months, we believe the USSR has had sufficient time to begin turning out series produced missiles.

19. In light of all the evidence, we believe that a Soviet IOC with a few—say, 10—series produced ICBMs is at least imminent, if in fact it has not already occurred. The evidence is insufficient, however, to support a precise estimate of IOC date. We believe that for

planning purposes it should be considered that by 1 January 1960 it will have occurred.[4]

20. The rate of operational buildup subsequent to IOC date would depend not only on the priority assigned, but also to a great degree on the planned force level. This will be discussed in the forthcoming NIE 11–8–59, "Soviet Capabilities for Strategic Attack Through Mid-1964."

21. *ICBM Performance Characteristics.* There is no direct information on the configuration of the Soviet ICBM and no conclusive intelligence regarding ICBM component testing, although Soviet statements indicate a positive relationship between the ICBM, space vehicles, and proven military hardware. Analysis of possible vehicles used in Sputnik [ ] indicates that the ICBM could be a one and one-half or parallel stage configuration but is probably not tandem. At this time we do not believe there is sufficient evidence to permit selection of a single most probable ICBM configuration.

22. [ ] Variations in the performance of Soviet ICBMs and space vehicles could be accounted for by modifications of one basic type of vehicle to accomplish specific purposes. It is also possible that some or all of the space vehicles do not specifically represent the basic ICBM, but were special purpose vehicles. While we cannot firmly relate any of these vehicles to the ICBM, the energy they required can be correlated to alternative ICBM warhead weights. An ICBM of a size sufficient to orbit Sputniks I and II would have a gross takeoff weight of about 350,000 pounds and could carry a warhead of 2,000–3,000 pounds in a heat-sink nosecone. An ICBM of a size sufficient to propel Sputnik III or Lunik would have a gross takeoff weight of about 500,000 pounds and could carry a warhead of 5,000–6,000 pounds. [ ]

23. While the evidence is not conclusive and we cannot eliminate the possibility of a lighter warhead, we believe the current Soviet ICBM is probably capable of delivering a warhead of about 6,000 pounds to a range of about 5,500 n.m. with a heat-sink nosecone configuration. A reduction in warhead weight from that used to 5,500 n.m. would permit an increase in range. For example, a range of about 7,500 n.m. could be achieved with a warhead of about 3,000 pounds with the same nosecone configuration. Since there is no firm evidence on whether the Soviet ICBM employs a heat-sink or ablative type nosecone, it must be noted that the ablative type would permit an even heavier warhead or extended range. Although we believe them to be within Soviet capabilities, neither radar camouflage of nosecone nor decoys have been detected in ICBM test firings to date.

24. We estimate ICBM guidance at IOC date to be a combination of radar track/radio command/inertial, although an all inertial system is possible (see paragraph 25). Soviet "state of the art" in precision radars, gyros and accelerometers leads us to estimate a theoretical CEP of about 3 n.m. at IOC at 5,500 n.m. range. Under operational conditions the theoretical CEP will be degraded by numerous factors, such as geodetic errors, insufficiently known weather and wind conditions in the target area, the inability of equipment to remain at peaked effectiveness for prolonged periods, variations in the tolerances of components, inexperienced personnel (especially at IOC and at new sites) and the pressure of combat conditions on the personnel. The

---

The Assistant to the Secretary of Defense, Special Operations; the Director for Intelligence, The Joint Staff; the Assistant Chief of Staff for Intelligence, Department of the Army; and the Assistant Chief of Naval Operations for Intelligence, Department of the Navy, believe that, in view of the orderly conduct of the Soviet ICBM test program (paragraph 16), as opposed to a "crash" program (paragraph 17), and in view of the fact that both the rate and number of ICBM firings, [ ] are lower than the intelligence community expected by this time (paragraph 16), the IOC will probably occur in the first half of 1960, with a possibility of its occurring in the latter part of 1959.

amount of degradation which would be introduced by such factors is unknown, but we estimate that CEP under operational conditions would be no greater than 5 n.m. at IOC date.

25. The guidance system and other factors would be improved so that under operational conditions a CEP of 3 n.m. in 1963 and 2 n.m. in 1966 is estimated as feasible. We have no knowledge as to Soviet intentions to retrofit inertial systems into ICBMs fabricated prior to operational adoption of an all inertial system, which could probably occur in the period 1960–1962.

26. Available evidence does not support the testing of more than one basic type of ICBM at Tyura Tam—the possible variations in range and warhead weight discussed in paragraph 23 could be accomplished with one basic missile.[5] Likewise, there is no evidence to indicate development of a second generation ICBM to replace that now being tested. If developed and tested in the future, such a missile would probably be designed to overcome certain operational difficulties and to permit simplified logistics. It might therefore be considerably smaller than the current system, taking advantage of improvements in the technology of construction, component design, warhead efficiency, fuels, and guidance.

27. *ICBM Ground Environment.* There is no firm evidence to indicate the Soviet concept of ICBM deployment or the nature of operational launching sites. From other ballistic missile systems it appears that mobility is a basic Soviet design consideration. The size, weight, complexity and mission of the ICBM, however, bring new factors to bear on launching system and site parameters.

28. As opposed to the advantages of hard or soft fixed site systems, a mobile system can reduce vulnerability by making site location and identification more difficult. Eliminating road mobile systems as being infeasible for the Soviet ICBM, we believe a rail mobile system, using special railroad rolling stock and presurveyed and preconstructed sites, to have certain advantages and disadvantages. So long as a multiplicity of sites existed, a rail mobile system would increase flexibility, decrease vulnerability and reduce the opportunity for enemy knowledge of occupied sites. On the other hand, missile system reliability might be reduced and sizable special trains would be required. The number and type of cars would depend on the size and configuration of the missile and the amount of fixed equipment installed at each of the prepared sites. The permanent installation at the launching site in such a rail system could be no more than a concrete slab on a special spur, but might include other facilities such as a small liquid oxygen facility, missile checkout building, missile erecting equipment, etc.

29. The available evidence suggests that the Soviet ICBM could be rail mobile; it is insufficient to establish whether the system as a whole will consist of rail mobile units, fixed installations, or a combination of the two. Whatever ground environment is selected, however, the Soviet rail network will play a central role in the operational deployment and logistic support of the ICBM system.

30. *ICBM System Summary.* In summary, we estimate that an ICBM is probably now in

[5] The Assistant Chief of Staff, Intelligence, USAF believes that the ICBM currently undergoing tests at Tyura Tam is a follow-on weapon. A possible correlation of 700/1,100 n.m. missile tests at the Kapustin Yar missile test center and ICBM/space vehicle firings at Tyura Tam can be made. Chronologically the 700 n.m. missile firings, the early Soviet space launchings (Sputnik I and II), and the successful ICBM firings from August 1957 to May 1958, could be related to the objective of developing an ICBM with a gross weight of approximately 350,000 pounds, carrying a 2,000 pound warhead to a range of 5,500 n.m. A similar chronological correlation emerges from analysis of the test firings of the 1,100 n.m. missile, the later Soviet space ventures (Sputnik III and Lunik) and the most recent run of successful ICBM test firings (January 1959 to date). If the initial success of the ICBM were derived from extensive 700 n.m. subsystem testing and experience gained from Sputniks I and II, the similar pattern of activity with respect to Kapustin Yar test firings of the 1,100 n.m. missile, Sputnik III, Lunik, and the most recent successful run of ICBM firings would suggest a follow-on R&D program of a missile designed for greater warhead weight and accuracy.

series production in the USSR, and that an IOC with a few—say, 10—series produced missiles is at least imminent. Probable characteristics of the system are estimated as follows:

US Designation	SS-6
IOC Date	See Paragraph 19
Maximum Range ...	5,500 n.m. with 6,000 lb. warhead
Propulsion	Liquid oxygen/kerosene, single-step final stage shutoff, and large verniers.
Configuration	One and one-half or parallel staging
Guidance	Probably radar track/radio command/inertial. All inertial could probably be available in 1960–1962.
Accuracy	CEP not greater than 5 n.m. at 5,500 n.m. under average operational conditions at IOC date; improvable to 3 n.m. in 1963 and 2 n.m. in 1966.
Maximum Warhead Weight	Probably 6,000 lbs. at 5,500 n.m. range
Ground Environment	Rail mobile and/or fixed installations

SUBMARINE-LAUNCHED MISSILE SYSTEMS

31. There is little evidence of research and development associated with specific missile systems for Soviet naval application, although there have been sporadic reports of possible launchings of missiles or rockets in the various Soviet fleet areas. [

]

32. Since 1955 there have been sightings of "W" class and smaller submarines with capsules and/or launcher-like structures on their decks. These included an excellent sighting in Leningrad in 1956 of a submarine with a capsule and launching ramp. It is probable that a few "W" class submarines have been converted to carry subsonic cruise type missiles having a maximum operational range of 150–200 n.m. and a low altitude cruise capability. Some smaller submarines have possibly been converted as well. Two such missiles can be carried in a deck capsule and launched from a ramp. Characteristics of the system are approximately as follows:

US Designation	SS-7
IOC Date	1955–1956
Maximum range of missiles	150–200 n.m.
Number per submarine	2
Launching condition	Surfaced
Guidance	Programmed with doppler assist, possibly with homing
Accuracy	2–4 n.m. CEP under operational conditions; 150–500 feet with homing.
Maximum Warhead Weight	2,000 lb.

33. Since 1956 there have been a few sightings and photographs of "Z" class submarines with greatly enlarged sails. Since 1958, three such submarines have been observed with two dome-shaped covers in the after portion of the enlarged sail. These submarines may have been modified for carrying and launching ballistic missiles. If so, an initial operational capability with at least three submarines has existed since mid-1958. Small numbers of modified "Z" class submarines are now in both the Northern and Pacific Fleet areas. Such submarines could carry two missiles each, but could probably launch them only while fully surfaced. The missile might have a range of about 200 n.m., a warhead weighing about 1,000 pounds, and a CEP under average operational conditions of 2–4 n.m. at maximum range.

34. There is inconclusive evidence that the Soviets are developing an advanced submarine/ballistic missile system. None of the small amount of evidence available concerns development of an associated missile itself. Based mainly on estimated Soviet requirements and technical capabilities, we believe

20. (continued)

the USSR will probably develop a submarine/ballistic missile system having the following characteristics:

US Designation	SS–9
IOC Date	1961–1963
Maximum range of missiles	500–1,000 n.m.
Number per submarine	6–12
Launching condition	Submerged or surfaced
Propellant	Solid or storable liquid
Guidance	All inertial
Accuracy	2–4 n.m. CEP under operational conditions
Maximum Warhead Weight	About 1,000 pounds

~~TOP SECRET~~

ANNEX A

ESTIMATED MISSILE RELIABILITIES

For several years after an IOC, the reliability of a missile system will probably improve, and then level off. Although we have little information on which to base an estimate of the operational reliability of Soviet missiles, the following are considered reasonable estimates.

US DESIGNATION	IN-COMMISSION RATE [1]	RELIABILITY	
		On launcher [2]	In flight [3]
SS-4	85	90	80
SS-5 at IOC	75	85	75
IOC plus 3 yrs	85	95	80
SS-6 at IOC	70	80	50
IOC plus 3 yrs	80	90	75
SS-7	Not applicable [4]	80	75
SS-9 at IOC		80	60
IOC plus 3 yrs	Not applicable [4]	90	75

[1] Percentage of national operational inventory considered "good enough to try" to launch at any given time.

[2] Percentage of those missiles in operational units considered "good enough to try" to launch that will actually get off the launcher when fired.

[3] Percentage of those missiles that get off the launcher that will actually reach the *vicinity* of the target, i.e., perform within the designed specifications of the missile system.

[4] In these categories, only those missiles considered "good enough to try" to launch will be loaded on submarines.

~~TOP SECRET~~ 9

~~TOP SECRET~~

ANNEX B

ESTIMATED REACTION TIMES

The reaction times of Soviet missile units would vary according to the type of missile, the location (on or off site), and degree of alert. In the absence of information we consider the following are reasonable estimates:

Reaction Times, Ground-launched Systems

a. For units in transit at the time of alert, the following times are estimated for the launching of the first missile after the unit has arrived at the prepared launching site:

SS-4—SS-5	2-4 hours
SS-6	4-12 hours

b. The following reaction times are estimated for the SS-4 through SS-6 when the missile unit is in place at a launching site under the alert condition indicated:

Case I —Crews on routine standby, electrical equipment cold, missiles not fueled but could have been checked out recently.
Reaction time 2-4 hours

Case II —Crews on alert, electrical equipment warmed up, missiles not fueled.
Reaction time 15-30 minutes

Case III—Crews on alert, electrical equipment warmed up, missiles fueled and occasionally topped. This ready-to-fire condition probably could not be maintained for more than 10-15 hours.
Reaction time 5-15 minutes

Naval Systems—While on station the reaction time for shipboard surface-to-surface missiles would be short. We estimate about 15 minutes for a submarine that must launch surfaced (SS-7), with an additional 7 minutes to launch a second missile, about 15 minutes or less for a submarine that can launch submerged (SS-9).

~~TOP SECRET~~ 10

21.

~~SECRET~~

No. 1391/64

CENTRAL INTELLIGENCE AGENCY

18 JUNE 1964

MEMORANDUM

SUBJECT: The Soviet Reconnaissance Satellite Program

A Soviet military reconnaissance satellite program appears to be well under way with possibly as many as 12 flights since 1962. The program uses recoverable vehicles launched from Tyuratam under the mantle of the Cosmos series. [redacted] The program is expensive, possibly costing as much as 500 to 700 million dollars so far, and places added demands on resources available for Soviet space programs. A requirement for precise targeting information on US targets, not obtainable through other collection means, seems to be the primary reason for the program. Also, Soviet collection of other military intelligence on the US could be usefully supplemented by satellite photography. Khrushchev's open acknowledgments of the program have been aimed at stopping U-2 flights over Cuba, but also imply a desire for a tacit understanding on reconnaissance satellites. The existence of the Soviet program tends to reduce the likelihood of a Soviet attempt to attack a US satellite.

* * * * * * * *

1. We have concluded that the Soviet military reconnaissance satellite program may have involved as many as 12 flights since 1962. The evidence is convincing that these were military reconnaissance satellites, although they may have had additional missions. Their launch times and orbits were ideally

---

Prepared jointly by the Directorate of Science and Technology and the Directorate of Intelligence.

~~SECRET~~

suited for reconnaissance coverage of the US during daylight hours, the payload was recovered, they were earth oriented and stabilized within the requirements of a sophisticated camera system, and telemetry from them reflected payload activity like that of a reconnaissance photographic payload.

2. A study of the 16 Cosmos satellites successfully launched from Tyuratam between 26 April 1962 and 10 June 1964 leads us to believe that four of them were military reconnaissance satellites, eight others probably were, and four probably were not.

3.

4. Moscow has held that the purpose of the Cosmos series, which began in March 1962, was to collect scientific data. It became clear, however, that different types of vehicles were being launched from two different rangeheads, Kapustin Yar and Tyuratam, and the characteristics of the 14 satellites successfully orbited from Kapustin Yar rule out a reconnaissance mission.

5. The 16 successful Cosmos operations from Tyuratam which we have examined are believed to have used

All were recovered in the Soviet Union three to ten days after launching. The most recent in the series, Cosmos 32, had an inclination of 51 degrees to the equator, while all previous Tyuratam Cosmos satellites had inclinations of 65 degrees. This change suggests that the Soviets are improving their reconnaissance program because the inclination of Cosmos 32 permitted greater coverage of the US each day.

-2-

~~SECRET~~

21. (continued)

6. The series launched from Tyuratam may have had other missions in addition to photographic reconnaissance.

7. We have identified most of the Tyuratam satellites

-3-

SECRET

21. (continued)

~~SECRET~~

f.

g.

h. Soviet statements: Khrushchev himself has alluded to Soviet satellite reconnaissance on several occasions. In 1963, he told Belgian Foreign Minister Spaak that the Soviets were engaged in photographing the United States and that he could produce the photographs to prove it Former Senator Benton also quoted Khrushchev as saying, during their recent meeting in Moscow, that Soviet space cameras have filmed US military installations.

8. If we are correct in concluding that most of the Cosmos satellites launched from Tyuratam have a reconnaissance mission, it would seem that Moscow is devoting a substantial share of its space effort to the collection of military intelligence. [According to preliminary estimates based on the costs of US scientific satellites, the cost of Tyuratam Cosmos operations to date may have amounted to the equivalent of about 700 million to one billion dollars, roughly 20 percent of total expenditures estimated for all observed Soviet space programs. As a rough proportion of this estimate, the costs of a military reconnaissance program including the 12 satellites launched so far would be on the order of 500 to 700 million dollars.]

-4-

~~SECRET~~

~~SECRET~~

9. Also important is the additional strain imposed on the human and material resources available for Soviet space programs by the demands of a reconnaissance program.

10. We believe that the USSR has made this large investment primarily for missile targeting purposes. Strategic missile systems require precise information on the geodetic relationship of the target to the launch point, particularly in the case of hardened targets. The precise targeting information needed on the hundreds of targets in the US is only obtainable by satellite photography.

11. Despite the USSR's comparatively easy access to much information on military weapons and installations in the US it has requirements for military reconnaissance satellites beyond those for targeting data.

a.

-5-

~~SECRET~~

~~SECRET~~

12. In view of Soviet activity in the reconnaissance satellite field, Moscow may be more tolerant of similar US programs than it has been in the past. Khrushchev's recent open acknowledgment of both US and Soviet efforts tends to bear this out. Although his immediate objective in these remarks has been to secure a cessation of U-2 flights over Cuba, they suggest a desire on his part for a tacit understanding with the US on reconnaissance satellites.

13. We believe that the Soviets intend to develop an antisatellite capability. [redacted] In our view, however, the existence of a Soviet reconnaissance satellite program tends to reduce the likelihood of a Soviet attempt to destroy or neutralize a US satellite.

-6-

~~SECRET~~

SOVIET CAPABILITIES FOR STRATEGIC ATTACK

THE PROBLEM

To estimate probable trends in the strength and deployment of Soviet forces for strategic attack and in Soviet capabilities for such attack through mid-1970.

SCOPE NOTE

This estimate covers those Soviet military forces which are suitable for strategic attack. Other major aspects of the Soviet military strength are treated in separate estimates on air and missile defense, on theater forces, on the nuclear program, and on the space program. Trends in the USSR's overall military posture and in Soviet military policy are examined in an annual estimate, the next issuance of which will be in the first quarter of 1965.

SUMMARY AND CONCLUSIONS

A. Major changes in Soviet programs for the development of strategic attack forces have become apparent during the past year. In 1962–1963, certain ICBM and ballistic missile submarine programs came to an end, and a pause ensued in the growth of these forces. At the same time, the pace of ICBM research and development increased markedly. More recently, the USSR has resumed ICBM deployment in a new and improved configuration, and the probable advent of a new submarine which we believe is designed to carry ballistic missiles probably marks the start of yet another deployment program. (*Para. 1*)

B. Soviet military policy in recent years has been to build up strategic offensive and defensive capabilities, maintain and improve large general purpose forces, and pursue research and development programs in advanced weapons. In our view, the primary concern of Soviet military policy for the next several years will continue to be the strengthening of the USSR's strategic deterrent. The evidence to date does not indicate that Soviet deployment programs are directed toward a rapid numerical buildup. We do not believe that the USSR aims at matching the US in numbers of intercontinental delivery vehicles. Recognition that the US would detect and match or overmatch such an effort, together with economic constraints, appears to have ruled out this option. (*Paras. 2–4*)

C. A stress on qualitative factors suggests that the Soviets see technological advance in weapons as a means by which they can improve their strategic position relative to the West. In the ICBM force, for example, major qualitative improvements currently being achieved include hardening and dispersal (which will sharply increase the number of aiming points), as well as better accuracy and larger payloads. (*Paras. 4–5*)

D. By the end of the decade, Soviet intercontinental attack capabilities will rest primarily upon an ICBM force of some hundreds of launchers, supplemented by a sizable missile-submarine fleet and a large but reduced bomber force. These forces will represent a marked improvement in Soviet retaliatory capability and a considerable strengthening of the Soviet deterrent. In the light of current and programmed US military capabilities, however, we do not believe that the Soviets will expect to achieve, within the period of this estimate, strategic attack capabilities which would make rational the deliberate initiation of general war. (*Para. 5*)

The ICBM Program

E. Major developments since mid-1963 include a proliferation of test facilities at Tyuratam, flight-testing of two third-generation ICBM systems (the SS–9 and SS–10), and the beginning of construction of hard, single-silo ICBM launchers, probably for one or both of the new systems. The deployment of second-generation ICBMs has probably ceased, and a pause between the second- and third-generation programs has slowed deployment. We believe that the Soviets now have about 200 operational ICBM launchers, and that the total number of operational launchers in mid-1965 will approximate the low side of the 250–350 range previously estimated. These figures do not include R&D launchers at Tyuratam.[1] (*Paras. 6–8, 10–18, 31*)

F. Research and development on third-generation systems has been generally successful. The SS–9 system appears to be an outgrowth of the SS–7 with improved accuracy and a larger payload. We have little information on the characteristics of the SS–10. Both new systems could enter service in 1965. We believe that work is underway on still other ICBM systems, which we cannot as yet identify. We continue to believe that the Soviets are developing a very large ICBM, capable of delivering [ ] We estimate that it could enter service in the period mid-1966 to mid-1967. In addition, the Soviets might be developing a new, small ICBM employing improved propellants. If they are, it could become operational as early as 1967. (*Paras. 19–26*)

G. The Soviets are now emphasizing deployment of single-silo hard launchers for ICBMs, and we expect this emphasis to continue. We expect third-generation deployment to include the expansion of both second-generation complexes and the initiation of additional new complexes. (*Paras. 9, 27*)

H. The growth of the Soviet ICBM force over the next several years will be influenced by a number of factors. In economic terms, the program must compete for funds with other military and space activities and with the civilian economy. In the technical field, we believe that research and development is proceeding on additional, follow-on ICBM systems, and we doubt that with these in the offing the USSR will fix upon any one or even two existing systems for urgent deployment on a large scale. We are also mindful that the interruptions that marked second-generation deployment programs may recur. In strategic terms, the Soviets evidently judge that an ICBM force in the hundreds of launchers, together with their other strategic forces, provides a deterrent. On the basis of the evidence now available, to us, we do not believe that they are attempting to deploy a force capable of a first-strike which would reduce the effects of US

[1] The Assistant Chief of Staff, Intelligence, USAF, considers the estimate of the numbers of launchers operational now and expected in mid-1965 is too low. He estimates that the Soviets now have about 240 operational launchers, including about 20 at Tyuratam and a 10 percent allowance for unlocated launchers. He believes the total number in mid-1965 will be between 275 and 325. See his footnote, page 11, para. 10.

retaliation to an acceptable level.[2] At the same time, we expect them to continue a vigorous R&D effort in the hope of achieving important technological advances, in both the offensive and defensive fields, which would alter the present strategic relationship in a major way. (*Para. 30*)

I. We estimate a Soviet ICBM force of 400–700 operational launchers for mid-1970; in our previous estimate, we projected this force level for mid-1969. By mid-1970, we believe that the force will include most or all of the launchers now deployed, some 125–200 single-silo SS-9/10 launchers, and 10–20 launchers for very large ICBMs. We believe that the attainment of as many as 700 operational launchers by mid-1970 would be likely only if the Soviets begin deploying a new, small ICBM at a rapid rate about 1967. The Soviet ICBM force which we estimate for mid-1970 will represent a substantial increase in numbers and deliverable megatonnage. Further, the trend to single silos will increase the number of aiming points represented by individual launch sites from about 100 at present to some 300–575 in mid-1970, the bulk of them hard. This will greatly improve the survivability, and hence the retaliatory capability, of the force.[3] (*Paras. 32–37*)

J. In the past few years the Soviets have improved the readiness and reaction time of their ICBM force. Our evidence now indicates that from the normal state of readiness, the soft sites which constitute the bulk of the present force would require 1–3 hours to fire. Hard sites would require about half an hour or less. A higher state of alert (i.e., 5–15 minutes to fire) can be maintained at most soft sites for a number of hours and at most hard sites for days. (*Paras. 38–40*)

K. There is ample evidence that the Soviets designed their soft ICBM systems to have a refire capability. We have re-examined the

[2] The Assistant Chief of Staff, Intelligence, USAF, considers that the Soviets may already have directed their intensive military R&D effort toward achievement of an effective first-strike counter-force capability before the close of this decade. Considering the length of time covered by this estimate and the number of unknowns involved, he believes this is a possibility which should not be disregarded.

[3] The Assistant Chief of Staff, Intelligence, USAF, considers the ICBM force by mid-1970 could range from approximately 600 to as high as 900 operational launchers depending on whether a new, small, easily deployed system is introduced. (See his footnote to table on page 18.) An ICBM force of this size would increase the number of aiming points represented by individual launch sites to approximately 400–700 in mid-1970.

factors likely to affect refire time, and conclude that it would require little longer to fire the second missile than the first. Our present estimate of refire time is 2–4 hours, considerably less than previously estimated. We believe that, on the average, two or more missiles are provided per soft launcher for initial firing, refire, and maintenance spares. We believe that hard ICBM sites do not have a refire capability. (*Paras. 41–43*)

L. We have little evidence on the hardness of Soviet ICBM sites. Given the many uncertainties in this area, only a very tenuous estimate can be made, but our best judgment is that Soviet hard ICBM sites have a hardness in the 300–600 psi range. This implies a design overpressure in the 200–400 psi range, somewhat higher than previously estimated.[4] (*Paras. 49–50*)

M. Qualitative improvements in the force can be expected as new ICBM systems enter service. Currently operational ICBMs have CEPs on the order of 1–2 n.m. The SS–9 will probably have an accuracy of 0.5–1.0 n.m. with radio assist, or 1.0–1.5 with all-inertial guidance. By mid-1970, the Soviets could achieve accuracies on the order of 0.5 n.m. or better. The SS–9 will probably carry a payload [ ] as compared with [ ] for second-generation ICBMs. We do not believe that the Soviets have yet developed penetration aids or multiple warheads, but they may do so in the future, particularly if the US deploys antimissile defenses. (*Paras. 44–48*)

MRBMs and IRBMs

N. Deployment programs for the 1,020 n.m. MRBM and the 2,200 n.m. IRBM are now ending, and almost certainly will be completed by mid-1965. We estimate that at that time the MRBM/IRBM force will have a strength of about 760 operational launchers, 145 of them hard. The bulk of the force (about 90 percent) is deployed in western USSR, with the remainder in the southern and far eastern regions of the USSR. This force is capable of delivering a devastating first strike or a powerful retaliatory attack against targets in Eurasia, and can attack such areas as Greenland and Alaska as well. Some of the

[4] The Assistant Chief of Staff, Intelligence, USAF, considers that, given the uncertainties involved, no meaningful estimate of the hardness of Soviet hard sites can be made. However, he believes that the design overpressure of Soviet hard sites is no greater than the 100–300 psi previously estimated.

MRBM/IRBM launchers are probably intended to support ground operations. (*Paras. 51–55*)

O. We doubt that the Soviets will expand their MRBM/IRBM force during the period of this estimate. It is possible, however, that operational capabilities will be improved by the introduction of a new missile system, which probably would be deployed in single-silos. Such a system, employing improved propellants, could become operational in the 1966–1968 period and would probably replace some of the soft launchers now operational. (*Paras. 56–59*)

Missile Submarine Forces

P. The Soviets now have operational some 40–50 ballistic missile submarines, including 8–10 nuclear powered. Most of these submarines are equipped with 350 n.m. missiles and must surface to fire. One or two are equipped with a new 700 n.m. submerged-launch missile, and others will probably be retrofitted. The USSR also has operational about 30 cruise-missile submarines, including 11–14 nuclear powered. The majority are equipped with 300 n.m. missiles designed for low altitude attack, primarily against ships. The remainder carry a newer 450 n.m. version of this missile, which probably has an improved capability to attack land targets. Current Soviet missile submarines carry relatively few missiles: the ballistic missile classes, two or three, and the cruise missile types, up to eight. The entire present force has a total of 120–140 ballistic missile tubes and 135–150 cruise-missile launchers. (*Paras. 60–71*)

Q. We believe that the Soviets have under construction a submarine which we estimate to be the first of a new nuclear-powered, ballistic missile class. We estimate that it will employ the submerged-launch 700 n.m. missile, and have a few more missile tubes than current classes. The first unit will probably become operational in 1965. Beyond this new class, we consider it unlikely that the Soviets will develop an entirely new follow-on ballistic missile submarine system within the period of this estimate, although they will probably continue to improve existing systems. We believe that they will also continue to construct cruise-missile submarines. By mid-1970 the Soviet missile submarine force will probably number 100–130 ships, about half of them cruise-missile submarines and about half ballistic. (*Paras. 72–75*)

R. In the past year, limited numbers of Soviet missile submarines have engaged in patrols in the open oceans. We expect a gradual expansion of this activity. By the end of the decade, Soviet missile submarines will probably be conducting regular patrols throughout the North Atlantic and Pacific, and possibly into the Mediterranean. (*Para. 76*)

Long-Range Bomber Forces

S. We have no recent evidence of major changes in the capabilities and structure of Soviet Long-Range Aviation (LRA). The force now includes some 190–220 heavy bombers and tankers and 850–900 mediums. It is being improved primarily through the continued introduction of Blinder supersonic dash medium bombers and through modification of older bombers for air-to-surface missile delivery, for aerial refueling, and for reconnaissance. Use of both medium and heavy bombers of the LRA in support of maritime operations has increased. (*Paras. 80–86*)

T. Considering noncombat attrition factors and the requirements for Arctic staging and aerial refueling, we estimate that the Soviets could put somewhat more than 100 heavy bombers over target areas in the US on two-way missions. Recent trends lead us to believe that medium bombers do not now figure prominently in Soviet plans for an initial bomber attack against North America. Nevertheless, should they elect to do so, we believe that at present the Soviets could put up to 150 Badgers over North American target areas on two-way missions. We have serious doubt about how effectively the Soviets could launch large-scale bomber operations against North America. We consider it probable that initial attacks would not be simultaneous, but would extend over a considerable number of hours.[6] (*Paras. 91–97*)

U. The Soviets will probably maintain sizable bomber forces, which will decrease gradually through attrition and retirement. Although continued Soviet work on advanced transports could be applied to military purposes, we think it unlikely that the Soviets will bring any follow-on heavy bomber into operational service during the period

[6] The Assistant Chief of Staff, Intelligence, USAF, considers this paragraph seriously underestimates the manned aircraft threat to the continental US. In the event war should eventuate and the USSR attacks the US with nuclear weapons, he believes this will be an all-out effort aimed at putting a maximum number of weapons on US targets. He therefore estimates that the number of heavy and medium bombers, including BADGERS on one-way missions, could exceed 500. See his footnote on page 32, para. 94.

of this estimate. We believe that Blinder medium bombers, some equipped with advanced air-to-surface missiles, will be introduced during much of the period of this estimate. By mid-1970, Long-Range Aviation will probably include some 140–180 heavy bombers of present types and 300–500 mediums, mostly Blinders.[6] (*Paras. 87–90*)

Space Weapons

V. Although the USSR almost certainly is investigating the feasibility of space systems for use as offensive and defensive weapons, we have no evidence that a program to establish an orbital bombardment capability is seriously contemplated by the Soviet leadership. We think that orbital weapons will not compare favorably with ICBMs over the next six years in terms of effectiveness, reaction time, targeting flexibility, vulnerability, average life, and positive control. In view of these considerations, the much greater cost of orbital weapon systems, and Soviet endorsement of the UN resolution against nuclear weapons in space, we believe that the Soviets are unlikely to develop and deploy an orbital weapon system within the period of this estimate. (*Paras. 98–103*)

[6] The Assistant Chief of Staff, Intelligence, USAF, believes the Soviets will continue to consider manned strategic aircraft an important adjunct to their ICBM force. He estimates that the USSR will introduce a follow-on heavy bomber. He further estimates the heavy bomber force will remain at about 200 or somewhat larger, depending on the timing of the expected follow-on bomber, and that by mid-1970 the medium bomber/tanker force will probably still include about 650–850 aircraft. See his footnote to table on page 31 following para. 90.

23.

~~TOP SECRET~~

SOVIET STRATEGIC AIR AND MISSILE DEFENSES

THE PROBLEM

To estimate the capabilities and limitations of Soviet strategic air and missile defense forces through mid-1967, and general trends in these forces through 1975.

CONCLUSIONS

A. Confronted by powerful Western strategic attack forces, the USSR is sustaining its vigorous effort to strengthen its defenses. We believe that the Soviets are responding to those challenges to their security that they can now see or foresee from aircraft, ballistic missiles, and earth satellites. (*Paras. 1-5*)

Air Defenses

B. The Soviets have achieved a formidable capability against aircraft attacking at medium and high altitudes, but their air defense system probably is still susceptible to penetration by stand-off weapons and low-altitude tactics. The Soviets probably foresee little reduction in the bomber threat over the next ten years. To meet this challenge, they are improving their warning and control systems and are changing the character of their interceptor force through the introduction of new high-performance, all-weather aircraft. In addition, there are recent indications that the Soviets are now employing light AAA in some areas for low-altitude defense. (*Paras. 3, 4, 8-19*)

C. The Soviets probably will continue to improve and to rely on the SA-2 as the principal SAM system. We believe that they will develop an improved or new SAM system for low altitude defense; such a system would probably be deployed more extensively than the SA-3. Deployment of a long-range SAM system probably is now

~~TOP SECRET~~

underway in the northwestern USSR and probably will be extended to other peripheral areas and to some key urban locations in the interior.[1 2] (*Paras. 20-26*)

Ballistic Missile Defenses

D. For nearly ten years, the Soviets have given high priority to research and development of antimissile defenses. We estimate that they have now begun to deploy such defenses at Moscow. These defenses could probably achieve some capability as early as 1967, but we think a more likely date for an initial operational capability is 1968. We do not yet know the performance characteristics of this system, or how it will function. (*Paras. 27-34*)

E. The Soviets will almost certainly continue with their extensive effort to develop ballistic missile defenses to counter the increasingly sophisticated threat that will be posed by US strategic missile forces. We cannot now estimate with confidence the scale or timing of future Soviet ABM deployment. We believe, however, that the Soviets will deploy ABM defenses for major urban-industrial areas. By 1975, they could deploy defenses for some 20 to 30 areas containing a quarter of the Soviet population and more than half of Soviet industry. (*Paras. 36-37*)

Antisatellite Defenses

F. The Soviets could already have developed a limited antisatellite capability based on an operational missile with a nuclear warhead and existing electronic capabilities. We have no evidence that they have

[1] Lieutenant General Joseph F. Carroll, USAF Director, Defense Intelligence Agency, Major General John J. Davis, the Assistant Chief of Staff, Intelligence, US Army, and Major General Jack E. Thomas, Assistant Chief of Staff, Intelligence, US Air Force, believe that the many uncertainties stemming from analysis of available evidence does not permit a confident judgment as to the specific mission of the new defensive systems being deployed in northwest USSR. They acknowledge that available evidence does support a conclusion that the sites in the northwest may be intended for defense against the aerodynamic threat. However, on balance, considering all the evidence, they believe it is more likely that the systems being deployed at these sites are primarily for defense against ballistic missiles.

[2] Rear Admiral Rufus L. Taylor, Assistant Chief of Naval Operations (Intelligence), Department of the Navy, and Lieutenant General Marshall S. Carter, USA, Director, National Security Agency, do not concur in the degree of confidence reflected in this judgment. Although they concur that the deployment activity is more likely a long range SAM system than an ABM system, they believe that the evidence at this time is such that a confident judgment is premature.

done so. In any event, we believe that the Soviets would prefer to have a system which could track foreign satellites more accurately and permit the use of non-nuclear kill mechanisms. We estimate that the Soviets will have an operational capability with such a system within the next few years. We believe, however, that the Soviets would attack a US satellite in peacetime only if, along with a strong desire for secrecy, they were willing for other reasons to greatly disrupt East-West relations.[3] (*Paras. 38-41*)

[3] Mr. Thomas L. Hughes, the Director of Intelligence and Research, Department of State, believes that the Soviets would conclude that the adverse consequences of destroying or damaging US satellites in peacetime would outweigh the advantages of such an action. He therefore believes it highly unlikely that they would attack US satellites in peacetime.

24.

SOVIET MILITARY RESEARCH AND DEVELOPMENT

THE PROBLEM

To assess the scope and nature of Soviet military research and development (R&D), to estimate the types of weapon and space systems likely to emerge from that effort in the next few years, and to discuss factors that will affect the course of Soviet military R&D over the longer term.

CONCLUSIONS

A. Military research and development (R&D) has been and will continue to be one of the highest priority undertakings in the USSR. The Soviets regard such an effort as imperative in order to prevent the US from gaining a technological advantage, to gain, if possible, some advantage for themselves, and to strengthen the technological base of Soviet power. Most Soviet military R&D is directed toward the qualitative improvement of existing kinds of weapon systems, but we believe that much is also devoted to the investigation of a broad range of new and advanced technologies having potential military applications.

B. With the rapid technological advance of the postwar era, there has been a great expansion in the funds, personnel, and facilities devoted to military R&D and the space program. We estimate that between 1950 and 1966 expenditures for these purposes increased tenfold. It is impossible to make a precise comparison of US and Soviet expenditures; our analysis suggests that if Soviet military R&D and space programs at their present levels were purchased in the US, they would generate an approximate annual expenditure more than three-fourths the amount of US outlays for the same purposes. And the Soviet effort rests on a considerably smaller economic base.

C. Soviet advanced research in fields applicable to military developments is probably now about equal to that of the West. Despite excellent theoretical work, however, Soviet military hardware frequently has not reflected the most advanced state-of-the-art in the USSR. In large part, this can be attributed to a conservative design philosophy which emphasizes proven technology and favors rugged, relatively simple equipment. In part, however, this Soviet choice may have been forced by deficiencies in manufacturing and fabrication techniques. Soviet production technology generally lags behind that of the US, although the Soviets are taking steps to correct these deficiencies.

D. It is almost certain that the Soviets have some type of R&D underway in every important field of military technology. Stringent Soviet security practices normally prevent us from detecting military R&D at the laboratory or drawing board stage. We can, however, detect major weapon systems during testing or early deployment. On the basis of evidence of development activity, our judgment of Soviet requirements, and other considerations, we can make estimates concerning the next generation of major Soviet weapon systems. We cannot estimate, however, the specific weapons which the Soviets will develop for introduction in the longer term, 10 or more years from now.

E. Soviet expenditures for R&D are continuing to grow, but the trend is showing a declining rate of growth, probably because the most costly stages of expansion have been finished. With the higher base level thus achieved, a slower growth rate still implies substantial annual increments. We estimate that total R&D expenditures—for military and civilian R&D and the space program together—will increase by about 7 or 8 percent annually through 1970. If, as we estimate, the Soviet space effort is leveling off, even this moderate growth rate would permit an increase in allocations to civilian R&D and continuation of a strong military R&D effort.

F. The Soviets will continue to press their search for new technologies and systems that offer the prospect of improving their strategic situation. We see no areas at present where Soviet technology is significantly ahead of that of the US. Considering the size and quality of the Soviet R&D effort, however, it is possible that the USSR could move ahead of the US in some particular field of strategic importance. The Soviet leaders would certainly seek to exploit any significant technological advance for political and military advantage, but in deciding to deploy any new weapon system they would have to weigh the prospective gain against the economic costs and the capabilities of the US to counter it.

25.

CONFIDENTIAL

PAGE:0336

13 MARCH 1986.

KEY JUDGMENTS: SOVIET LASER CHEMISTRY RESEARCH AND APPLICATIONS

SINCE THE EARLY 1960S THE SOVIETS HAVE PIONEERED THE FIELD OF LASER CHEMISTRY IN WHICH A LASER IS USED TO INFLUENCE OR DIRECT A CHEMICAL REACTION. TWENTY YEARS OF CONTINUOUS RESEARCH HAS GIVEN THE SOVIETS SCIENTIFIC RECOGNITION AS WORLD LEADERS IN THIS SCIENCE AND A TECHNOLOGICAL BASE FOR DEVELOPING SIGNIFICANT INDUSTRIAL APPLICATIONS IN ELECTRONICS, CHEMICAL ENGINEERING, PROCESS CONTROL, AND GENETIC ENGINEERING.

---

1. KEY JUDGMENTS: SOVIET LASER CHEMISTRY RESEARCH AND APPLICATIONS

THE FOLLOWING KEY JUDGMENTS ARE REPRINTED FROM A

CONFIDENTIAL

25. (continued)

CONFIDENTIAL

PAGE:0337

RECENTLY PUBLISHED SCIENTIFIC AND TECHNICAL INTELLIGENCE REPORT PRODUCED BY THE OFFICE OF SCIENTIFIC AND WEAPONS RESEARCH.

WE BELIEVE SOVIET BASIC RESEARCH IN LASER CHEMISTRY IS EQUAL TO OR AHEAD OF US RESEARCH IN MOST AREAS. OUR JUDGMENT IS FORMED PRIMARILY FROM ANALYSIS OF OPEN-LITERATURE PUBLICATIONS BY SOVIET SCIENTISTS LASER CHEMISTRY IS A TECHNOLOGICAL BASE FOR THE DEVELOPMENT OF NUCLEAR POWER AND WEAPONS, ELECTRONICS, CHEMICAL ENGINEERING, PROCESS CONTROL, AND GENETIC ENGINEERING.

IN LASER CHEMISTRY, LASER LIGHT IS USED TO PROMOTE CHANGES IN THE PHYSICAL OR CHEMICAL PROPERTIES OF MATTER. THESE CHANGES CAN PRODUCE NEW CHEMICAL COMPOUNDS, HIGHER YIELDS IN PROCESSES FOR MAKING CONVENTIONAL COMPOUNDS, OR COMPOUNDS WITH PROPERTIES NOT EASILY OBTAINED THROUGH CONVENTIONAL CHEMISTRY. LASER CHEMISTRY CAN ALSO BE USED TO SEPARATE VERY SIMILAR ATOMS OR MOLECULES AND TO DETECT THE PRESENCE OF THESE SPECIES IN EXTREMELY SMALL QUANTITIES. THE SOVIETS HAVE PERFORMED EXTENSIVE RESEARCH IN ALL FIELDS OF LASER CHEMISTRY.

ALTHOUGH THE SOVIETS LEAD THE UNITED STATES IN MANY AREAS OF BASIC RESEARCH, THEY HAVE BEEN SURPASSED BY THE UNITED STATES IN THE INDUSTRIALIZATION OF APPLICATIONS OFFERING THE GREATEST NEAR TERM ECONOMIC POTENTIAL. WE BELIEVE THAT THE SOVIETS HAVE LAGGED BEHIND THE UNITED STATES IN INDUSTRIALIZATION PRIMARILY BECAUSE OF A LACK OF COOPERATION BETWEEN SOVIET BASIC RESEARCH INSTITUTES AND INDUSTRY--NOT BECAUSE THE SOVIETS ARE TECHNICALLY LIMITED IN THEIR ABILITY TO APPLY ADVANCES FROM BASIC RESEARCH. THE SOVIETS, HOWEVER, HAVE NOW ESTABLISHED A WELL-DEFINED, GOAL-ORIENTED PROGRAM, WHOSE INITIAL SUCCESS COULD GREATLY INCREASE THE RATE OF INCORPORATION OF BASIC SOVIET LASER CHEMISTRY RESEARCH INTO INDUSTRY. IF THIS PROGRAM IS SUCCESSFUL, THE SOVIETS COULD IMPROVE THE DEVELOPMENT OF APPLICATIONS BY 1995.

LASER CHEMISTRY AS APPLIED TO ISOTOPE SEPARATION PROMISES TO BE A MORE EFFICIENT AND ECONOMICAL WAY OF SEPARATING OR ENRICHING MANY NUCLEAR ISOTOPES--IMPORTANT IN BASIC RESEARCH, MEDICAL RESEARCH, NUCLEAR POWER, AND NUCLEAR WEAPONS. THE SOVIETS LEAD THE WEST IN THE BASIC RESEARCH OF LASER ISOTOPE SEPARATION (LIS). THEY HAVE BUILT THE WORLD'S FIRST TWO PILOT PLANTS FOR THE SEPARATION OF LIGHT ISOTOPES, AND WE BELIEVE THEY ARE NOW CAPABLE OF OPERATING THESE PLANTS AND INDUSTRIAL-LEVEL SEPARATION PLANTS FOR LIGHT ATOMS AND LOW MOLECULAR WEIGHT MOLECULES. THEIR RESEARCH, HOWEVER, MAY NOT BE AS APPLICABLE TO THE SEPARATION OF URANIUM AND PLUTONIUM ISOTOPES AS THAT PURSUED IN THE UNITED STATES. IN OUR JUDGMENT, THEY WILL NOT BE ABLE TO OPERATE AN INDUSTRIAL PLANT FOR THE ENRICHMENT OF URANIUM BEFORE THE YEAR 2000.

CONFIDENTIAL

25. (continued)

PAGE:0338

THE SOVIETS, ACCORDING TO OPEN SOURCES, HAVE PROPOSED USING LASER ISOTOPE SEPARATION TO PRODUCE HIGH PURITY CARBON-13. A POTENTIAL APPLICATION FOR LARGE QUANTITIES OF CARBON-13 IS FOR USE IN CARBON-DIOXIDE LASER WEAPONS. THE SOVIETS, ACCORDING TO A SCIENTIFIC PUBLICATION, ARE AWARE OF THE ADVANTAGES OF CARBON-13 AND MAY BE MOTIVATED TO DEVELOP A CARBON-13 LIS PROCESS TO MEET MILITARY OBJECTIVES.

LASER CHEMISTRY AS APPLIED TO ULTRAPURIFICATION IS USED TO REMOVE TRACE IMPURITIES FROM A BULK MATERIAL. WHEN APPLIED TO MATERIALS WHERE HIGH PURITY IS REQUIRED, SUCH AS SEMICONDUCTORS OR PHARMACEUTICALS, IT CAN DRAMATICALLY INCREASE THE VALUE OF THE MATERIAL. THE SOVIETS LEAD THE WEST IN THIS TYPE OF BASIC RESEARCH. USING LASER PURIFICATION, THEY HAVE DEVELOPED HIGH-QUALITY ELECTRONICS-GRADE SEMICONDUCTOR MATERIALS IN ORDER TO REDUCE A PRESENT SHORTAGE OF THESE MATERIALS. WE BELIEVE THAT BY 1990 THE SOVIETS COULD OPERATE A PILOT PLANT.

LASER CHEMICAL SYNTHESIS OFFERS GREATER CONTROL OVER THE CHEMICAL REACTION PATHS AND PRODUCTS THAN CONVENTIONAL

NNNN

CONFIDENTIAL

CONFIDENTIAL

PAGE:0001

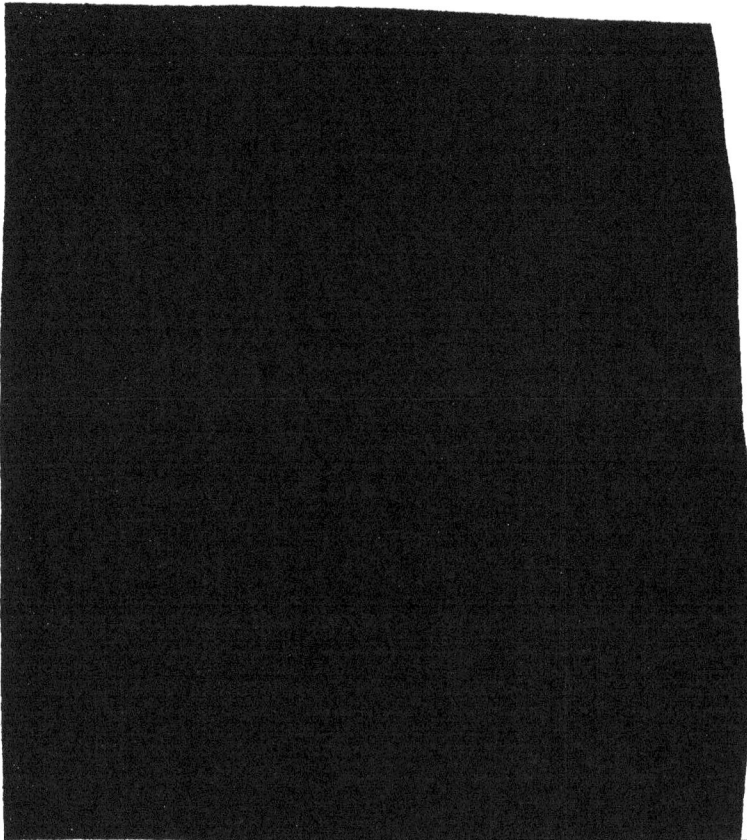

CHEMISTRY. IT THUS HAS POTENTIAL TO PRODUCE UNIQUE COMPOUNDS, TO INCREASE THE SELECTIVITY AND YIELDS OF INDUSTRIAL REACTIONS, AND TO PERFORM CONTROLLED CHEMICAL REACTIONS ON SURFACES AND IN LIVING ORGANISMS. THE SOVIETS LEAD IN THE BASIC RESEARCH OF LASER CHEMICAL SYNTHESIS, AND WE BELIEVE THEY WILL ESTABLISH A PILOT PLANT FOR LASER-INDUCED CHEMICAL SYNTHESIS BY 1995. 

LASER SURFACE CHEMISTRY IS IMPORTANT IN THE PRODUCTION OF ADVANCED MICROELECTRONIC COMPONENTS AND THE COATING OF ADVANCED MATERIALS. SOVIET LASER SURFACE CHEMISTRY RESEARCH IS PURSUING CONCEPTS EQUAL TO OR MORE ADVANCED THAN THOSE IN THE WEST. THIS BASIC RESEARCH, HOWEVER, OFTEN HAS POINTED TOARD APPLICATIONS THAT ARE TOO ADVANCED TO OFFER SOVIET INDUSTRY PRACTICAL SOLUTIONS TO EXISTING PROBLEMS. AS THE SOVIET ELECTRONICS INDUSTRY DEVELOPS IN THE COMING DECADE, HOWEVER, WE BELIEVE LASER SURFACE CHEMISTRY WILL PLAY A MORE

CONFIDENTIAL

25. (continued)

CONFIDENTIAL

PAGE:0002

SIGNIFICANT ROLE.

ONE AREA OF LASER PHOTOCHEMISTRY IN WHICH THE SOVIETS MAINTAIN A SIGNIFICANT LEAD IN BOTH BASIC AND APPLIED RESEARCH IS LASER PHOTOBIOLOGY, POTENTIALLY USEFUL IN GENETIC ENGINEERING AND BIOLOGICAL WARFARE RESEARCH. THIS EFFORT IS WELL ORGANIZED WITH PHYSICISTS, CHEMISTS, BIOLOGISTS, AND MEDICAL DOCTORS WORKING JOINTLY IN THE RESEARCH. THE SOVIETS HAVE ACHIEVED SELECTIVE LASER CHEMISTRY RESULTS ON BIOLOGICAL MOLECULES AND HAVE MUTATED BACTERIA AND VIRUSES SELECTIVELY.

THE SELECTIVITY OF LASER CHEMISTRY PROVIDES A HIGHLY SENSITIVE METHOD FOR DETECTING AND MEASURING TRACE QUANTITIES OF ATOMS OR MOLECULES. IT HAS A WIDE RANGE OF APPLICATIONS FROM PROCESS AND QUALITY CONTROL IN INDUSTRY TO THE DETECTION OF POLLUTANTS OR CHEMICAL WEAPONS IN THE ATMOSPHERE. THE SOVIETS, WHO LEAD IN THE BASIC RESEARCH OF LASER ANALYTICAL CHEMISTRY, ARE PLACING SPECIAL EMPHASIS ON THOSE APPLICATIONS THAT IMPROVE BOTH THE PROCESS CONTROL AND AUTOMATION OF THE SEMICONDUCTOR INDUSTRY.

COMPARISON OF SOVIET AND US ACHIEVEMENTS IN LASER CHEMISTRY

RESEARCH AREA	BASIC RESEARCH	APPLIED RESEARCH	PILOT PLANTS	INDUSTRIAL PLANTS
LIGHT ISOTOPE SEPARATION	USSR GREATER THAN US	USSR GREATER THAN US	USSR GREATER THAN US	USSR GREATER THAN US
URANIUM/ PLUTONIUM SEPARATION	US EQUALS USSR	US GREATER THAN USSR	US GREATER THAN USSR	NONE
ULTRAPURIFI- CATION	USSR GREATER THAN US	US GREATER THAN USSR	US GREATER THAN USSR	US GREATER THAN USSR
DIRECT PHOTOCHEMISTRY	USSR GREATER THAN US	US GREATER THAN USSR	US GREATER THAN USSR	NONE
LASER-INDUCED CHEMISTRY	US EQUALS USSR	US EQUALS USSR	US EQUALS USSR	NONE
LASER SURFACE CHEMISTRY	USSR GREATER THAN US	USSR GREATER THAN US	US GREATER THAN USSR	US GREATER THAN USSR
LASER PHOTOBIOLOGY	USSR GREATER THAN US	USSR GREATER THAN US	USSR GREATER THAN US	NONE
LASER ANALYTICAL CHEMISTRY	USSR GREATER THAN US	USSR GREATER THAN US	US EQUALS USSR	US GREATER THAN USSR

NNNN

CONFIDENTIAL

Secret
NOFORN

Soviet Quest for Supercomputing Capabilities

Key Judgments

Information available as of 1 April 1986 was used in this report.

Soviet development of supercomputers—required for large-scale scientific computing (LSSC)—lags that of the United States by about 10 years. Through the year 2000, Soviet LSSC is virtually certain to remain at least five and probably 10 to 15 years behind the West. At present, we believe that the Soviets have no machines in the true supercomputer class. The best Soviet scientific computers are slower by at least a factor of 20 than their Western counterparts, and Soviet claimed computer capabilities are greatly exaggerated. Rapid future Soviet progress in LSSC is likely to depend on the technology transfer of both software and hardware from the West. Accordingly, we expect substantially increased Soviet efforts at industrial espionage—particularly efforts directed at software acquisition.

Lack of LSSC handicaps many important aspects of Soviet weapons programs, especially in the nuclear and aerodynamic fields. To compensate for their inability to do effective computer modeling of weapon systems, Soviet developers must make trade-offs involving:

- More extensive experimental testing programs.
- Larger engineering design teams.
- Longer system development time.
- Greater development expense.
- Reduced system performance and reliability.

In some fields, such as reentry vehicle design, the Soviets have been successful in making such trade-offs; in other fields, their progress has been severely hindered.

Soviet LSSC lags in both software and hardware. Although the Soviets have great strength in some well-established areas of traditional pure mathematics, the USSR has made few contributions to theoretical computer science. Those contributions that they have made—in the area of algorithms—have not been exploited in the USSR. The lack of a "computer culture" in the Soviet Union has reduced the Soviets' ability to encourage and support research in advanced software. In hardware, the best Soviet machines fall far short of Western supercomputers. Their reliability is poor, their processing rate is slow, and their memory sizes are limited. By the early 1990s, the Soviets could have a true supercomputer, the El'brus-3, in production; at present, however, system development is only in the very early stages.

Secret

In our judgment, Soviet propaganda boasting of computer capabilities may be designed to undercut attempts to restrict Communist Bloc access to Western supercomputers by making such safeguards appear unnecessary. In specific computer software areas, the Soviets have acquired and exploited significant Western programs and will probably increase their efforts to steal or purchase software. Hardware acquired by the USSR includes machines up to—but probably not above—the VAX "supermini" class. Soviet efforts to access or acquire a true supercomputer such as a Cray-1 are likely to be strenuous. Unrestricted access to Western supercomputer technology would help the Soviets close the gap in this field, perhaps cutting their development time in half. ▇▇▇

Two long-term trends may help the Soviets in LSSC development during the next 10 to 15 years. First, as computer science research progresses, the labor-intensive nature of software development probably will be reduced; research into automatic programing and ultra-high-level computer languages may make it possible to set up and solve complex LSSC problems much more easily than at present. It will be difficult to keep this technology out of Soviet hands, and acquisition of it may eventually help reduce the Soviet lag in LSSC capability. Second, as Western computer hardware technology advances, more computer power will become available in smaller, cheaper packages. In 10 to 15 years, it is possible that desktop computers with power equal to that of today's supercomputers will be available for under $10,000. We believe that such hardware will also be virtually impossible to keep away from the Soviet Union. ▇▇▇

In both hardware and software, even if the gap between the West and the USSR remains constant or widens, the Soviets will still be making rapid progress in absolute terms. In 10 to 15 years, we believe the top Soviet scientific institutions will probably have equipment comparable to that of the best US national laboratories at present. Average research institutes may reach that level a few years later. ▇▇▇

27.

23630

Central Intelligence Agency

Washington, D.C. 20505

DIRECTORATE OF INTELLIGENCE

19 June 1986

THE KRASNOYARSK RADAR: CLOSING THE FINAL GAP IN COVERAGE FOR BALLISTIC MISSILE EARLY WARNING

Summary

The large phased-array-radar (LPAR) located near Krasnoyarsk, USSR has been an ABM Treaty issue since it was first detected in July 1983 because of its inland, rather than peripheral, siting. Responding to US demands about its inconsistency with the ABM Treaty, the Soviets have repeatedly argued that the radar is for satellite detection and tracking.

Our analyses indicate, and [ ] *that the primary mission of this radar is ballistic missile detection and tracking. Further, we believe the Krasnoyarsk LPAR closes the final gap in the Soviet ballistic missile early warning (BMEW) and tracking network that includes LPARs and the older Hen House type radars.*

We believe the siting of an LPAR near Krasnoyarsk was motivated primarily by the requirement to close this BMEW gap and at the same time achieve more favorable RV-impact prediction accuracy at the expense of warning-time. Although the Soviets lose some tracking time because of the inland location, track times are comparable to those of the rest of their BMEW system. We believe the

----

This typescript memorandum was prepared by and of the Office of Scientific and Weapons Research. OSWR, contributed to this report. Questions and comments are welcome and may be directed to the Chief, OSWR on

SWM 86-20036

WARNING NOTICE
INTELLIGENCE SOURCES
OR METHODS INVOLVED

SECRET

CL BY
DECL OADR
DERIVED FROM

~~SECRET~~

specific location of the radar was determined on the basis of logistical requirements for construction and maintenance, and construction and operations costs.

28.

The Soviet Weapons Industry: An Overview

Summary

Over the last two decades, the Soviet Union has delivered weapons to its military at a level unequaled anywhere in the world. Over 50,000 tanks, 80,000 light armored vehicles, 9,600 strategic ballistic missiles, 50,000 aircraft, 650,000 surface-to-air missiles, and 270 submarines have been procured since 1965.

In the process, the Soviets have built the largest weapons industry in the world. Roughly 50 major design bureaus control the development of 150 to 200 weapons at any one time. Weapons are assembled in about 150 major production complexes scattered throughout the Soviet Union. Designers and producers are supported by thousands of organizations in Soviet academia and industry.

Since the 1920s, the entire complex has been operated in a way that exploits the priority given to defense and the advantages of a command economy, and minimizes the impact of Soviet technical weaknesses. Soviet weapons acquisition has been characterized by:

- Centralized management by party and government organizations, demonstrating continuity and stability in personnel and programs.
- Final leadership authorization of weapon programs and their funding early in the acquisition process.
- Relatively simple, low-risk weapon designs, emphasizing standard components and existing technologies.
- Easily manufactured systems, which can be fabricated by a technologically unsophisticated industrial base with semiskilled or unskilled labor operating general purpose conventional machine tools and equipment.
- Long production runs yielding large numbers of weapons.
- Weapon advances that emphasize incremental upgrades instead of the development of completely new systems or subsystems.

Developments in the economy, technology, and the foreign threat are inducing the Soviets to modify these strategies. The slower growth of the Soviet economy in the past decade and harsh constraints on the availability of key resources have led the Soviet leaders to stress efficiency more than in the past. At the same time, dramatic improvements in Western weapons and advances in their own and foreign military research and development

(R&D) have led them to seek greater advances in weapon performance and capabilities. Changes are under way in the Soviet defense industrial establishment that respond to these new conditions:

- *In resource allocation.* The Soviets appear to be evaluating more carefully the priority accorded the defense industries. Defense will continue to have a high priority, but the increasing costs and complexities of producing advanced weapons are inducing them to seek more cost-effective ways to meet military requirements. In addition, writings and statements indicate the Soviets recognize that their long-term defense needs require more balanced development in Soviet industry, services, and the technology base.

- *In weapon development.* The Soviets are shifting from well proven to more advanced technologies and from simple to more complex weapon designs. They will continue to rely on traditional, proven approaches to develop most of their weapons. But in several areas—such as strategic defense—they will find it more and more difficult to meet new threats by relying on those strategies. Development cycles for some systems may lengthen as a consequence, particularly in the test phase.

- *In production.* The Soviets are manufacturing advanced weapons in smaller quantities and at lower rates. Improved weapon performance and greater multimission capabilities, along with greater production problems and the higher procurement and maintenance costs of new weapons, are encouraging the Soviets in some cases to reduce the numbers produced. The danger of obsolescence from a more rapidly changing threat and military technology base will further encourage shorter production runs. Retrofit programs, which enhance and prolong the combat worthiness of older systems, are probably intended to partly compensate for this.

- *In the industrial base.* The high-technology support sector of the weapons industry—radioelectronics, telecommunications, specialty materials, and advanced production equipment—will generally continue to grow more rapidly than weapon and equipment producers. Throughout the defense industries, the Soviets are using incentives and investment policy to encourage the renovation and modernization of established facilities instead of new plant construction.

iv

- *In administration.* Small-scale changes in planning and management are being implemented. The Soviets are modifying industrial organization and revising plan targets, prices, and incentives to encourage innovation and quality over quantity. They will not undermine the central planning system by providing managers with real autonomy, however, and the defense industries will continue to be the most thoroughly scrutinized part of the Soviet economy.

- *In seeking help from abroad.* The Soviets are stressing and supporting the buildup of the scientific-technical base of their East European allies and will seek more imports of technology and equipment from them. They will also continue to rely heavily on acquisition of Western technology.

Changes in the Soviet armed forces in the 1990s will drive—and be driven by—changes in the weapons industry. Alterations in doctrine, force structure, logistic organization, maintenance requirements, and manpower utilization are likely to accompany the evolution in the products of the defense industries. In some cases, the long-term impact of increasingly sophisticated weapons may be a reduction in total numbers maintained in active inventories. Overall force effectiveness is likely to increase, nonetheless, as the mobility, survivability, and lethality of new weapons improve.

Certain aspects of the weapons industry are unique in the Soviet economy, but many of its problems confront the civilian sector as well. Although the defense industrial ministries have never been completely insulated from civilian industry—an indispensable supplier of materials, components, and subassemblies—the lines between the two sectors have become increasingly blurred as weapons have grown in complexity. Since the last years of the Brezhnev era, the Soviets have been implementing policies to speed the modernization of both the civilian and defense industries.

The Soviet defense industries face considerable challenges in their mission to produce sufficient quantities of highly advanced weapons for the forces of the next decade. Nevertheless, expansion in high-technology industries, advances in precision machining and other fabrication technologies, and continued aggressive exploitation of Western technology will allow the Soviets to overcome some of the difficulties with which their domestic R&D base is currently struggling. Moreover, the Soviets' speed in introducing generic equivalents of Western technologies into their own systems and their ability to surge ahead along a narrow front of military technologies will help them remain competitive in deployed military capabilities.

v

In any event, the Soviet weapons industry will remain a potent force in the 1990s. It has been a vital ingredient in Soviet military power, which has been the primary instrument of the Soviet leadership in achieving national security, political leverage, and prestige throughout the world. The weapons industry will continue to be at the forefront of Soviet technology and industrial prowess, and it will absorb a large share of the best Soviet resources. Its leaders will continue to wield considerable influence on Soviet policy. And—because of growing economic constraints and the potential of advancing military technology—its performance is likely to be an even greater determinant of Soviet military power than is the case today.

29.

23295

Central Intelligence Agency

Washington, D.C. 20505

CIA | SW | 88-20026 | A

DIRECTORATE OF INTELLIGENCE

1 August 1988

US STEALTH PROGRAMS AND TECHNOLOGY: SOVIET EXPLOITATION OF THE WESTERN PRESS

Summary

The Western press has reported extensively on US Stealth -- or very low observable (VLO) systems -- since the mid-1970s. Western reporters often intertwine fact and analysis when writing about US programs. This blending of fact and analysis probably keeps US Stealth programs shrouded in mystery and perpetuates false rumors about the capabilities of Stealth technology. We believe the majority of Stealth technology articles found in the press reiterate well-established signature-reduction techniques that have appeared in technical journals and books.

The Soviets read the Western press to learn about US Stealth programs and technology. They likely used this information to develop comparable offensive systems, to focus research and development efforts toward the design of defenses to counter the Western Stealth threat, and to guide their covert intelligence collection efforts. Although the Soviets use the press to learn about US military systems, we estimate that the special access controls surrounding the US Stealth programs have reduced the amount and quality of militarily significant reporting appearing in the press

The Soviets likely have a good understanding of US Stealth programs and technology from successful Western technology acquisitions, their research and development efforts, and their analysis of the Western press. The relationship among Soviet Stealth acquisitions, the press, and the Soviet weapons development cycle leads us to conclude that the Soviets may be at the prototype stage of an indigenous Stealth program.

Background

The Soviets have a multi-channel Western technology acquisition effort that relies upon a network of covert intelligence operations, trade diverters, international trade agreements, and open source collectors. This well-funded collection effort is targeted primarily against US defense contractors, their affiliates overseas, and their competitors [ ] the Soviets seek information about future Western military systems to develop comparable offensive systems, to focus research and development efforts towards the design of defenses to counter Western threats, and to estimate the relative technology level of the Soviet Union vis-a-vis the West.

10 SWX

The Soviets use the Western press to guide their covert intelligence collection efforts and trade

This memorandum was prepared by , Office of Scientific and Weapons Research. It contains information available as of 1 August 1988. Comments and questions may be directed to the Chief , OSWR

SW M 88-20026
CL BY
DECL OADR
DER FROM

SECRET

1269

30.

Secret

The Flat Twin ABM Radar: Not as Capable as Previously Believed

Summary

Information available as of 1 August 1991 was used in this report.

New analysis of the Soviet Flat Twin ballistic missile defense radar shows that it is not as capable as previously believed.[ ]

[ ] Our analysis[ ] indicates severe constraints imposed on the Flat Twin by its antenna. This strengthens our belief that a widespread, fast-paced Soviet ABM deployment using the Flat Twin is unlikely because of the number of radars required, as well as the extreme difficulty of modifying the Flat Twin to make it perform effectively.

Our analysis of the Flat Twin's antenna indicates that the Flat Twin is much less capable in off-boresight scanning for track and search than we had previously estimated[ ] indicate that the Flat Twin has a maximum scanning capability of about ±15 degrees in azimuth and elevation for tracking.[ ] also indicates that the Flat Twin can search less than ±10 degrees. This reassessed search capability is considerably less than the earlier estimate of ±45 degrees

Because of the Flat Twin's scanning limitations, a widespread ABM system using the Flat Twin would require an overwhelming number of radars. A system deployed at Moscow and 40 of the most important areas in the Soviet Union would require about 500 to 570 Flat Twin radars. These numbers are about 30 percent higher than our previous assessment. Although the Soviets would require fewer Flat Twin radars to defend their 125 high-priority deployment sites under the START treaty, the number required is still considerable. Under the START treaty limit of about 4,900 US ballistic missile warheads—the level to be achieved by 1996—our modeling indicates that a Soviet defense would require about 510 to 600 Flat Twin radars. Under a potential future START treaty permitting about 2,450 US ballistic missile warheads, we calculate that the number of Flat Twin radars required for defense would be reduced to about 380 to 450.

Given the Flat Twin's limitations as a widespread ABM system, we believe that the Soviets would use a new type of ABM radar. We would expect a new radar to have a greatly improved scan angle, a better multiple-target-tracking capability, and greater detection range. Thus, a significant reduction in the number of radars required in a widespread ABM system would result[ ]

Reverse Blank

Secret

SW 91-10069
October 1991

Assessing Soviet Economic Performance

Assessing Soviet Economic Performance
Author's Comments: James Noren

The CIA documents excerpted in this section illustrate the range of CIA's coverage of economic intelligence that supported US policymakers during the Cold War. The first document, "Long-Run Soviet Economic Growth," used an innovative analytical approach to address a much-debated question in the 1950s-1960s. Soviet agriculture, the Achilles' heel of Soviet economic development, was also an ongoing focus of CIA analysis. "The New Lands Program in the USSR" suggests the depth of research devoted to this subject. It was arguably the most important initiative of the 1950s.

CIA work on Soviet military spending was necessary to research on the Soviet Gross National Product (GNP). US defense planners enthusiastically read such material, asking for disaggregated estimates like those in the third document, "Soviet Military Expenditures by Major Missions, 1958-65." Monitoring Soviet crop prospects also attracted intense interest, especially after the USSR began to buy grain after poor harvests. "The Soviet Grain Deficit" is a typical report intended for the Washington audience. Searching for the causes of the slide in economic productivity, CIA tried to find alternative relations between output and inputs of labor and capital in the USSR. "Investment and Growth in the USSR" identifies one plausible source of the problem. CIA analysts also raised questions about the impact of technology transfer on Soviet capabilities during the Cold War. "Soviet Economic and Technological Benefits from Détente" is an example of the many papers issued in response to this question.

As a warning of the Soviet Union's impending descent into economic stagnation, "Soviet Economic Problems and Prospects," issued in 1977, was a paper of first importance. Reprinted by the Joint Economic Committee of the US Congress, it set out the reasons why the Soviet economy was in trouble and why its future was so grim. In addition, CIA singled out problems in Soviet oil production as a major factor in the outlook for the economy. See the selection, "The Impending Soviet Oil Crisis." The next document "Organization and Management in the Soviet Economy: The Ceaseless Search for Panaceas," represents CIA's consistently negative appraisal of Soviet attempts at economic reform, one prong of Moscow's efforts to jump-start the Soviet economy.

CIA's involvement in heated policy issues was evident in the Reagan administration's determination to stop the Siberia-to-Western Europe gas pipeline. The Agency's unwelcome evaluation of the chances for success were set out in "Outlook for Siberia-to-Western Europe Natural Gas Pipeline," a paper typical of the numerous assessments of various proposed sanctions and embargoes. The final selection, "Gorbachev: Steering the USSR in the 1990s," described the impasse Gorbachev's economic policies reached by 1987, considered the options open to him, and concluded that he could be deposed because of failure to deliver on his promises.

31.

CIA/RR 53
(ORR Project 10.406)

S-E-C-R-E-T

LONG-RUN SOVIET ECONOMIC GROWTH*

Conclusions

Soviet economic growth is defined as the increase in the ability of the USSR to produce goods and services and may be measured in terms of the increase in Soviet gross national product. It is determined by the quantities of the factors of production available -- land, labor, and capital -- and by the efficiency with which they are used -- technology, management, the scale of production, and other elements which can be treated only qualitatively.

It is unlikely that the gross national product of the USSR will grow at an annual average rate of 5 percent or more over the period to 1975. The most probable average annual rate of growth will be between 4.2 and 4.8 percent, depending on the Soviet policy decisions concerning the allocation of the Soviet gross national product among various consuming sectors, primarily investment, consumption, and defense. The chief deterrents to a higher rate are the problems involved in increasing the output of the agricultural sector above that projected in this report. This difficulty is illustrated by the differences in the projected levels of nonagricultural and agricultural production for 1975: whereas nonagricultural output is expected to be 170 to 260 percent greater than in 1953, agricultural output is expected to be only 60 to 80 percent greater than in 1953.

The limits of this range are set by making assumptions as to the largest and smallest probable growth in consumption and in agricultural production. Two methods are used in projecting gross national product in this report.

The above estimates are based, not upon a sample projection of the gross national product, but upon projections of the principal factors determining production. To obtain nonagricultural output, the quantity and quality of labor, the stock of capital, and the net effect of all other factors (technology, management, and so on)

* The estimates and conclusions contained in this report represent the best judgment of the responsible analyst as of 13 December 1954.

S-E-C-R-E-T

are projected. In the case of the agricultural sector, an assumed level of output serves as a basis for estimating labor and capital requirements.

A rough comparison of the projected gross national product of the USSR and that of the US is helpful in assessing the meaning of estimates developed in this study. This comparison cannot be precise, because it involves not only all the inaccuracies of projecting both the USSR and US data but also the inaccuracies of international comparison.

The best estimate is that the Soviet gross national product will increase from $103 billion in 1953 to $290 billion (4.8 percent per year), assuming low consumption, and $250 billion (4.2 percent per year), assuming high consumption, in 1975. It is estimated that the US gross national product will increase from $350 billion in 1953 to $735 billion (3.4 percent per year in 1975). The gap (in absolute terms) between the US and Soviet gross national product is expected to increase, even though the Soviet gross national product is expected to become a larger percentage of the corresponding US value by 1975.

A basic assumption of this report is that international trade will increase only slightly and will not contribute to the growth of the USSR substantially more than it currently does. If, however, the Soviet policy makers decide to supplement the agricultural output of the USSR by imports to a significant extent, the rate of growth of the Soviet gross national product could be higher.

Another basic assumption of this report is that expenditures for defense will be geared to a continuation of the cold war. If, however, defense expenditures are less than projected, it is possible that total production in 1975 would be higher than estimated.

It also should be pointed out that the contributions to the growth of the USSR made by the Satellites have not been explicitly considered. These effects have, however, been considered implicitly to the extent that they have affected Soviet growth in the past.

This report necessarily assumes there will be no basic changes in the Soviet political system.

Finally, it should be noted that the projections of Soviet output in 1975 are limited to the extent that all economic projections

S-E-C-R-E-T

over a long period of time are limited. They are based on what is known about the past developments and present conditions and what can be deduced from this information and reasonable assumptions about the future. They are limited to the extent that currently unknown future events affect the quantities which this report attempts to estimate.

- 3 -

S-E-C-R-E-T

32.

CIA/RR 87 S-E-C-R-E-T
(ORR Project 20.827)

THE NEW LANDS PROGRAM IN THE USSR*

Summary

The "new lands" program in the USSR involves great amounts of capital investment and manpower and a vast area of land. In less than 2 years, 30 million hectares,** an area 25 percent larger than the acreage sown to wheat in the US in 1955, have been brought into cultivation, and eventually 40 million hectares may be reclaimed. The new lands program has been developed without major dislocations in the Soviet economy. A large part of the necessary total investment has been made, and in the future the program will impose no major strains on the economy.

On the basis of soil and climate, the major area of the new lands program may be divided into three zones.*** The Northern Zone includes the territory between the Ural and the Altay Mountains extending from the boundary of Kazakh SSR to the bogs and forests north of the Trans-Siberian Railroad. This zone is the northern part of the Asiatic spring wheat belt. The Southern Zone, the southern part of the Asiatic spring wheat belt, extends from the northern boundary of Kazakh SSR southward into the arid steppe. The Western Zone, the northeastern part of the Asiatic spring wheat belt, is largely in the European USSR and includes the southern Ural region, the northwest Kazakh SSR, and a part of the middle Volga region. The new lands program is also operative in several other relatively small areas of virgin and long-fallow land, chiefly in the southern regions of the European USSR, East Siberia, and southern Kazakh SSR.

The soils in much of the area covered by the three major zones are suitable for the production of grain. From north to south the soils are similar to those in the prairie provinces of Canada, one of the world's greatest wheat producing regions. In the new lands area of the USSR, gray-brown soils in the north merge with black soils to the south. Farther to the south are dark chestnut soils, merging with light chestnut soils in the extreme south.

---

* The estimates and conclusions contained in this report represent the best judgment of ORR as of 1 November 1956.
** One hectare equals 2.471 acres; 30 million hectares, therefore, equal about 74 million acres.
*** See Figure 1, following p. 2, below.

S-E-C-R-E-T

Virtually all of the more suitable soils in the new lands probably were under cultivation in 1953. There had been unsuccessful attempts at farming, and large acreages were abandoned because of excessive salinity and alkalinity. Much of the land reclaimed in 1955, when 30 million hectares were plowed for planting in 1956, was very poor.

More important than the poor quality of much of the soil in the new lands are the hazards of climate, particularly in the Southern Zone, where a major part of the reclamation is taking place. Rainfall is the most critical factor. In the Northern Zone, average rainfall is about the same as that in the Canadian spring wheat belt. Annual rainfall in the Southern Zone averages less than 12 inches, a minimum below which the cultivation of crops is hazardous. The absence of mountain barriers between the three major zones and the Central Asian deserts to the south and the Arctic to the north exposes the new lands to the drying desert winds, which may cause severe droughts, and to the Arctic winds, which may bring snow as early as August.

The new lands area of the USSR is a spring crop region in which grain -- mainly wheat -- is the major crop. Available data do not permit an estimate of the acreages and yields of specific grain crops in the new lands, but it may be assumed that yields of wheat are indicative, within a reasonable margin of error, of the yields of all grain crops.

On the basis of a 16-year series of yield data for wheat grown in the areas now affected by the new lands program, a long-term average yield, weighted by the distribution of acreages in the new lands in 1954, has been estimated. The estimate indicates that with an average distribution similar to that of 1954 an average yield of 6.6 centners* per hectare may be expected in the new lands. On the basis of the 1955 distribution of acreage, however, the long-term average yield which may be expected in the new lands is slightly lower, 6.2 centners per hectare; a larger percentage of the new lands brought into cultivation in 1955 was in the Southern and Western Zones, which have poorer soils and climate.

* One centner equals 220.46 pounds. A yield of 6.6 centners per hectare is equal to a yield of about 588 pounds -- 9.8 bushels -- per acre.

32. (continued)

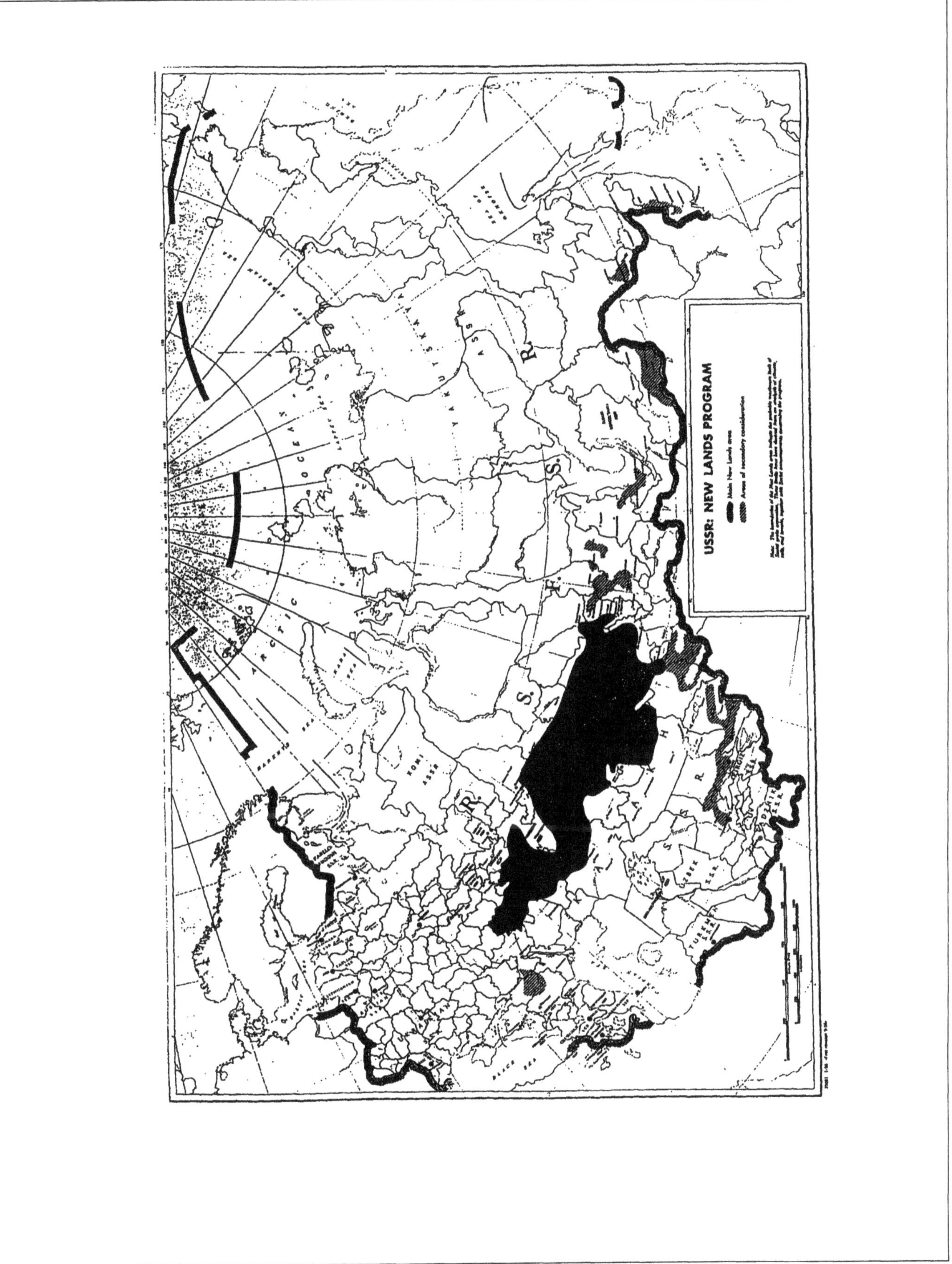

S-E-C-R-E-T

Wide annual variability in yields is to be expected in the new lands, particularly in the Southern and Western Zones, because of the extreme fluctuation from year to year in the amount and distribution of rainfall. This variability in yields is well illustrated by the yields obtained during the first 2 years of the program.

Almost all of the 4.3 million hectares of new land sown in 1954 was sown to wheat. Growing conditions were unusually favorable in 1954, and there was a very good grain crop. The yield is estimated at 10.5 centners per hectare, 60 percent above the long-term average yield of 6.6 centners per hectare and about 35 percent above the estimated 1954 average yield per hectare in the USSR as a whole. The average yield of 10.5 centners per hectare, when applied to the 4.3 million hectares sown to grain in the new lands in 1954, indicates gross production of about 4.5 million metric tons,* about 5 percent of the estimated total Soviet production in 1954.

During the 1955 crop year, most of the new lands suffered from a drought, and the estimated yield of 4.3 centners per hectare was less than one-half of the yield obtained in the extraordinarily good year of 1954. The yield in 1955 is about 70 percent of the long-term average yield of 6.2 centners per hectare and is about 55 percent of the estimated 1955 average yield per hectare in the USSR as a whole.

When applied to the 18.5 million hectares sown to grain in the new lands in 1955, the average yield of 4.3 centners per hectare indicates an estimated gross production of almost 8 million tons, about 8 percent of the estimated total Soviet production in 1955. Because of the much larger area sown in 1955, production of grain in the new lands in that year -- in spite of unfavorable weather -- was substantially greater than in 1954.

Soviet planners know that continued productivity of the new lands depends on a system of crop rotation, including fallow. Present plans call for the introduction of rotation systems after an initial period of 2 to 6 years of continuous cultivation. In the majority of these systems, grain crops in any one year will occupy three-fourths of the land in rotation, and fallow and perennial grasses will occupy the remaining one-fourth.

* Tonnages throughout this report are given in metric tons.

- 3 -

S-E-C-R-E-T

The proposed Soviet systems of crop rotation appear to include an exceptionally high proportion of land sown to grain. In Canadian practice, only one-third to one-half of the land in rotation is sown to grain, and the remainder is fallow or sown to perennial grasses. Canadian experience indicates that the Soviet systems may deplete the soil of the new lands if abnormally heavy cropping to grain is continued for many years. It is possible, however, that Soviet agricultural planners may not press exploitation of the soil to the point of depletion before they modify the proposed systems of rotation; there is evidence that the systems of rotation to be used have not been determined finally.

Official Soviet statements about expected successes in the new lands seem to be unrealistically optimistic. The statements about expected production, for example, imply an average yield over a period of years of 10 to 11 centners per hectare, a yield which is about one-third higher than the estimated 1950-55 average yield for the USSR as a whole. On the basis of the historical yield series for the area, 6 centners per hectare would be a more reasonable estimate of the long-term average yield that can be expected in the new lands.

Khrushchev has stated that he expects the annual average production of the new lands to be not less than 33 million tons (implying a yield of 11 centners per hectare on an area of 30 million hectares). Canadian experience in crop rotation indicates that to have 30 million hectares continuously sown to grain requires that there be 60 million to 90 million hectares in the rotation system, but no program of acreage expansion of this magnitude has been implied by Soviet officials. At the end of 1955, only about 30 million hectares had been reclaimed.

Recent Soviet statements provide a basis for a more realistic estimate of potential production in the new lands. These statements indicate that the current intention is to reclaim about 40 million hectares. Experience in Canada shows that of these 40 million hectares, 13 million to 20 million could be sown to grain. With a yield of 6 centners per hectare, an average production from the new lands of 8 million to 12 million tons could be expected. This production would represent about 10 to 15 percent of the estimated average production in the USSR for the period for 1950 through 1953, the 4-year period before the inauguration of the new lands program. A gross production of 8 million to 12 million tons of grain -- after deduction for seed and waste -- indicates a net availability for direct human consumption of 6 million to 9 million tons. This quantity would supply the grain requirements of 30 million to 40 million people.

- 4 -

S-E-C-R-E-T

A part of the new lands program is the development of the livestock industry. The Soviet government plans to use the large areas of pasture and the increased production of straw, chaff, hay, and corn as food for great flocks and herds on each of the newly established state grain farms and state livestock farms and on the expanded collective farms. Each new state grain farm is to have between 2,500 and 5,000 head of cattle, up to 15,000 head of sheep, and 1,000 head of swine. As of 1 October 1955 the new state farms of Kazakh SSR, almost entirely within the Southern Zone of the new lands, had 89,500 head of cattle, 243,500 head of sheep, and "many pigs." These figures represent an average of about 265 head of cattle and 722 head of sheep per new state farm. Although the stocking of state grain farms has been progressing, as of 1 October 1955 livestock numbers were far short of ultimate goals.

The immediate source of livestock for stocking new state farms is apparently the privately owned livestock of collective farm households and the herds of existing livestock farms. As private ownership in animal husbandry decreases, state farms may replace collective farms as the centers of animal husbandry in the new lands. The completion of this transition, however, will depend on great improvement in the food base and heavy investment in water supplies and in shelter -- requirements which it will take many years to complete.

The new lands program is being implemented with the participation of about 10,660 collective farms, 1,740 machine tractor stations (MTS's), and an undetermined number of state farms, including 425 new state farms organized during 1954-55. In the initial phase of the new lands program the larger share of the reclamation tasks fell to existing MTS's and collective farms, which could most easily exploit the readily accessible land near them. These farm units have been relatively more important in the RSFSR, where 1,457 MTS's and about 8,960 collective farms are engaged in the program.

In establishing the 425 new state farms for the exploitation of virgin and long-fallow land in the remote areas of the new lands the Soviet authorities not only have been influenced by the suitability of the land for large-scale grain farming and by the inadequate labor resources in the region but also have been motivated by the desire to expand the state sector of agriculture. Their success in approaching

- 5 -

S-E-C-R-E-T

this goal is indicated by the doubling of the grain acreages of state farms in the USSR between 1954 and 1956 as a result of the disproportionately large role assigned to state farms in the new lands program. The creation of new state farms in the isolated areas of the new lands also assured the channeling of a larger share of agricultural products through the state distribution system.

Agriculture in the new lands is to be highly mechanized. Initial requirements for machinery have been met by heavy allocations of agricultural machinery to the new lands at the expense of deliveries to established agricultural areas and by loans of machinery from those areas. Loans of equipment were particularly important in facilitating the harvesting and delivery of grain to points of concentration.

The high priority assigned to the new lands is shown by the fact that deliveries of tractors to the established agricultural areas in 1954 dropped to one-half of the annual average delivery in the 3 preceding years. In 1955, however, deliveries of tractors to the established areas increased to 85 percent of this 3-year average in spite of the continuing priority accorded the new lands. Present plans call for the delivery to state farms in Kazakh SSR during 1956 of more than two-thirds as many tractors and combines as were delivered to them during 1954 and 1955.

The major effect of deliveries of agricultural machinery to the new lands probably has been a delay in the reequipment of agriculture in the established areas, particularly the grain areas, and therefore to impose temporarily a greater workload on the existing machinery park in those areas. After 1956 the mechanization problem of the new lands program will be largely one of replacement.

The tractors, combines, trucks, and other farm machinery operating in the new lands require large quantities of diesel fuel, gasoline, and lubricants. The percentage of the total Soviet production of petroleum products required for the exploitation of the new lands in 1955 is estimated to have been as follows: diesel fuel, 4.8 percent; gasoline, 4.8 percent; and lubricants, 1.9 percent. Although these quantities of petroleum products are large, they do not impose a serious strain on the resources of the USSR.

The agricultural manpower requirements of the new lands program are estimated to be 1.33 million workers, about 2.4 percent of the total agricultural labor force in the USSR. In addition, about 400,000 workers are required for the construction and maintenance of ancillary service facilities associated with the program. The manpower requirements of the new lands, therefore, are relatively small. In fulfilling these requirements, however, some specialists and skilled workers have been recruited from industry, a reversal of the usual procedure in the USSR.

Barring major changes in the new lands acreage goals the program will not be a continuing drain on the national supply of manpower, and once the initial requirements for manpower are met, maintenance of the labor force should not be a major problem.

Announced and estimated requirements for carrying out the new lands program include housing and communal facilities for about 2.8 million persons; almost 2,300 kilometers of rail line (to be completed in 1957); more than 6,000 kilometers of motor roads; granary capacity of more than 773,000 tons; and nonresidential farm buildings for 425 new state farms, new and expanded MTS's, and expanded collective farms.

It is estimated that the total cost of state construction required for the new lands program in 1954-56 is about 13 billion rubles. In addition, the cost of construction of collective farms is estimated to be 5 billion to 15 billion rubles and the cost of construction of private housing to be about 5 billion rubles.

Although expenditures for construction have been large in the new lands, they do not appear to have had a serious impact on construction in other sectors of the Soviet economy. There have been many lags in agricultural construction, and a shortage of storage facilities and elevators caused some losses of grain after the harvest of 1954. It does not appear, however, that the underfulfillment of construction plans has seriously hindered the new lands program.

At the beginning of the new lands program in 1954 the new lands, particularly the Southern Zone, had very few railroads, and most motor roads were not suited to year-round use. It was inevitable that there would be serious transport problems until the transportation system was expanded and improved. In 1954 a high volume of construction materials, fuel, and machines congested the rail system, and in September and October, outbound traffic was snarled by the increased load resulting from the very large grain crop. During 1955 the transportation problems were not so severe, because of the opening for temporary service of several new rail lines in the new lands.

The present program of transportation construction appears to be adequate to meet the eventual needs of the new lands program. Although there were confusion and delays during the harvest season of 1956, the transportation system probably will be adequate in the future.

The new lands program has increased allocations from the Soviet state budget to the agricultural sector of the economy, but there have been no consequent reductions in the allocations to other major sectors. In relation to total allocations to agriculture and to total state investment the budget expenditures on the new lands appear to be large but not excessive. The most costly year of the new lands program probably was 1955, when the planned allocations to the new lands were approximately 20 percent of total planned allocations to agriculture. In the same year, investment in the new lands probably was less than 5 percent of total planned state investment (in terms of fixed capital) in the national economy and less than 40 percent of the 1955 total state investment in agriculture.

The development of the new lands program exemplifies some of the major strengths and weaknesses of the Soviet system. Strength is indicated by the speed with which resources were marshalled and the initial objectives attained. An important weakness of the new lands program is that it appears to have been initiated and developed without a sound preliminary analysis of the best ways to proceed and without a realistic estimate of the production of grain that could be expected. Suitable systems of crop rotation and the total area that is to be reclaimed apparently have not yet been determined.

Khrushchev's expectation of obtaining 33 million tons of grain annually cannot be realized. Over a long period the new lands probably will not yield much more than one-third of this amount. The evidence indicates that an annual yield of only 8 million to 12 million tons, 10 to 15 percent of the annual average production of grain in the USSR in 1950-53, can be expected.

Speed was apparently of great importance to the USSR in the development of the new lands. The program was initiated and implemented very rapidly. Although the USSR will need more grain in the future to feed an expanded population and although an increase in agricultural production is necessary if levels of living are to rise substantially, there was no immediate food crisis in 1954, and the haste of the program cannot be explained on economic grounds. The new lands program was dramatic and, with the probability of initial success, was well designed to win popular approval. The decision to embark on the program may have been influenced greatly by the uneasy internal Soviet political situation in 1954.

The production of grain in the new lands is dependent on the weather and other natural factors, and it may fluctuate widely. In any one year, production may be considerably above or below average. In order to maintain yields, the USSR will have to develop systems of crop rotation more suitable than those that have been discussed publicly. If the stated intention to sow three-fourths of the area to grain each year is put into practice, declining yields and large-scale wind erosion may eventually result.

Although the new lands can produce, on a long-term basis, only about one-third of the target quantity mentioned by Khrushchev, it is likely that the program will not be abandoned unless production falls to a very low level.

I. Introduction.

A. General.

In spite of the continual, optimistic claims of the USSR that socialized agriculture is the most advanced type of agriculture in the world, the Soviet government, since the inception of collectivization in 1928, has been unable to provide a satisfactory diet for an increasing population. At times, especially in the early years of collectivization and during World War II, the USSR has even been plagued by severe shortages of food.

33.

~~S-E-C-R-E-T~~

SOVIET MILITARY EXPENDITURES BY MAJOR MISSIONS*
1958-65

Summary and Conclusions

Allocation of the estimated military expenditures of the USSR to the four major missions -- strategic attack, air defense, ground, and naval** -- in accordance with their requirements suggests that important changes in emphasis are occurring within the Soviet armed forces.*** The share of mission outlays (that is, the summation of all the outlays that are directly allocable to the missions) that is absorbed by the ground mission is expected to decline from 51 percent to 36 percent between 1958 and 1965.† During the same period the share for the air defense mission is expected to rise from 22 percent to 30 percent. The share allotted to the strategic attack mission also will increase, but for a limited time only -- it is expected to climb from 11 percent in 1958 to 25 percent in 1962 and then to fall back to 18 percent in 1965. The share represented by the naval mission is expected to decline only modestly, but it is estimated that by 1959-60 it was smaller than the shares going to the other missions. In 1958 this share claimed 17 percent of total mission outlays but during 1959-65 is expected to claim only 14 to 16 percent.

Total outlays for Soviet military programs during 1958-65 for these four missions, for unallocable overhead for the four missions -- command and support -- and a residual have been allocated as follows:

---

* The estimates and conclusions in this report represent the best judgment of this Office as of 15 March 1961.

** For definitions of the missions, see I, B, p. 6, below, and Appendix B.

*** It should be noted that the likelihood of error in the allocation of expenditures indicated in the discussion that follows is greater for 1964-65. Outlays for all missile programs could not be specified beyond 1963 in sufficient detail to assign them to individual missions. The missions most likely to be understated because of such unallocable missile expenditures (which are consigned to the residual) are air defense and strategic attack. Conceivably the decline in the later years of the period in the share absorbed by the strategic attack mission would be overcome if these missile expenditures could be allocated.

† All aggregates and percentages appearing in this report are based on unrounded figures.

~~S-E-C-R-E-T~~

S-E-C-R-E-T

	Ground Mission	Air Defense Mission	Strategic Attack Mission	Naval Mission	Command and Support	Residual
Outlays (billion 1955 rubles*)	302	176	139	111	111	363
Percent of total	25	15	12	9	9	30

The large size of the residual is caused primarily by the inability to allocate 239 billion rubles of expenditure for research and development for 1958-65 and 28 billion rubles for certain guided missile programs after 1962.

An analysis of the expenditures presented in the chart, Figure 1,** also shows the striking reallocation of expenditures within the mission structure. The most dramatic examples are the 34-percent decline in expenditures for the ground mission and the 127-percent increase in outlays for the strategic attack mission that are expected to occur from 1958 through 1962. Expenditures on air defense are expected to climb erratically during 1958-65, whereas expenditures for the naval mission are expected to fall slightly. As a result of these changes, by 1965 the ground mission no longer will hold its historically dominating position in the structure of Soviet military expenditures.

These developments indicate the effect that changing weapons technology may be having on Soviet military planning. Increasing expenditures on strategic attack reflect the replacement of the manned bomber by long-range missiles and missile-launching submarines. Similarly the substitution of missiles and highly sophisticated warning and control systems for fighter aircraft and antiaircraft artillery in air defense will require a growing share of total mission expenditures. Within the naval mission the introduction of missile-launching destroyers and nuclear submarines (torpedo) will keep outlays for this mission from falling too drastically.

As is demonstrated in the chart, Figure 2,** there also are changes in the composition of the expenditures. In all missions except strategic attack, required outlays for personnel are expected to decline,

* All expenditures expressed in this report are in terms of 1 July 1955 rubles. From 1958 to 1965 the weighted ruble/dollar ratio for defense expenditures using Soviet weights varies between 3.6 rubles to US $1 and 4.1 rubles to US $1.

** Following p. 2.

- 2 -

S-E-C-R-E-T

whereas expenditures for operation and maintenance will tend to increase. The changes in relative standing among the missions reinforce these trends in that the ground mission demands proportionately higher outlays for personnel and proportionately lower outlays for operation and maintenance than do the air defense and strategic attack missions. Increasing expenditures for nuclear weapons will offset a declining level of procurement for other categories of equipment.

Finally, when the programs and activities underlying the missions are expressed in 1959 US dollars (that is, what they would cost if purchased in the US at prevailing prices of 1959), they have an annual value of roughly $30 billion during 1958-61 and some $26 billion annually thereafter. This pattern reflects, in part, the estimated change in the composition of Soviet military expenditures toward areas that would be relatively less expensive in equivalent dollar terms -- for example, nuclear weapons as opposed to manpower. Total Soviet military programs and activities, when similarly expressed in US dollars, remain somewhat more constant, at an annual level of roughly $40 billion.

SECRET

CENTRAL INTELLIGENCE AGENCY
Directorate of Intelligence
March 1970

INTELLIGENCE REPORT

Investment And Growth In The USSR

Introduction

One of the principal features of Soviet economic development has been the government's policy of investing the maximum possible amount of the national product. This report explores the possibility that this traditional investment policy is no longer capable of providing the rate of economic growth desired by the Soviet leadership. After World War II, this policy for a time met with much the same sort of success in promoting high rates of economic growth as it had before the war. In the process, however, the investment rate (investment in buildings and equipment expressed as a share of gross national product) increased from 12% in 1950 to 23% in 1960. Since 1960, it has grown more slowly -- to about 26% in 1969.

The steady rise in the investment rate during the 1950s brought about a very rapid increase in the stock of capital in the economy. At the same time, output grew almost as rapidly, so the ratio of capital to output remained at a fairly low level. According to Simon Kuznets, a leading student of comparative economic development, "... the distinctive feature of the USSR record is that so much capital formation was possible without an increase in the capital-output ratio to uneconomically high levels."* He was referring to growth prior to 1958. The USSR now seems to have lost that distinction.

---

* Economic Trends in the Soviet Union, *Ed. A. Bergson and Simon Kuznets, 1963, p. 357.*

Note: This report was produced solely by CIA. It was prepared by the Office of Economic Research.

SECRET

SECRET

In the 1960s the growth of output of industry, construction, and national income, as announced by the Soviet government, slowed dramatically. The growth in capital stock also declined, but not as much as the growth of output. The resulting fall in the ratio of output to capital was noted by Soviet politicians and technicians alike. Such a decline in the return on capital investment threatened the basic Soviet strategy of economic development. The economic difficulties of this period contributed to Khrushchev's fall from power in 1964 and led to the promulgation of Kosygin's reforms in 1965. At first, Khrushchev's successors tended to treat the decline in the output/capital ratio as a temporary phenomenon resulting from Khrushchev's bad management. More recently, they have reluctantly recognized that a turning point has been reached in the method of achieving economic growth.*

The role of investment and capital in Soviet economic growth is explored in this report by means of an aggregate production function. A production function is a relation between inputs -- usually capital and labor -- and the resulting output, or production. Production functions of one kind or another are often used for medium-range economic forecasting, but in previous work

* *The gist of the leadership's remarks to the December (1969) plenary meeting of the CPSU Central Committee has been reported as follows: "The definite reasons for our difficulties are essentially connected with the fact that we have entered a stage of development that no longer permits us to work in the old manner but demands new methods and new solutions .... The raising of the effectiveness of social production has indeed become the key problem, primarily because the main factors in our economic growth have changed. If we were previously able to develop the national economy primarily by quantitative factors, i.e., by increasing the number of workers and by high rates of accumulation of capital investments, then henceforth we must count primarily on qualitative factors of economic growth, on raising the effectiveness, the intensification of the national economy."* (Pravda, *13 January 1970, p. 1.)*

- 2 -

SECRET

on the USSR both the general form and the precise characteristics of the relationship between output and inputs have been usually assumed or specified by analogy with Western practice.

In this report a relatively new form of production function is fitted statistically to the Soviet postwar experience. This function -- known as the Arrow-Chenery-Minhas-Solow function after some of the economists who first proposed it -- has the characteristic of allowing for rapidly diminishing returns to capital. This function is compared with production functions previously used for forecasting Soviet economic growth. The various functions are then used as a basis for discussion of the following questions:

a. What return on investment can be expected in the USSR in the coming years?

b. Can the USSR rely on an upswing in the growth of investment -- perhaps at the expense of military expenditures -- to restore the rates of economic growth achieved in the 1950s (or mid-1960s)?

The production functions in this report are based on the past performance of the Soviet economic system -- in particular, on the past efficiency of its economic organization and on the past rate of adoption of new technology. If the USSR were to be more successful than in the past in its efforts to reform economic management or to expedite the process of introducing new technology, its performance would exceed that which the production functions project. Finally, it should be noted that the various future trends in investment and military expenditures assumed in the report are not predictions but are projections to illustrate the effects of possible alternative programs.

The production functions cover both the non-agricultural non-service sectors of the economy as a whole and industry alone. Agriculture is excluded because year-to-year changes in production

SECRET

are affected so much by variation in weather as well as in the amount of land cultivated. Services such as education, health, and housing are excluded because output in these sectors is measured by the amount of inputs of either labor or capital; no separate measure of output exists.

The statistical basis for the production functions described in this report is found in CIA estimates of GNP originating in the non-agricultural and non-service sectors of the Soviet economy (or, alternatively, in industry) in 1950-68. The data on labor inputs (expressed in man-hours) and on capital services (reflecting annual average fixed capital stock) are derived almost entirely from published Soviet sources.

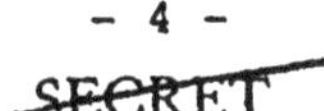

Conclusions

43. The finding of this report is that Soviet economic growth since 1950 is best described by a production function in which strongly diminishing returns to new investment occur. This function, known as the ACMS function, fits the growth of the Soviet industrial and non-agricultural non-service sectors better than a Cobb-Douglas production function of the kind formerly used. In trying to achieve the highest possible volume of investment, Soviet economic policy has forced the capital-labor ratio continuously upward, and this strategy accentuates the effect of diminishing returns. Under these conditions, the ACMS production function estimated for the USSR -- with its relatively low substitutability of capital for labor -- generates a gain in output per unit increase in capital stock that falls off sharply over time. This pattern of growth accurately matches the observed Soviet slowdown since the 1950s.

44. If the relation of output to inputs in the USSR is of the character described by the ACMS function, the situation confronting the Soviet leadership is indeed discouraging. A continuation of the growth of man-hours and capital

stock at the same rate as in the 1960s would result in a projected average annual rate of growth of output in the non-agricultural non-service sector of only 4.0% a year during 1969-80 -- far less than the 7.0% a year achieved in 1961-68 or the 8.6% in 1951-68. In a turnabout from its earlier economic history, the USSR would have to deal with a series of planning periods in which the growth of the labor force -- not the growth of capital stock -- is the real constraint on the rate of growth of output.

45. Should returns to investment -- or what amounts to the same thing, the substitutability of capital for labor -- actually be somewhat higher than the value projected by the ACMS function, the prospects would be brighter. Nevertheless, diminishing returns to new investment would be a serious problem for the leadership over a wide range of plausible functions. Studies of Western economies have found the substitutability of capital for labor to be lower than that inherent in the Cobb-Douglas production function, so a like finding for the USSR is credible.

46. Given a diminishing rate of growth of output with respect to capital, a transfer of a billion rubles from other end uses to investment was found to have a smaller and smaller effect on growth over time. This would be true for a simple transfer of funds from defense to investment. But high-quality resources, particularly scientific and technical manpower, now employed in defense might have a more than proportional effect on growth. Even so, it is doubtful if the potential of these resources could be fully realized without some drastic shake-up in the management of civilian R&D and investment.

47. The implications of such strongly diminishing returns to new investment for Soviet policy are pointed. Having assembled a huge stock of capital, the USSR needs to adopt a different strategy for growth. According to Simon Kuznets,

> Modern economic growth is distinguished by the fact that the rate of rise in per capita product

> was due primarily to improvements in <u>quality</u>, not quantity of inputs -- essentially to greater efficiency -- traceable to increases in useful knowledge and better institutional arrangement for its utilization.*

48. A change of priorities favoring a higher rate of capital formation will not insure even a continuation of present rates of economic growth. While the USSR recognizes that it is behind the West technologically and that it is not closing the gap, the policies necessary to spur technological progress are not obvious. The discussion above suggests that the USSR will have to choose between accepting a lower (and possibly still declining) rate of growth and attempting to improve the managerial efficiency of the system on a broad front. The dilemma for Soviet leaders is that no one has suggested a sure-fire program of reform that will spur economic progress and also insure the degree of central control that the leadership considers to be essential.

* *Modern Economic Growth -- Rate, Structure, Spread*, 1966, p. 491.

35.

CONFIDENTIAL

1/997

February 1974

Soviet Economic and Technological Benefits from Detente

US-Soviet detente has already brought a succession of economic and technological benefits to the USSR: grain to offset a crop failure, access to technology, and equipment previously denied, and long-term credits to finance imports. If detente continues, these gains will accumulate. Nevertheless, overall Soviet economic growth is unlikely to be affected appreciably. Machinery imports from the United States will be small relative to total Soviet investment, and the USSR will continue to have problems in assimilating new technology. The USSR, moreover, has alternative sources of goods and technology if US-Soviet relations sour. Moscow could benefit substantially, however, if it is able to acquire key military-related technology under the umbrella of detente.

The size and terms of the grain purchases from the United States undoubtedly were influenced by the detente atmosphere. The prices paid for the grain were favorable, and Commodity Credit Corporation credits helped the USSR at a time when it was incurring its largest hard currency deficit in history. The US-Soviet maritime agreement also saved the USSR hard currency, as the USSR was able to move several million metric tons of grain on its own bottoms rather than on third-country ships.

Under detente, export controls were relaxed, and some highly prized US equipment and technology became available to the USSR for the first time. Third-generation computers and components and equipment for their manufacture were high on the Soviet shopping list. If science and technology agreements just signed with US computer firms are implemented, Moscow could modernize its computer industry and thus boost productivity in both military and civilian industry. If negotiations for advanced semiconductor production are successful, the Soviets also could be helped in developing complex electronics systems and instrumentation for advanced weapons.

Heavy industry has also received technological aid from the United States. For the Kama truck complex, the Soviets have been able to buy US equipment and technology for the most advanced foundry in the world as well as other equipment not available elsewhere. US technology probably can also help to alleviate the many serious problems confronting Soviet oil and gas industries, particularly exploration and drilling in permafrost and offshore.

---

i

CONFIDENTIAL

~~CONFIDENTIAL~~

To a substantial degree, these machinery purchases -- like the grain imports -- have been facilitated by US long-term credits, both Eximbank and private. The terms of the Eximbank credits are comparable with or better than those offered in Western Europe and Japan, contributing to the already-existing world competition in promoting exports to the USSR.

US-Soviet trade in technology still has a large potential for growth. Cooperative ventures with US companies for the development of Soviet resources offer important advantages to the USSR. US companies are able to provide the USSR with advanced equipment, technology, and know-how to carry out the large internal development projects currently scheduled. Equally important, the Soviets need to tap US financial markets for government-backed credits if the massive Soviet imports needed for such projects are to be financed at reasonable interest rates.

So far in the detente period, the USSR has obtained US technology mainly through the trade channel. At the same time, however, a network of officially sponsored government-to-government bilateral agreements has been built up which could provide the Soviet economy with a good deal of US technology on an exchange basis. The US-USSR Science and Technology Agreement has led to the conclusion of more than 20 agreements between Soviet agencies and private firms. Most of the agreements call for general cooperation, joint research and development, and exchanges of delegations, information, processes, know-how, and licenses. Most agreements are also in high-technology industries of prime interest to the USSR such as electronics, chemicals, energy, and construction.

The growing imports of machinery and equipment together with cooperative ventures and bilateral agreements will transfer a substantial amount of Western technology to the USSR -- whether in the form of informal (and sometimes inadvertent) disclosure of know-how, exchanges of technical data, or finished products. But the ultimate economic effect of technological transfer through either machinery imports or informal contacts and bilateral exchanges depends on how rapidly the technology is assimilated. Soviet R&D and economic administration have been weakest in carrying technology from research through the development and testing stages into production. Many of the reforms in economic administration, science, and education in the past decade attempted to deal with just this problem, but the reforms seem to have petered out. The Soviet economy must do better in this area if imports of US technology are to have a substantial effect.

Other factors will also reduce the impact of US-Soviet trade and technological relations on the USSR. First of all, US leverage is limited because the USSR can go elsewhere for credits and roughly equivalent machinery and technology, except in a few sectors or for a few giant projects. Second, the scale of such relations -- although increasing -- will remain small relative to total production or trade. For example, imported US equipment will be equal to no more than 1% of the total value of equipment scheduled to be installed in Soviet industry in 1971-75.

ii

~~CONFIDENTIAL~~

~~CONFIDENTIAL~~

The effect on military capabilities is another matter. Some US technology could help the Soviets considerably in developing new weapons, especially in modernizing their strategic weapons systems. Although thus far the trade, contacts, and technical agreements associated with two years of detente have not transferred discernible amounts of military technology, the changes in US-Soviet relations under detente have the potential to upgrade Soviet military capabilities. While continuing their efforts to acquire such technology by espionage and theft and by purchase from other countries who evade COCOM controls, the Soviets will attempt to acquire military-related technology directly from the United States by opening up new channels of transfer and widening existing channels. Whether the full potential of transfer is realized depends in part on the care with which US firms, scientists, engineers, and technicians treat the developing contacts. In this regard, the guidelines set and administered by the US Government will be influential in determining private attitudes and decisive in limiting the transfer of military-related technology.

iii

~~CONFIDENTIAL~~

36.

~~CONFIDENTIAL~~

THE SOVIET GRAIN DEFICIT

Principal Findings

Our current estimate of Soviet grain production for FY 1976 of 170 million tons falls about 58 million tons short of requirements.

The USSR has so far purchased approximately 16 million tons of foreign grain in FY 76. In addition, Moscow undoubtedly will draw down grain stocks which we believe do not exceed 10-15 million tons and may be considerably less. These two factors, taken together narrow the difference between available supply and requirements to a minimum of 27 million tons.

The Soviets presumably will have to take a combination of unpalatable steps: (a) negotiate for further large amounts of grain from the United States -- the only large supplier in sight; (b) import additional quantities of soybeans from the United States and Brazil; (c) cut livestock feed rations to the 1972 level while maintaining livestock numbers, saving up to 13 million tons; and (d) slaughter additional livestock (a 5% reduction in herds would save about 6 million tons).

Because of the continuing high priority given to increasing meat production, the latter two options will be taken as a last resort.

CLASSIFIED BY
EXEMPT FROM GENERAL DECLASSIFICATION SCHEDULE OF E. O. 11652, EXEMPTION CATEGORY:
§ 5B(1), (2), (3) or (4) (circle one or more)
AUTOMATICALLY DECLASSIFIED ON
Date Impossible to Determine
(unless impossible, insert date or event)

~~CONFIDENTIAL~~

CONFIDENTIAL

Production and Requirements

Soviet grain requirements this year are expected to far exceed supply. Direct grain needs are estimated to be about 196 million metric tons. In addition, due to unusually large losses this year of hay and other forage crops -- normally supplying about two-thirds of the USSR's livestock feed* -- at least 11 1/2 million more tons of grain may be required to feed livestock.** The lost forage added to the normal grain requirements brings 1975/76 total grain needs to roughly 208 million tons. (See Table)

The quantity of grain required, however, cannot be directly balanced with the estimated gross output. The USSR reports grain production on a "bunker" weight basis that is, as the grain comes from the combine before preliminary cleaning and drying is done*** and before handling and transportation losses occur. At the same

---

* Important forage crops include silage (12% of total feed units in 1970, the year of most recent data), green chop (9%), potatoes and feed roots (3%), hay (10%), straw (6%), and pasture (22%).

** Since the nutritive content (or "feed-unit" value) varies by type of grain, the conversion from forage into grain equivalent depends on the type of grain available for feeding. Because corn is the most likely feed grain to be imported we have expressed the forage crop shortfall in "corn equivalent." The calculation is based on hay and silage losses only. It does not include an estimate of possible loss of pasture feed.

*** Bunker weight includes excess moisture, trash, dirt, weed seeds and grain admixtures, all of which are reduced to acceptable standards in several stages from farm to user.

-2-

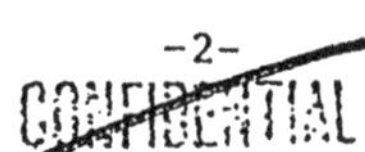

CONFIDENTIAL

time, uses shown in the table are given on a cleaned and standardized basis. Therefore, to be comparable, gross production must be discounted to exclude waste and losses.

Although the discount varies from year to year, evidence indicates that grain production -- as measured in standard condition -- has been from 4% to 12% less than reported during 1961-70. The average exaggeration for the 10-year period has been about 8%. In addition, roughly 3% of the reported production is lost in handling and transportation.

If our current production estimate of 170 million tons is realized, and if we have correctly estimated (1) normal requirements, (2) "losses" caused by exaggerated production data and in handling, and (3) the possible grain deficit caused by forage losses, the total gap will be 58 million tons (208 million m.t. minus 150 million m.t.) as shown in the table.*

So far, during FY 76 the USSR has contracted for about 16 million tons of foreign grain. In addition,

---

* Another way to look at this adjustment is the following: a Soviet grain requirement of 208 million tons would be covered by a grain production, as reported by the Soviets, of 233 million tons. The resulting deficit of 63 million tons is reduced to 58 million tons when adjusted for losses. The 150 million tons of usable grain from a gross production of 170 million tons is derived by deducting 58 million tons from the total requirements of 208 million tons. Because of rounding, this total is slightly below the 151 million tons derived by deducting 11% (19 million tons) from a gross production of 170 million tons.

36. (continued)

CONFIDENTIAL

USSR: Estimated Production and Requirements of Grain

Million Metric Tons

Fiscal Year	Estimated Production (1)	Waste and Losses a/ (2)	Requirements: Total (3)	Feed (4)	Food b/ (5)	Seed (6)	Industrial (7)	Export (8)	Deficit
1975/76	170	19	208	115 c/	60	27	3	3	58 d/

a. Waste and loss rate of 11% applied to production. This includes an estimated 3% handling loss factor and an estimated 8% waste factor resulting from excess moisture and extraneous matter included in the bunker weight measurement of grain (see text). The average exaggeration for the period 1961-70 came to about 8%.

b. Our estimates of the quantity of grain required for food are based on production data for flour and groats.

c. Including an allowance of 11-1/2 million tons of corn equivalent for losses of forage crops.

d. This deficit of 58 million tons is derived by "inflating" the total requirements of 208 million tons to a total of 233 million tons, the amount of grain required to be reported in official Soviet terms (see text) -- 208 divided by .89 -- and subtracting the gross production of 170 million tons (column 1). Because of rounding, a nominal deficit of 57 million tons is obtained by subtracting the net availability of 151 million tons (gross production - column 1 - minus waste and losses - column 2) from requirement of 208 million tons (column 3).

-4-

CONFIDENTIAL

CONFIDENTIAL

the Soviets undoubtedly will draw on its stocks, which we believe do not exceed 10 to 15 million tons.* This would narrow the gap between expected current supply (expected production net of losses and waste, plus current purchases of 16 million tons, plus the use of 15 million tons of stocks) and requirements to 27 million tons.

This estimate of the remaining gap between grain requirements and production is more likely to be too low than too high.

- An unofficial Soviet spokesman has admitted publicly that grain production would be "as low as in 1972," when it totalled 168 million tons. This suggests that production is expected to be no higher than 170 million tons, but could be lower.
- Our estimate of current requirements is conservative. It allows for only a moderate increase in livestock feed supplies considering the trend in livestock numbers.
- As mentioned above, we believe our allowance for drawdown of stocks to be high.

---

* Stocks could be substantially less. Less is known about Soviet grain stocks than any other aspect of the supply and demand situation. The quantity held in reserve is a state secret, protected by law. Estimates must be derived by balancing uses against production and imports using less-than-adequate data and requiring arbitrary assumptions for some important factors.

-5- CONFIDENTIAL

37.

SECRET

The Impending Soviet
Oil Crisis

The Soviet oil industry is in trouble. Soviet oil production will soon peak, possibly as early as next year and certainly not later than the early 1980s. The maximum level of output reached is likely to be between 11 and 12 million barrels per day (b/d)–up from the 1976 level of 10.4 million b/d. Maximum levels are not likely to be maintained for long, however, and the decline, when it comes, will be sharp.

The Soviets have two basic problems: one of reserves and one of production. Barring an extremely unlikely discovery of a massive new field close to an existing field, new deposits will not be found rapidly enough to maintain acceptable reserves-to-production ratios, and those fields that account for the bulk of Soviet production are experiencing severe water encroachment. As a result, increasingly large quantities of water must be lifted for each barrel of oil produced, and high-capacity submersible pumps–obtainable only from the United States–will be required if production declines are to be staved off even temporarily.

During the next decade, the USSR may well find itself not only unable to supply oil to Eastern Europe and the West on the present scale, but also having to compete for OPEC oil for its own use. This would be a marked change from the current situation, in which exports of oil to the West annually provide 40 percent of total Soviet hard currency earnings. The USSR has large reserves of coal and natural gas, but those scheduled for exploitation over the next decade are east of the Urals, far from consuming centers in the western USSR. Distance, climate, and terrain will make exploitation and transport difficult and expensive. Exports of gas will increase, but will not compensate for the loss of earnings from the export of oil. Although some substitution of coal and gas for oil in domestic use will be possible in the long run, the effect of such substitution will be minimal

Note: Comments and queries regarding this memorandum are welcome. They may be directed to
the Office of Economic Research

37. (continued)

in the short run. Neither hydroelectric power transmitted from the east nor construction of nuclear electric plants (mainly in the western USSR) can be expected to afford much relief in the Soviet energy situation for more than a decade.

38.

Soviet Economic Problems and Prospects

Central Intelligence Agency
Directorate of Intelligence

July 1977

Summary

The Soviet economy faces serious strains in the decade ahead. The simple growth formula upon which the economy has relied for more than a generation--maximum inputs of labor and capital--will no longer yield the sizeable annual growth which has provided resources needed for competing claims.

In the past, rapid growth enabled Moscow simultaneously to pursue three key objectives:

- catching up with the US militarily;
- steadily expanding the industrial base; and
- meeting at least minimal consumer expectations for improved living conditions and welfare.

Reduced growth, as is foreshadowed over the next decade, will make pursuit of these objectives much more difficult, and pose hard choices for the leadership, which can have a major impact on Soviet relations with Eastern Europe and the West.

This study examines the causes of the slowdown in growth, its implications, the policy choices open to the Soviet leadership, and their possible impact on defense, the consumer, foreign trade, and US relations.

Causes of the Slowdown

Factors tending to slow down the rate of growth have been apparent for some time.

- The drying up of rural sources of urban labor force growth;

- A slowdown in the growth of capital productivity;

- An inefficient and undependable agriculture which may be hit hard by a return of the harsher–but probably more normal–climatic patterns that prevailed in the 1960s;

- A limited capacity to earn hard currency to pay for needed technology imports and intermittent massive grain purchases.

These problems are not new. The Soviet leadership has tried to offset their effect by improvisation and palliatives, without impairing the priority development of defense production. They did not succeed, however, in preventing a steady fall-off in economic growth from its earlier high rate.

Looking toward the next five to ten years, these long-standing problems are likely to intensify, and will be joined by two new constraints which will greatly aggravate the resource strain: a sharp decline in the growth of the working age population and an energy constraint.

Labor force. In the 1980s the rate of growth of the labor force is expected to drop sharply (to less than 1 percent beginning in 1982) because of the depressed birth rates of the 1960s. Moreover, additions to the labor force will come mostly from ethnic minorities in Central Asia who do not readily move to the northern industrial areas.

In anticipation of this labor force constraint, the Soviet government is planning for an accelerated growth in the productivity of both labor and capital in the current 5-year plan (1976-80). But for years productivity gains have been slowing, and this trend is likely to continue given the sharply rising resource costs facing the economy. The more readily accessible fuel and mineral reserves west of the Urals are being rapidly depleted, while the abundant but more remote resources of Siberia and Central Asia require enormous investment outlays.

Energy. The most serious problem is a looming oil shortage. Soviet exploration and extraction policy has long favored increasing current output over developing sources of future output. As a result, new oil deposits have not been discovered rapidly enough to offset inevitable declines in older fields. Consequently, production will begin to fall off in the late 1970s or early 1980s. The current level of oil production is close to the estimated maximum potential of 11 million to 12 million b/d. By 1985 oil output is likely to fall to between 8 million and 10 million b/d.

The decline in output may or may not be a temporary phenomenon. The USSR is counting on large new supplies of oil and alternative energy sources—coal, natural gas, and hydroelectric power—coming onstream beyond the mid-1980s. But most of these energy sources lie east of the Urals, far from major industrial and population centers: their development would take years and require massive capital investment.

In the near-term, however, even if the development of alternative energy sources is pushed to the maximum, overall energy output will grow at a sharply declining rate. Under a plausible set of assumptions, it would decline from 4 percent in 1976-80 to slightly above 1 percent in 1981-85. Since Soviet energy consumption increases in close parallel with the growth of the economy, a sharp slowdown in energy production would seriously constrain economic growth unless Moscow finds ways of conserving large amounts of energy or covers its shortfall by becoming a net oil importer. The Soviet government appears to be aware that it has an energy problem but has not yet made the difficult choices which will be needed to deal with it. The longer the delay in adoption of a top-priority energy program, the greater will be the economic impact in the 1980s.

Policy Choices

Measures for grappling with these varied problems must meet two tests: first, they must be designed to remedy particular elements of the problem—the labor force, productivity, and energy constraints; second, they must be shaped with the recognition that the problems are interrelated, and that measures aimed at easing one problem may aggravate another.

Even on the first level, it will not be easy to find solutions that will do more than alleviate the component problems. Powerful remedies are either not readily available or not politically feasible.

The labor force constraint could be eased somewhat by such measures as retaining older workers longer in the labor force, shortening secondary education, and reducing military manpower by cutting the term of service. But such measures would have only a one-time impact.

iii

Moscow's options for raising the rate of growth and productivity of plant and equipment are even more constrained.

• They could convert industrial capacity from defense to the production of investment goods. They would be reluctant, however, to impair their defense production capability. Moreover, specialized defense resources are not easily transferred on short notice.

• They could stretch out R&D programs and production schedules and slow the rate of expansion of defense-oriented industrial capacity, but this would have limited effect in the short run.

• They could institute incentive-enhancing reforms of economic management. Such reforms, however, will be resisted by powerful vested political and bureaucratic interests.

Even a combination of these measures—such as a leveling off of defense production, coupled with measures to obtain additional manpower—would probably raise economic growth only slightly.

Options for dealing with the energy problem are similarly constrained. Opportunities for conservation are less obvious in the USSR than in the West—for example, there are few automobiles and most are for commercial or industrial use. Consequently, conservation measures alone are unlikely to yield large oil savings. The leadership thus will probably have to rely on some combination of the following measures:

• importing substantial amounts of oil from non-Communist countries;

• cutting oil exports to Eastern Europe; and

• severely rationing oil to domestic users.

Moving from a position of major oil exporter to that of a net importer would be particularly painful. Last year Soviet oil exports of $4.5 billion accounted for almost one-half of its hard currency earnings. If current trends are projected with no change in present policies, Soviet oil import requirements by 1985 could cost $10 billion at today's prices. Even with high priority measures to boost other exports, including gold sales, oil imports at that level would absorb most of the Soviet hard currency earnings in the 1980s, and largely foreclose the import of other goods from the West, including badly needed Western technology.

Cutting oil exports to Eastern Europe would ease this problem by forcing Eastern Europe to share the burden of the oil shortage. Any substantial cut in the Soviet oil supply commitment to Eastern Europe, however, would worsen that area's already difficult economic situation.

Placing the burden of the oil shortage on the domestic economy would mean curtailing oil rations to producing enterprises. Such cuts would almost certainly impede production, though the impact would be less severe if reductions were more gradual as part of a long-term energy-saving program.

Implementing the foregoing solutions is complicated by the fact that the problems are interrelated and the solutions impinge upon each other. For example, pressure on enterprises to save labor will be much less effective if they must also save energy. If the energy shortage is eased by allocating foreign exchange to import oil, the resulting decline of imports of foreign machinery and technology would adversely affect productivity and economic growth within a few years. Failure to import large amounts of energy equipment and technology from the West would substantially worsen the USSR's prospects for raising oil and gas production in the longer-term.

We conclude that a marked reduction in the rate of economic growth in the 1980s seems almost inevitable. At best, Soviet GNP may be able to continue growing at a rate of about 4 percent a year through 1980, declining to 3 - 3 1/2 percent in the early and mid-1980s. These rates, however, assume prompt, strong action in energy policy, without which the rate of growth could decline to about 3 1/2 percent in the near-term and to 2 - 2 1/2 percent in the 1980s.

These are average figures; in some years performance could be better, but in others, worse, with zero growth or even declines in GNP a possibility if oil shortages and a bad crop year coincide.

Potential Impact on Defense The slowdown in economic growth could trigger intense debate in Moscow over the future levels and pattern of military expenditures. Military programs enjoy great momentum and powerful political and bureaucratic support. We expect defense spending to continue to increase in the next few years at something like recent annual rates

v

of 4 to 5 percent because of programs in train. As the economy slows, however, ways to reduce the growth of defense expenditures could become increasingly pressing for some elements of the Soviet leadership.

On Consumers The reduced growth potential means that the Soviet consumer will fare poorly during the next five to 10 years compared to recent gains. Under the projected growth rates, per capita consumption could grow no more than 2 percent a year in contrast to about 3.5 percent since 1965. As a result, there will be no progress in closing the gap in living standards with the West or, for that matter, with most of Eastern Europe. Moreover, rises in wages over the next ten years combined with a slower growth in the availability of consumer goods would result in higher prices, more widespread shortages, and increasing consumer frustration.

On Relations with the US Moscow's economic problems in the 1980s will affect its relations with the West, especially the United States. Since the USSR's ability to pay for imports from the industrial West in the early and mid-1980s will be strained, Moscow may seek long-term credits (10-15 years), especially to develop oil and gas resources. Much of the needed energy technology would have to come from the US.

Stresses upon the Leadership

These serious problems ahead seem most likely to prompt Soviet leaders to consider policies rejected in the past as too contentious or lacking in urgency. Some leaders might be persuaded that basic organization and management reforms in industry are necessary. But that will raise the spectre that such reform would threaten political control. Consideration of other options—such as accelerating investment at the expense of defense or consumption, or reducing the armed forces to enhance the civilian labor force—could also result in strong leadership disagreements. Soviet responses to these problems could be further complicated by the fact that leadership changes will almost surely take place during the coming period. Even a confident new leadership would have difficulties in coming to grips with the problems ahead

39.

Organization and Management in the Soviet Economy: The Ceaseless Search for Panaceas

Central Intelligence Agency
National Foreign Assessment Center

December 1977

Introduction

Over the past decade, the USSR has been engaged in an effort, unprecedented in scope and intensity, to improve organization, management, and incentives in the economy. Most of the measures adopted stem directly from the program of reform outlined by Kosygin in 1965; other approaches, such as the effort to computerize everything computerizable, are ancillary to it. The effort as a whole is aimed at raising economic efficiency as measured by labor and capital productivity and improving the quality and mix of output.

The wide-ranging approaches may be conveniently grouped under five rubrics: (1) planning; (2) organization; (3) incentives, including those for improving quality of products; (4) computerization; and (5) miscellaneous programs. The first sections of this paper (1) review developments in each area over the past decade, with particular attention to changes during 1973-77, and (2) indicate the apparent future directions as reflected in the Directives for the 10th Five-Year Plan (1976-80) and the general literature.[1]* Final sections assess the success of the overall program in achieving its objectives up to now, its likely effects in the near term, and the prospects for effective reforms in the longer term.

Developments During 1965-77

Planning

Kosygin's program called for implementation of his economic reforms strictly within a framework of centralized planning, which was, however, to be improved in fundamental ways. First, the role of long-term plans was to be upgraded. To this end, the Five-Year Plan (FYP) was made legally binding

* For a discussion and list of source references, see the appendix.

and was to be a directive for enterprises. Annual plans are now drawn up taking into account the annual breakdowns set in FYPs, and incentive arrangements are supposed to allow for the degree of progress toward meeting FYP targets.

In addition, FYPs are being formulated within the framework of a 15-Year Plan (1976-90). During 1970-72, a great deal of work was set in motion to draft this plan. However, the effort was delayed by bureaucratic wrangling over planning methodology and probably also by the sheer magnitude of the task and the difficulty in getting agreement on long-range forecasts. Meanwhile, the Academy of Sciences and the State Committee for New Technology have drafted a "Comprehensive Program of Scientific-Technical Developments and Socioeconomic Consequences, 1976-90" with some 200 targets.[2] However, the draft of the overall 15-Year Plan is still in process of formulation.[3] At the 25th Congress of the Communist Party of the Soviet Union (CPSU) in 1976, Brezhnev again stressed the importance of long-term plans and the urgent need to improve their quality.

Second, the "scientific basis" for planning was to be radically upgraded. In practice, this has meant the more extensive use of mathematical forecasting models, input-output data, and optimizing techniques in planning. Although the traditional plan-formulation process remains intact, these approaches seem to be used extensively (notably in the economic research institutes) in preliminary planning work, in testing the consistency and balance of various kinds of plans, in calculating plan variants, and in making decisions about location, distribution, and mix of product in particular sectors. The "Comprehensive Program" for 1976-90, which used these techniques, aided the drafting of the 10th FYP, thus allegedly raising its "scientific basis."

Third, the system of plan indicators was to be directed more specifically toward solving problems of efficiency and product quality. As a result, an exhaustive discussion has taken place over the "correct" way to measure the efficiency of labor, capital, materials, new technology, computerized management systems, and much else. While the arguments have raged, the State Planning Committee (Gosplan) has introduced many new indicators of efficiency and product quality in national and enterprise plans. The national plan for 1976-80 and the annual plan for 1977 include over 500 such targets, and reporting is required in respect to their fulfillment.[4] At present, Gosplan is drafting proposals for further revision of these plan indicators to stress the use of long-term norms. In particular, a reorganization of the planning of wages and investment on the basis of such norms is under active consideration.

Fourth, some planning authority was to be delegated to the enterprise level, with the aim of spurring initiative on the periphery. To accomplish this objective, the number of directive targets set centrally for enterprises was initially cut sharply as part of the economic reform. However, all important targets were retained; in the process of implementing the reforms, new ones (labor productivity, product quality, contract fulfillment) were added through formal changes in the rules; and in practice the ministries have set many others.

Finally, to the end of "improving planning," an extensive discussion has taken place concerning so-called "complex" planning, a "system approach" to planning, and the "program-goals" approach in planning. The discussion seems to concern mainly the planning of regional complexes (such as Baikal-Amur) and the planning of integrated programs aimed at fostering scientific-technical progress (such as mechanization of labor). Judging from a barrage of discussion and criticism,[5] satisfactory integration of national and regional planning remains an elusive goal. Despite the increased role given to republic and local planning agencies, regional planning seems to amount mostly to adding up the relevant sectoral plans, which continue to have priority. Much work was done by economists and planners during the Ninth FYP (1971-75) to develop "complex" approaches and efficiency calculations for various kinds of regional and functional complexes. The 10th FYP includes a number of such "complex programs"—for fuel and energy, building materials, development of agriculture and associated branches, the non-Black Soil area, and Eastern regional raw materials. The Plan Directives call for further "improvements" in plan formulation via use of the program goals and "comprehensive" approaches. A revised set of methodological instructions to accomplish these and other improvements in plan making is to be published in 1978.[6]

Prospects

Despite the revival of some discussion of economic reform in the Party press in 1976, the likelihood of radical changes in the established system of economic organization and management is remote at present. In respect to organization, discussions are taking place on the desirability of creating supraministries of some kind to manage groups of related activities. No concrete steps have yet been taken in this direction, and the whole idea is likely to encounter strong bureaucratic opposition. The scheme is reminiscent of Khrushchev's piling up of coordinating bodies and, even if implemented, is likely to do more harm than good.

The leadership seems fully committed to pushing the merger of producing units into ever-larger entities. In the industrial sector, this movement is in full swing and is scheduled to be completed by 1980. It is unlikely that large gains in efficiency will come from this source. The initiative and independence of individual producing units will be severely restricted in favor of greater power for the production associations. What is more important, it seems clear that the associations and their components will be operating within an essentially unchanged economic environment. Hence, their behavior is likely to resemble that of their predecessor independent enterprises. Moreover, the associations are likely to receive detailed and tight supervision from the industrial associations, as well as the ministries, which are ultimately responsible for the performance of their sectors and whose powers are actually being strengthened. The ministries are the organizations that administer the system of rewards and penalties for the associations. In agriculture, the giant collective and state farms, which are coming to resemble one another more and more, will remain the basic form of organization. Sizable extension of the private sector in agriculture and services does not seem likely, even though present policy shows more tolerance toward this activity.

No fundamental reform of economic incentives is currently under active discussion. At the 25th Party Congress, Brezhnev stressed the importance of rewarding enterprises and workers for "final" (net) results, rather than gross output, and experiments to test such measures are continuing. Although further modifications of success criteria are likely, the benefits will be inconsequential, as long as incentives remain tied to fulfilling plans for whatever target or targets. The cutting of this Gordian knot is not being seriously advocated, at least in the open press. Because rewards are linked directly to fulfilling plan targets, variously defined, the relationships among units in the entire chain of suppliers, shippers, manufacturers, and distributors are administrative, rather than economic, in nature. The behavior of each unit is oriented toward meeting its own particular plan targets, rather than satisfying its clients. This perverse effect of incentives is reinforced by the fact that each link also is aware that its clients lack alternative suppliers, shippers, or customers—there is no competition.

In the Directives for the 10th FYP, the present conservative leadership has opted for continuance of the status quo. Although experimentation with organizational forms and incentive schemes is continuing, they do not entail any esssential modification of the traditional system. Since the Soviet Union's persistent difficulties with efficiency, technical progress, and product quality are rooted in the nature of the bureau-administered economic system itself, these problems are likely to persist and to defy solution through modification of organizational forms and administrative rules. These chronic difficulties will be reflected in a continuing sluggish growth of productivity.

In the long run, radical economic reforms involving the introduction of market arrangements in some form might help alleviate these chronic problems and raise the rate of productivity growth. To be effective, such reforms would have to include abolition of directive plans for enterprises, replacing the rationing of most producer goods with markets, freeing most prices, and introduction of profit-based incentives. Transition to such a "market socialism" would surely cause serious economic disruptions in the short run, including inflation and unemployment. Moreover, such a move would disturb established balances in both political and economic power. It would be strongly opposed by the state bureaucracy, where jobs, careers, and political influence would be at stake, as well as by the Party bureaucracy, whose control over economic decisionmaking and resource allocation would be threatened. Faced with uncertain long-run benefits, probable high short-run costs, and certain strong opposition, a Soviet leadership of any foreseeable composition would probably opt against taking such risks. The political leadership probably would consider such a radical move, only if faced with a severe economic crisis, such as stagnating or declining production or serious popular unrest. As long as present organizational arrangements continue to yield modest, even if declining, rates of growth, the leadership will probably prefer to put up with the familiar deficiencies of the systems, rather than to launch major changes with unknown payoffs and known political risks.

Secret

Outlook for the Siberia-to-Western Europe Natural Gas Pipeline

Key Judgments

We believe that the USSR will succeed in meeting its gas delivery commitments to Western Europe through the 1980s. Moscow has a wide range of options to accomplish this end:

- Deliveries could begin in late 1984, as scheduled, by using existing pipelines, which have excess capacity of at least 6 billion cubic meters (m^3) annually.

- Using some combination of Soviet and West European equipment, deliveries through the new export pipeline could probably begin in late 1985 and reach nearly full volume in 1987—about one year later than if the sanctions had not been imposed.

- At substantial cost to the domestic economy, the USSR could divert construction crews and compressor-station equipment from new domestic pipelines to the export pipeline or even dedicate a domestic pipeline for export use to ensure capacity adequate to meet contractual delivery obligations.

The task confronting the Soviets is made easier by the nonlinear relation between compressor power requirements and gas throughput in pipeline operations. By obtaining the 20 or so turbines built with the GE-made rotors already in Western Europe and operating compressor stations without standby units, Moscow could deliver through the new pipeline about three-fifths of the planned annual throughput of nearly 30 billion m^3. Turbines using an additional 40 rotors—the number Alsthom-Atlantique contracted before the US embargo to build for the Soviet Union under GE license—could boost throughput to nearly 90 percent of capacity. For reliability of pipeline operation and periodic maintenance, however, the Soviets would probably use some of the available turbines as standby units, thereby limiting throughput to about three-quarters of capacity.

Completion of the pipeline has become a top-priority objective for the Soviet leadership. On the economic side, they look forward to some $5 billion a year in new hard currency earnings from gas in the early 1990s (after repayment of pipeline borrowing) to partially offset declining oil export revenues. In their view, moreover, the United States' imposition of

Information available as of 6 August 1982 was used in the preparation of this report.

iii

Secret

SOV 82-10120
EUR 82-10078
August 1982

22200

Secret

sanctions has made completion of the pipeline a matter of national prestige and has provided an opportunity to foment dissension in the Western alliance.

The West Europeans see Soviet gas as a relatively low-priced substitute for uncertain Middle Eastern oil and also view the Soviet pipeline equipment orders as easing their substantial unemployment problems. In addition, they hold that increased East-West economic interdependence will lead to more responsible Soviet behavior. They are deeply angry about the US decision, especially the extraterritorial and retroactive features of the measures, which they regard as a serious infringement of their sovereignty.

As a result, the West Europeans are seeking ways to defeat or circumvent the extended US sanctions. Paris has ordered French firms to honor their Soviet contracts, and [

] Rome has said that pipeline contracts will be honored but has not yet ordered Italian firms to do so.

Taking all this into account, we think the likely Soviet choices for completing the export pipeline—in descending order of probability—are:

- Shipment of completed turbines built with the 20 or so GE rotors already in Western Europe.
- Production of the 40 GE-designed rotors by the French firm Alsthom-Atlantique under its existing contract with the Soviets—the move already announced by Paris.
- Production by Alsthom-Atlantique of 60 additional GE rotor sets, to be supplied to the West European turbine manufacturers.
- Western assistance in manufacturing rotors for Soviet-designed megawatt turbines.
- Soviet redesign of pipeline compressor stations, substituting a combination of smaller turbines or other drivers of either foreign or Soviet design.

Only the last outcome—primary reliance on their own resources—would cause the USSR much difficulty. The costs to them will be much higher if they have to build their own gas turbines and compressors for the export pipeline. Specifically, diverting from the domestic pipeline program Soviet equipment sufficient to equip the export line could reduce gas delivery to the domestic economy by as much as 30 billion m³ annually for a year or two. Other Soviet equipment options would have considerably smaller impact on domestic gas supply.

Secret

41.

Secret

Gorbachev: Steering the USSR Into the 1990s ▇

Key Judgments

Information available as of 30 June 1987 was used in this report.

In the next year, Soviet leader Mikhail Gorbachev and his Politburo will have to agree on adjustments to the current (1986-90) five-year plan to cope with emerging shortfalls and to correct imbalances. Meanwhile, the future of economic reform is being worked out, and the Soviet leaders will be attempting to formulate their resource allocation guidelines for the 1991-95 plan. The USSR's planning cycle calls for these guidelines to be given to the economic planners by about mid-1988. This will be a tough call because not all the returns will be in from measures already implemented. ▇

Adjusting the 1986-90 Plan

The present five-year plan has virtually no slack that would permit more attention to one of the major sectors of the economy without some impact or offsetting adjustments in other areas. For example, the growth in overall volume of investment, while higher than in the two previous five-year plans, still appears low in comparison with the production targets. Taken at face value, the plan indicates that the Soviets expect a sharply increasing ratio of output per ruble of investment. But if the efficiency gains from the "human factor" campaign do not materialize, the leadership will have to decide whether to push for faster investment growth in the present plan to keep its industrial modernization program on track. Such a step could force the USSR to consider permitting a buildup of debt to the West to finance more imports. And sustained higher rates of investment would not be feasible, in our view, without holding military procurement relatively flat. ▇

Similarly, allocations to the consumer in the current five-year plan, particularly goals for consumer durables, have been held down against a promise of better things to come in the 1990s as the hoped-for benefits of industrial modernization are realized. The leadership, however, will have to be careful to avoid the kinds of shortages that in the past have had a dampening effect on labor incentives—particularly because so much of the present plan appears to bank on increasing productivity through a motivated work force. ▇

v

Secret

Secret

Reforms

In the case of reforms, what has been accomplished so far amounts to a set of partial measures. Soviet leaders will need to consider adjustments to those measures already implemented and how to implement the more comprehensive changes in the organization and management of the economy that Gorbachev called for at the Central Committee plenum in June 1987. It will be particularly important for the leadership to avoid the kind of backsliding that has brought past reforms to a standstill. Gorbachev has been searching for a formula that encourages more initiative at lower levels while permitting control to be maintained from the center. This is a delicate balance at best; early in the 1965 and 1979 reforms, for example, the ministries began to reassert their control over enterprises by multiplying the number of plan targets and limiting their use of discretionary funds. And the natural inclination of local party officials will be to exercise the same kind of petty tutelage over enterprises that they have in the past. Preventing this will require a fundamental restatement of the responsibilities of ministries and party organizations.

According to guidelines approved by the Central Committee on 26 June 1987, the next phase in improving organization and management will involve curbing the powers of central economic authorities, developing genuine wholesale trade, reforming the price system and financial and credit institutions, and introducing stronger incentives for enterprises to use their increased independence in ways that satisfy the guidelines set out in the state plan. Gorbachev could also expand the permissible boundaries of private production and allow greater wage differentiation. Even with the best leadership intentions, improving worker incentives will depend mainly on whether workable arrangements in these areas can be developed and on how the labor force reacts to them. Elastic work rules and narrow wage differentials have become an important part of the "social contract" in the Soviet Union.

Formulating Resource Guidelines for 1991-95

The leadership's perception of progress on the industrial modernization program—especially in the machine-building sector—will be a critical factor in its outlook on the next five-year plan. If by next year this program does not appear to promise growth large enough to give generous increments to consumers and defense as well as investment, the leadership will

Secret

be forced to decide whether civilian machine building should get more funding in the 1991-95 plan. Another factor that could contribute to pressures for higher investment than originally envisaged for 1991-95 would be a dwindling of the impetus to growth from tightening labor discipline and weeding out poor managers. And a key unknown may be whether the construction and machine-building base will be adequate in scale and quality to support a large increase in investment without a cutback in the defense plan submitted by the General Staff.

Foreign Help

So far, Gorbachev has had little success in obtaining help for his economy from abroad—either from Eastern Europe or the West. The Soviets have had trouble getting their East European allies to shoulder more of the burden of the USSR's resource development and the Warsaw Pact's force modernization. Meanwhile, although the extent to which the leadership planned on increasing imports from the West during the 1986-90 plan period remains an unsettled question, Moscow's ability to buy more Western machinery or farm products has eroded badly because of the decline in world energy prices and the lower value of the dollar. At this juncture, the Soviets appear to be counting heavily on joint ventures with Western firms. They are currently negotiating with about 100 Western companies, although only a few of these negotiations appear to be in their final stages.

The Potential Pitfalls . . .

A wide range of special interests and sensitivities will impinge on Politburo decisions over the next few years. First of all, military support for the modernization of civilian industry could erode substantially if the external threat assessment now being offered by military leaders becomes starker because arms negotiations fail to constrain NATO defense programs and bilateral US-Soviet relations worsen. In the reform arena:

- A relaxation in the tautness of the economy would help innovation and ease a transition to new economic arrangements, but Gorbachev stands in the way. From his first days in power he has stepped up the pressure on workers, managers, and bureaucrats.

vii Secret

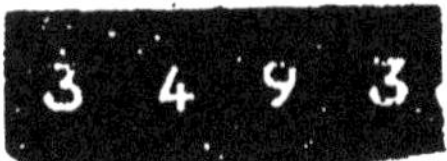

- Ministries are not likely to easily accept a lesser role in administering the economy. They probably will try to entrap their enterprises in a new web of rules and requirements, while ideological conservatives will fight an expansion of private economic activity.
- Genuine elections for party-state offices would evoke the specter of factionalism and be seen as a threat to the top-down direction of the society and the economy that has characterized "democratic centralism" for 60 years.

. . . And A Helpful Environment

The investment/defense decisions to be made would, of course, be generally much easier if economic growth turned upward sufficiently to ease the resource bind and diminish some of the fears of the fence sitters in Gorbachev's Politburo. At the same time, arms control agreements and improved US-Soviet relations that reduced both the momentum of NATO military programs and the influence of the Soviet military-industrial complex would give Gorbachev more room to maneuver. Soviet success in these areas would in turn raise Western interest in granting credits to Eastern Europe and establishing joint ventures in both the USSR and Eastern Europe.

Somewhat paradoxically, however, better economic performance and a favorable international climate would both strengthen and weaken the case for more ambitious economic reform. Reform is easier to implement when annual GNP growth is high, but the urgency attached to a reform program tends to fade when the economy is doing relatively well.

Gorbachev's Next Steps

At considerable risk to his political future, Gorbachev is gambling that his policies will rejuvenate the USSR's economy and society. The problems he is encountering have not yet derailed his program or diminished his determination to change the system radically. But even his supporters are concerned that he will need to win new victories before long if he is to sustain the momentum for change he has generated.

Secret

Thus, we believe that Gorbachev cannot work out the next steps toward renewal at his leisure. Developments during the past year have increased the chances that he will act boldly to sustain the momentum of his program. Because he seems determined to protect a modernization program that is already underfunded and because the milestones for fashioning the 1991-95 economic plan are fast approaching, Gorbachev is likely to seek arms control agreements in the final years of the Reagan administration rather than wait for the next election. Moreover, the weaknesses of the reform measures undertaken thus far are likely to become clearer over the next few years. We think Gorbachev is likely to move forward rather than retreat and push through more radical reforms so that they will be in place for the 1991-95 plan period. In this context, Gorbachev sees publicity and elections at lower levels as a way of exposing and disciplining those who will not or cannot implement his program. In the economy, workers probably will have a greater say in choosing trade union officials, foremen, and even managers.

The Consequences of Failure

Gorbachev has already asked the military and the population to curb their appetites in return for more later. If his programs do not work out, other leaders could appeal to these constituencies. The risks in a more radical reform and a rewrite of the social contract are that confusion, economic disruption, and worker discontent will give potential opponents a platform on which to stand. Gorbachev's position could also be undermined by the loosening of censorship over the written and spoken word and the promotion of limited democracy. If it suspects that this process is getting out of control, the party could well execute an abrupt about-face, discarding Gorbachev along the way.

Reverse Blank

ix

Secret

3495

Estimating Soviet Military Intentions and Capabilities

TASS-SOVFOTO

Estimating Soviet Military Intentions and Capabilities
Author's Comments: Raymond Garthoff

The documents in this volume dealing with CIA's analysis of military affairs during the Cold War were selected with several considerations in mind. First, they provide illustrative examples of analyses of Soviet intentions and military doctrine, as well as of military forces and capabilities. Second, they include materials on strategic forces and theater or general purpose forces for nuclear and non-nuclear warfare. For reasons of space, however, some subjects regrettably are not covered, such as Soviet naval forces and civil defense. Third, they provide a balance, including CIA Directorate of Intelligence analyses on current Soviet military affairs (and "post-mortems" on past analyses and estimates), as well as CIA-drafted National Intelligence Estimates forecasting future developments.

Finally, the documents selected highlight new materials, omitting many relevant documents released earlier and published in previous collections. As a result, less attention is given to the 1960s and 1970s, and to the early period of concern over possible Soviet initiation of war in the late 1940s and early 1950s, the "missile gap" of the late 1950s, the Cuban missile crisis of 1962, the "Team B" competitive analysis on strategic estimates in the late 1970s, and the end game of the Cold War in the late 1980s.

THE SOVIET STRATEGIC MILITARY POSTURE, 1961–1967

THE PROBLEM

To reassess the broad outlines of the USSR's military doctrine and posture in the light of recent information on Soviet strategic thinking, present military capabilities, and R&D in major weapon systems, and to estimate future trends in Soviet military strategy and force structure.[1]

THE ESTIMATE

CURRENT TRENDS IN SOVIET MILITARY THOUGHT

Basic Principles

1. Soviet thinking about military policy has proceeded from a general outlook which stresses that historical forces are moving inexorably in the direction of communism. This movement is carried forward by the struggle of "the masses," led by the Communist parties, to overthrow the existing social-economic order, rather than by the direct use of the military power of the Communist Bloc. These beliefs lead the Soviets to view their armed forces as a means to deter Western military action against the Sino-Soviet Bloc, to inhibit the West from intervening militarily in other areas, to maintain security within the Bloc, to lend weight to their political demands and to demonstrate the success and growing power of their cause. At the same time, they wish to have the forces to fight a war effectively should one occur. However, their political outlook, their military programs of recent years, and intelligence on their current intentions, all suggest that the Soviet leaders do not regard general war as desirable or a Western attack on them as probable.

Strategies and Forces

2. Within this general framework, the specific concepts which underlie Soviet decisions about force goals and strategic planning are difficult to discern. These principles can only be deduced, and incompletely at that, from overt Soviet statements, which are carefully framed with an eye to both security and propaganda; from such classified Soviet information as can be obtained; from the choices reflected in the actual military programs undertaken by the

[1] Detailed estimates of the present and future strengths and capabilities of the Soviet and Bloc armed forces can be found in Annexes A and B of NIE 11-4-61, "Main Trends in Soviet Capabilities and Policies, 1961–1966," dated 24 August 1961, in NIE 11-8/1-61, "Strength and Deployment of Soviet Long Range Ballistic Missile Forces," dated 21 September 1961, and in NIE 11-2-61, "Soviet Atomic Energy Program," dated 5 October 1961.

It should be noted that the present estimate does not touch on Chinese Communist military developments or possible actions. These might come to affect Soviet military policies and programs during the period under consideration.

USSR; and from the strategic situation which objectively confronts them.

3. It is worth noting that, while the Soviets have made impressive advances in modern weapon systems, a number of factors have hampered the process of integrating these advances into their strategic doctrine. One of these factors is the influence of a long military tradition, strongly reinforced by their experience in World War II, stressing massive movement, protracted campaigns, and the paramount significance of ground combat and the occupation of enemy territory. Another is security barriers within the military establishment, which appear to be far more stringent than in the US. Perhaps the most serious fetter, however, has been the rigid politico-military concepts which Stalin dogmatically imposed upon military thought. It was not until the mid-1950's, for example, that Soviet doctrine began to relax the principle that strategic surprise and the force of the initial blow are relatively unimportant to the outcome of a war between major powers, a position Stalin took in order to divert attention from the USSR's nearly catastrophic unpreparedness at the outset of World War II.

4. The pace of military thought, however, has quickened sharply in the last two or three years, primarily at the initiative of Khrushchev. At about the time when he set in motion a modernization of the Soviet force structure, including a substantial reduction in personnel, the regime began deliberately to encourage controversial discussion among senior officers in an effort to spark original and creative thought. As a result, strategic doctrine is a lively and argumentative field of professional study in the USSR today.

5. Such high-level discourse as we know about does not revolve around the questions of alternative attack strategies and target systems which are at the center of US military attention. Instead, the chief argument ranges "conservative" against "modern" views. Adherents to the first view assert that, despite the advent of new weapons, general war is likely to be protracted, ground combat on a mass scale will continue to be of major importance, and victory will require the combined action of forces of all types, including a multimillion man army. Adherents to the second view charge that their opponents are making only minimal and inadequate adaptations of earlier doctrine to accommodate new weapons. This group argues that a general war is likely to be short, with victory decided primarily in the initial nuclear exchange. Current official doctrine, as it appears in statements by the Minister of Defense, appears to be an amalgam of both these views.

6. The high-level discussions of which we are aware are remarkably deficient in sophisticated analysis of such concepts as first and second strike capability or counterforce strategy. The problems of attacking hardened and mobile strategic forces go completely unmentioned in such information as we have on Soviet targeting for long range attack. While most recommended target lists include nuclear retaliatory forces and control centers, they generally give equal importance to strikes against urban centers and their enemy's broad warmaking potential.

7. We think it certain that the strategic thought which underlies operational planning in the long range striking forces themselves is more sophisticated than this. But we have not acquired detailed Soviet discussions of doctrine for the operations of long range missile and bomber forces. Planning in these forces has certainly been obliged to consider such factors as warning and reaction times and the specific characteristics of different weapon systems and enemy targets. [ ] indicates that at least some of these factors have been taken into account, but not in ways that suggest very advanced concepts for dealing with the problems involved.

8. On the whole, the information we have suggests that Soviet military thought generally is still preoccupied with the problems of integrating nuclear and missile weapons into general doctrine and is only beginning to cope with the detailed comparative analysis of alternative strategies and force levels. Nor is this preoccupation completely surprising,

since the achievement of an ICBM capability, even in the early stages of its deployment, represents to the Soviets a profound change in their strategic situation. For over a decade, they confronted an opponent who possessed a formidable strategic capability but against whom their own long-range striking capabilities were relatively limited. Now, for the first time, they have a weapon system capable of delivering nuclear attacks against the US with little warning by a means against which there is no present defense.

9. The USSR probably has not elaborated any comprehensive doctrine covering the contingencies of limited and local war between Soviet and Western forces. Public Soviet statements regularly insist that such wars would quickly and inevitably expand into general nuclear war. These statements are clearly intended to deter the West from embarking upon conflict on the Bloc periphery or attempting penetrations of Bloc territory; they are not necessarily to be taken as expressions of Soviet military policy. Confidential sources do not reveal what detailed contingency plans the Soviets have for such a case. We believe, however, that the USSR would wish to avoid direct involvement in limited combat on the Bloc periphery and, if such conflict should occur, would wish to minimize the chances of escalation to general nuclear war. Consequently, it would not in most circumstances take the initiative to expand the scope of such a conflict. Although the degree of Soviet commitment and the actual circumstances of the conflict would determine their decision, we believe that in general the Soviet leaders would expand the scope of the conflict, even at greater risk of escalating to general war, only if a prospective defeat would, in their view, constitute a grave political reverse within the Bloc itself or a major setback to the Soviet world position.

10. Soviet doctrine apparently does not contemplate conflict with Western forces in areas of contention at a distance from Bloc territory. Conflicts involving local anti-Western or Communist forces are treated under the rubric of "national liberation wars." Such forces are credited, on ideological grounds, with the inherent strength to overcome "imperialist" attempts at military intervention. The Soviet support rather vaguely proffered is intended to be of a general deterrent character, but does not envisage overt Soviet military involvement. Despite the Soviet tendency in recent years to adopt an aggressive political stance in conflicts all over the world, the Soviets have not developed the naval forces and other special components which would give them a capability for military operations at great distances from the Bloc.

CURRENT STRATEGIC POSTURE

11. The strategic nuclear force the USSR has developed in recent years could permit the launching of large-scale initial attacks on short notice against a large number of Eurasian targets and a more limited number of North American targets. However, the Soviet leaders cannot at present have any assurance that their own nation and system could escape destruction from retaliatory Western attacks even if the USSR struck first. The Soviet leaders evidently believe their current strategic forces provide a strong deterrent against Western initiation of general war and are sufficient to support a more assertive foreign policy, particularly by virtue of the threat they pose to allies of the US in Europe and Asia. But there is no implication in Soviet behavior that they consider themselves in a position deliberately to attack the West, or to undertake local moves which carried with them a serious risk of bringing on general war. These views do not exclude Soviet use of available strategic attack forces to launch a preemptive blow should they conclude that the West was irrevocably committed to an imminent attack.

12. There have been considerable improvements in the Soviet air defense establishment, primarily through the widespread deployment of surface-to-air missiles at major cities and other key installations. Soviet defenses are now reasonably adequate against medium and high-altitude attack by subsonic Western bombers. We believe that the system as a

whole, however, is far less adequate to cope with sophisticated penetration tactics, low altitude penetrations or supersonic cruise-type missiles. It has no present capability against ballistic missiles. Most important, because of the susceptibility of their defenses to saturation and degradation, the Soviet leaders almost certainly cannot be confident of the degree to which they could cope with the diverse types and scales of attack the West could direct against the Bloc.

13. In addition to forces designed for long-range attack and for defense against such attack, the USSR continues to maintain large theater field forces. The Soviets regard these forces as part of the deterrent to general war, and their military doctrine considers such forces as essential to the conduct of general war should it occur. The Soviet theater forces now in being could institute large-scale attacks in peripheral areas, but the success of such operations in a general war would depend heavily on the outcome of the initial nuclear exchange. The Soviet leaders also regard these forces as a deterrent to any limited action against Bloc territory or on its periphery, serving at the same time as an essential means of maintaining Communist regimes in the Satellites.

14. Based on the current Soviet naval posture and available writings on doctrine, we believe that the mission of the Soviet Navy is to carry out a variety of tasks in a protracted general war, including the support of theater forces in such a war. The USSR has developed some capability to deliver nuclear attacks against land targets, including some in the US, by means of short-range submarine-launched missiles. However, the bulk of the Soviet submarine forces, predominantly torpedo attack types, would engage in interdiction operations in a long war in which the US attempted to maintain extensive logistic support to overseas areas. The Soviet Navy would also conduct defense against hostile naval forces possessing long-range attack capabilities, which the Soviets evidently regard as a major strategic threat. Its capabilities against US missile submarines in the open seas remain severely limited.

Military Research and Development

15. The Soviets are engaged in intensive efforts in weapons research and development to acquire new systems which, by their psychological, political, and military impact, would shift the world relation of forces to their advantage. In making their decisions, Soviet planners will have to consider such problems as rapid technological change, long lead times, developments in opposing forces, and increasing costs of weapon systems. Despite the rapid growth in Soviet economic resources, there will continue to be competition among military requirements as well as with the demands of important nonmilitary programs. Over the last two years, for example, Khrushchev has apparently linked his military arguments for reducing the size of Soviet forces with a further argument that additional funds could in this way be made available for raising living standards. Nevertheless, the USSR is allocating funds generously to military R&D, concentrating major efforts on improving the forces for long range attack and for defense against such attack by the West.

16. Much of the military R&D about which we have recent evidence is designed to fill obvious gaps in the Soviet strategic posture. In the field of long range delivery systems, an intensive program of test firing has been underway to develop second generation ICBM systems, which we believe include missiles of reduced dimensions and lighter weight, more easily deployed than the massive first generation Soviet ICBM. Some of the recent ICBM testing may represent development of systems for delivering warheads with yields on the order of 100 MT. Both a 2,000 n.m. ballistic missile and a supersonic "dash" medium bomber have been developed, and there is some evidence of R&D efforts in follow-on heavy bombers.

17. The principal current Soviet R&D program for strategic air defense, and perhaps the major Soviet military developmental program, is a large-scale effort to achieve defenses against

ballistic missiles. It has been clear to us for more than a year that the Soviets are assigning very substantial resources to this effort. In October 1961, Marshal Malinovsky stated that the USSR had "solved the problem" of intercepting a ballistic missile in flight. From intelligence sources, we believe that the Soviets are making good progress in development work for an antimissile system. This effort has resulted in the acquisition of important data, including data on high altitude nuclear effects, and has also involved the testing of at least some system components. Other known R&D in the air defense field over the recent past has included improved radars for early warning and fighter control, a surface-to-air missile system for use against low-altitude penetrators, and new fighter interceptor systems.

18. Soviet research and development activities also reflect efforts at qualitative improvement in the theater field forces and naval forces. The emphasis has been on mobility and firepower for theater forces, and short and medium-range missiles are now available for their support. Soviet field forces, at least in East Germany, have been allocated surface-to-air missiles for defense against medium and high altitude air attack. Within the next two or three years they will probably also have available missiles for defense against low flying aircraft as well as against ballistic missiles of short ranges. With the advent of US missile submarines, the Soviet Navy has recently placed increased emphasis on new weapons and techniques to extend ASW capabilities to the open seas. We believe, however, that over the next five years, the USSR will have only a limited capability to detect, identify, localize and maintain surveillance on submarines operating in the open seas.

Recent Nuclear Tests

19. The preliminary information now available indicates that the 1961 nuclear test series has given the Soviets increased confidence in current weapon systems, advanced their weapon design significantly, added greatly to their understanding of thermonuclear weapon technology, and contributed vital weapon effects knowledge. Soviet thermonuclear weapon technology in particular appears to be sophisticated and advanced. The 1961 test series will permit the Soviets to fabricate and stockpile, during the next year or so, new weapons of higher yields in the weight classes presently available.

20. Of the 44 shots detected in the 1961 series, 5 to 10 appear to have been proof tests of complete weapon systems, many of them with yields in the megaton range. We believe the Soviets have proof-tested weapon systems of the following types: short or medium range ground-launched ballistic missiles with yields up to about 2 MT and short-range submarine-launched ballistic missiles with yields of about 3 MT. In addition, they have proof-tested bombs with yields up to about 6 MT and have probably delivered more than one such bomb on a single bomber mission. The warheads tested in these various weapon systems are believed to be in stockpile. Those few proof-tested warheads thus far analyzed appear to reflect 1958 technology.

21. Weapon effects tests were apparently conducted underground, underwater, near the surface of the water, and at various altitudes up to 100–200 n.m. Those at very high altitudes will contribute valuable effects information needed for Soviet development of antiballistic missile defenses, but were probably not complete systems tests.

22. The majority of the 1961 shots were developmental tests aimed at improving future Soviet nuclear weapons capabilities. Some of the fission weapons tested revealed extensive Soviet efforts to increase efficiency, and to reduce weapon size and weight. Two very large yield tests in this series are particularly significant in that they indicate a high degree of sophistication in weapon design.

a. [ ] Preliminary estimates give

[ ] If the actual weight is 10,000 pounds, a 25 MT warhead could be delivered by the first generation Soviet ICBM to a range of about 5,500 n.m.

b. The 58 megaton device probably was actually a 100 MT weapon tested at reduced yield. Used as tested, the device could be of value to a Soviet strategy designed to minimize the fallout from very high-yield weapons. Weapons of this size and weight (probably 20,000–30,000 pounds) could be delivered by aircraft such as the BEAR, or could be emplaced offshore. If the actual weight is 20,000 pounds, such a warhead could be delivered by the first generation Soviet ICBM to a range of about 3,500 n.m. We believe that a more powerful vehicle than the first generation ICBM would probably be required to deliver such a warhead against most targets in the US.

c. A few handmade versions of these very high-yield weapons could be available now or in the near future, but series production would probably require a year or more. However, if they are to be employed as first generation ICBM warheads, we would expect tests of ICBMs with modified dummy nosecones prior to operational deployment.

23. Tests of other thermonuclear weapons, which apparently comprised the bulk of the shots in the recent series, indicate a continuing and highly successful Soviet effort to improve efficiencies, improve yield-to-weight ratios, and reduce fissionable material requirements. These tests show a concentration on weapons with yields between about 1.5 and 5 MT (corresponding to weights between about 1,000 and 3,500 pounds), which are suitable for delivery by all Soviet bombers and offensive missiles. The preliminary analysis indicates that [ ] significant progress in thermonuclear weapons design has been achieved.

PROBABLE MAJOR DEVELOPMENTS IN SOVIET FORCES TO THE MID-1960's

24. Major Soviet concern will continue to focus on the strategic weapons balance. In this area, a critical question is whether or not the Soviet leaders will consider it feasible and desirable to: (a) seek a capability to destroy the US nuclear delivery forces prior to launching, by means of a first strike; (b) seek no more than a capability to deliver nuclear attacks on population and industrial centers; or (c) seek nuclear attack forces of a type and size which will be somewhere between these two concepts.

25. We believe the Soviets already view the first of these concepts as no longer practicable. This is partly because of the thousands of Soviet missiles and launchers that would be required to destroy all the fixed bases of the US nuclear force programed for 1963–1967, especially the hardened US ICBM sites. Equally important, US warning capabilities, fast reaction times, and mobile forces such as airborne bombers and missile submarines already tend to offset Soviet capabilities to attack fixed bases. These latter factors would compound the uncertainties inherent in any Soviet strategy for destroying US nuclear forces prior to launch, regardless of the size of Soviet long-range striking forces.

26. As to a capability to attack cities alone, there is evidence from recent statements and writings that some Soviet military men regard destruction of population and industry, not merely as something to be threatened for purposes of deterrence and intimidation, but also as a major determinant in the outcome of a general war. In view of the weight of nuclear attack the US can launch and the impossibility of achieving a fully effective defense, however, we believe that the Soviet leaders have decided that a capability to destroy only urban and industrial centers, while a powerful deterrent, would be inadequate should general war occur.

27. Consequently, we believe that the Soviets will seek a larger strike capability. This will

probably be one large enough to bring under attack the SAC bomber bases and other soft and semihardened US military installations against which their ICBMs are an efficient weapon system. Further, in determining force goals, they may also wish to provide themselves with an ICBM force large enough to permit them to attack some hardened US targets, and to have a more substantial residual striking capability after a US attack. Although the Soviets would probably not regard a capability on this order as adequate for deliberate initiation of general war, it would put them in a position to strike preëmptively at an important segment of the US nuclear delivery forces should they reach a decision that such action was required.

28. Taking these considerations into account, we believe that the USSR will have an ICBM force of several hundred operational launchers in the period 1964–1967. The deployment complexes presently in operation and under construction, while protected by concealment from ground observation, some dispersal, and surface-to-air missiles, are unhardened and vulnerable to overhead observation. In view of Soviet concern for US reconnaissance and attack capabilities, we believe that the Soviets will move to increase the survivability of their ICBM force. In the mid-1960's, the bulk of the force will probably be protected by greater dispersal and possibly by semihardening, and some of the later launchers will probably be fully hardened. More than one missile will probably be available for most launchers.

29. In addition, through 1967, we forecast that the USSR will retain a mix of long range weapon systems. This will include a heavy bomber force which will probably remain relatively small but increase in quality, and an expanding force of missile submarines. Medium bomber strength will probably drop to a few hundred by the mid-1960's, but a considerable portion of these will be supersonic "dash" types, perhaps equipped for standoff missile delivery and for armed reconnaissance. After about the next year, ballistic missile forces other than ICBMs will be characterized by shifts to improved, longer range systems rather than by sheer numerical expansion.

30. In addition to strengthening defenses against manned bombers and cruise-type missiles, we believe that a major Soviet objective of the mid-1960's will be to achieve defenses against long-range ballistic missiles before the US has acquired a comparable capability. In Soviet eyes, this would enable them to claim an important advantage over the US. For political as well as military reasons, the Soviets probably would wish to deploy antimissile defense in at least a few critical areas even if the available system provided only a limited, interim capability. Considering these factors and the present status of the Soviet research and development program, we estimate that in the period 1963–1966 the Soviets will begin at least limited deployment of an antimissile system. Soviet cities will probably have priority for deployment of any AICBM defenses available through 1967. We believe that throughout this period, the Soviets are likely to have only a marginal capability for interference with US satellites.

31. We believe that the Soviet leaders will continue to retain large theater and naval forces. The extent to which these forces are reduced in the next few years will depend in part on the prevailing international situation, but we now believe it may rest equally on the course of the internal Soviet discussion regarding the nature and duration of a large-scale war fought with nuclear weapons. In general, we believe that economic and political factors, together with the further growth of nuclear capabilities, will at some point persuade the Soviet leaders to revert to the military manpower reductions begun in 1960 but suspended in 1961. Ground divisions and tactical air forces will probably be reduced and older ships retired or mothballed, but the USSR will retain sizable forces calculated to be sufficient for all types of warfare, nuclear and conventional, limited and general. Moreover, the Soviets will not abandon the reservist and

mobilization system designed to augment their forces rapidly should the need arise.

32. The recent nuclear test series does not in itself provide clear guidelines as to possible changes in force structure or strategic concepts. We believe that long-range striking forces have been given priority in the allocation of available nuclear materials, and that limitations in the Soviet stockpile have consequently restricted the nuclear capabilities of other forces. The broad range of proof tests, weapon effects tests, and developmental tests in the 1961 series suggests an effort to improve the nuclear capabilities of all arms of the Soviet military establishment. We had anticipated that in any event the limitations on allocation of nuclear weapons to air defense, theater, and naval forces would have eased by the mid-1960's and this trend may be hastened by the recent tests. These forces will then have a greater variety of nuclear weapons at their disposal.

33. It now appears that the trend in nuclear weapon yields of long-range missile and bomber systems will be upwards. The use of higher yield weapons would tend to reduce Soviet numerical requirements for delivery vehicles to accomplish given objectives, although for attacking military targets the accuracy and reliability of the Soviet weapon systems are generally more critical than warhead yield. Warheads in the 25 MT class, which could probably be made available in quantity within a year or so, would enhance the capabilities of the first generation Soviet ICBM against hardened targets. It is reasonable to believe that some of the new ICBMs now under intensive testing are designed to carry warheads of very high yield. Nevertheless, we continue to believe it unlikely that the Soviets would try to acquire the very large number of ICBM launchers needed for effective attack on all the hardened ICBM sites planned by the US. For the present, the very high yield devices are probably intended to support deterrence and psychological warfare, although we have no doubt that military uses are also intended.

POLICY AND STRATEGIES TO THE MID-1960's

34. From the developments likely to occur in Soviet forces, and from implications found in current discussions of military doctrine, we conclude that, over the ~~next~~ five years or so, the Soviets are unlikely to develop a military strategy and posture aimed at the deliberate initiation of general war. They are likely to continue to believe that their policy goals cannot be achieved by this means. Therefore, their first priority, since they evidently do intend to pursue forward policies involving some level of risk, will be to have a credible deterrent against initiation of war by the West. They will recognize that deterrence may fail, and if completely convinced in some situation of high risk that the West was about to launch a general nuclear attack, would attempt to pre-empt. Their strategy for the conduct of general war will probably call for delivering large-scale nuclear blows against Western striking forces and national centers of power, protecting the Soviet homeland against nuclear attack to the extent feasible, and subsequently committing their remaining forces to extended campaigns probably aimed initially at the occupation of Western Europe.

35. The Soviets will want a formidable military posture primarily to prevent such a war, but they will also want it as a support to vigorous policy initiatives short of war. These latter will include in particular the sponsorship of revolutionary activity directed at advancing Communist or pro-Soviet groups to power in any part of the world where the opportunity exists or can be created. It is this sort of struggle below the level of direct military engagement with the major Western Powers which will almost certainly continue to be the Soviets' principal reliance in seeking the expansion of their power.

36. It is conceivable, however, that by the mid-1960's the Soviets will come to regard the deterrence which they can exert upon the West as strong enough to permit them, without excessive risk, to use their own forces in local military actions. They will certainly continue to have field forces on a scale to permit this in areas peripheral to Soviet Bloc

territory, and these will be forces of increased mobility and flexibility. They are also capable of acquiring the naval strength, air transport, and special forces to conduct local military action in more remote areas. On the whole, however, we believe that the Soviets are unlikely to adopt such a course as a matter of general policy, in part because of the risks involved but also because in their view there is likely to be increasing opportunity to advance their cause by nonmilitary means.

37. The use of Soviet forces in local military actions outside the Bloc, if attempted, would be unlikely to take the form of naked military aggression. Instead, any use of Soviet forces outside the Bloc would take the form of support to revolutionary actions by local Communist or pro-Soviet forces, where a pretext could be made that Soviet intervention was intended to forestall intervention by the "imperialists." We believe there is some possibility that such a strategy will emerge by the mid-1960's and will be applied to vulnerable areas bordering on the Soviet Bloc. We think it more likely, however, that the Soviets will continue to rely on local political revolutionary forces, operating without overt Soviet military support but under the protection of an increasing deterrent power, to achieve a more gradual expansion of the area of Soviet control.

CAPABILITIES OF THE SOVIET THEATER FORCES

THE PROBLEM

To estimate the role and capabilities of the Soviet theater forces, especially against the NATO area in Europe, at present and over the next two years or so.

FOREWORD

1. As considered in this estimate, the components of the Soviet theater forces include: the ground forces and their weapons; tactical aircraft and missiles; supporting and logistical elements such as transport aircraft; and major portions of the surface naval and submarine fleets. The roles and capabilities of those Soviet forces which would perform other primary military missions, notably long-range striking forces and air and missile defense forces, are the subject of other National Intelligence Estimates.

2. In recent years, Soviets have debated at greater depth than in the past the probable nature of a general nuclear conflict between the Bloc and the West, and the information available to us reflects this increased attention. In this estimate, particularly in Chapters I and IV, we consider mainly the employment of Soviet theater forces in general nuclear war, taking some account of the way in which Soviet plans might be affected if operations were begun on short notice, or after a period of preparation. In Chapter V, we consider at much shorter length the possible employment of these forces in limited nuclear or conventional warfare under the threat of escalation.

3. It should be emphasized that, in discussing Soviet theater forces and their capabilities, we do not take account of the actions of opposing Western forces. In particular, we do not assess the

effect on Soviet theater forces of an initial, strategic nuclear exchange. We believe, however, that the effect of such an exchange could be a principal factor governing the ability of Soviet theater forces to carry out their assigned missions in a general war.

SUMMARY AND CONCLUSIONS [1]

A. Soviet military doctrine for general nuclear war stresses the use of all types of forces, and not strategic forces alone, from the outset of hostilities. The requirements for general nuclear war, as the Soviets see them, include forces prepared for action during a relatively brief strategic exchange, and forces suitable for protracted theater warfare involving extensive campaigns. Although this position imposes heavy demands on Soviet resources, it is still being sustained after extensive debate within the political and military leadership. We believe that for at least the next few years the Soviets will continue to regard large theater forces as essential. *(Paras. 1–5)*

B. Soviet doctrine continues to assume the full-scale employment of theater forces from the outset of a general war, with the ultimate objective of annihilating enemy military capabilities and occupying territory. The prospect of nuclear warfare has led to many modifications but no radical revisions in operational doctrine for theater forces. Efforts are being made to adjust organization and training to the requirements of rapid advance and flexible maneuver, to coordinate the employment of tactical nuclear support for Soviet forces, and to ensure destruction of the comparable nuclear means of the enemy. The traditional Soviet concept of combined arms operations has provided a basis for gearing modernized tactical air and missile support to the motorized and armored ground forces. *(Paras. 6–11)*

C. The ground elements of Soviet theater forces, containing nearly two million men and representing the largest part of the total military establishment, are well-trained and equipped with excellent materiel. Present trends point to a continuing emphasis on firepower and mobility. We estimate that there are

[1] The Assistant Chief of Staff, Intelligence, USAF, dissents from major aspects of this estimate. For his views, see pages 7–10, immediately following the SUMMARY AND CONCLUSIONS.

about 145 line divisions, approximately 80 of them considered to be combat ready and the remainder at low and cadre strength. The strongest concentrations are in East Germany and in the western and southern border regions of the USSR. If the Soviets were able to mobilize for 30 days before the initiation of hostilities, they could expand their total forces to about 100 combat ready and 125 nonready divisions, although there would be deficiencies in training, equipment, and supporting units. (*Paras. 13–16, 46–49*)

D. Short-range rockets and road mobile missiles with ranges up to 350 nautical miles are now in the artillery support structure of major Soviet theater commands. Tactical Aviation has been sharply reduced in quantity, and a prime current deficiency is the small number of modern aircraft, particularly fighter bombers. However, there have been qualitative improvements in aircraft and their armament, and this trend will continue. In addition, tactical ballistic and antiaircraft missiles are now available, and theater support could also be afforded by MRBMs and IRBMs in western USSR. These developments provide a net increase in the firepower available to support theater forces in the event of general war, but at the expense of some flexibility. (*Paras. 17–21*)

E. Organic air transport is now sufficient to airlift simultaneously only one airborne division or the assault echelons of two such divisions; we believe that this capacity may be doubled in the next several years. Amphibious assault capabilities are extremely limited, and there are no indications of significant future improvements. (*Paras. 29–30, 33–34*)

F. Tactical nuclear support is still limited in quantity and quality, but it has improved markedly over the past few years. Soviet military planners are now in a position to think in terms of committing up to a few hundred nuclear weapons, virtually all with yields in the kiloton range, to a typical *front* operation.[2] Limitations on the quantity and variety of nuclear weapons available to theater forces will have eased by the mid-1960's. The Soviets are probably developing subkiloton weapons, but we have no present evidence of work on delivery systems designed spe-

[2] A *front* is roughly comparable to a Western army group.

cifically for such weapons. We believe that chemical warfare munitions are available in quantity and would be used extensively in conjunction with nuclear and conventional weapons in general war. (*Paras. 25–27, 45*)

G. Although tactical nuclear delivery systems are integral to Soviet theater forces, the nuclear weapons themselves do not appear to be in their custody. Such weapons are normally stored in depots operated by the Ministry of Defense and located within the USSR. Soviet procedures for controlling these weapons ensure the national leadership that they will not be used without authorization. Existing procedures, together with deficiencies in logistical support, appear to penalize the Soviets in terms of operational readiness and rapid response for tactical nuclear weapons employment. (*Paras. 22–24*)

H. The Soviets probably consider the East European Satellite forces to be a sizable but problematic asset, because of their varying levels of effectiveness and reliability. In the event of war, however, the USSR would probably employ some Satellite forces in combined combat operations, by integrating selected Satellite divisions, corps, or even field armies directly into major Soviet commands. Other Satellite units would be retained under national command for security, reserve, and other functions. (*Paras. 36–37, 41–42*)

I. The principal operations of Soviet theater forces in general war would be directed against NATO in Europe. The Soviets plan to move massive forces rapidly toward the Channel coast in the initial days of such a war. This campaign would probably be augmented by operations in Scandinavia, operations toward the Mediterranean, and operations toward the exits of the Baltic and Black Seas. The Soviet submarine fleet would contribute to the campaign against Western Europe by interdiction operations against the highly important Atlantic supply lines. Other peripheral areas, notably the Far East, apparently have lesser priority for theater force operations. Soviet capabilities to conduct theater force operations against North America are limited to minor airborne and amphibious attacks against Alaska and other Arctic bases. (*Paras. 44, 59*)

J. Although Soviet theater forces are formidable, especially in the area facing NATO in Europe, they continue to have certain limitations beyond those of tactical nuclear support. In the initial period of a general war, a significant portion of the tactical fighters would need to be assigned to interceptor as well as to ground attack missions. In offensive operations, the highly mechanized group forces are in constant danger of outrunning their logistic support. Finally, existing command and control systems do not permit the Soviets to exercise their traditional strict supervision over subordinates in the widely extended deployment required on the nuclear battlefield. (*Para. 45*)

K. The Soviets currently have 22 line divisions and 1,200 tactical aircraft stationed in East Germany and Poland. In a situation in which surprise or pre-emption were overriding considerations, they could launch an attack against Western Europe without prior buildup. If circumstances permitted, however, the USSR would seek to assemble a considerably larger striking force, primarily of Soviet but probably including some Satellite units. This force could comprise three *fronts* with a total of 50–60 divisions and 2,000 tactical aircraft. We estimate that under noncombat conditions, such a striking force could be built up in East Germany and western Czechoslovakia within 30 days, and a theater reserve could be provided for backup. The ability of these and other Soviet theater forces to carry out their assigned general war campaigns could be governed principally by the effects of the initial nuclear exchange. (*Paras. 53–58*)

L. The adjustments in Soviet theater forces in the past few years have not materially impaired their capabilities to conduct nonnuclear operations. The USSR's highly mechanized forces have favorable characteristics for the dispersed operations required because of the constant possibility of escalation to nuclear warfare. Over the past two years, the nonnuclear firepower of ground units has not been significantly altered, but the supporting nonnuclear firepower which can be delivered by tactical aircraft has decreased. There are indications that the Soviets have recently given recognition to the possibility of nonnuclear war with NATO forces in Europe. They probably intend to retain capabilities for conventional warfare against NATO, but they do not appear to have revised their expectation that any major conflict with NATO would be nuclear from the start or would probably escalate. (*Paras. 63–66*)

M. The Soviets have evidently not elaborated any doctrine for limited nuclear warfare by theater forces, involving the use of tactical weapons only. We think they would be severely handicapped in any attempts to conduct such warfare at present. Moreover, thus far the Soviets appear to think that limited nuclear conflict in the NATO area would almost certainly escalate to general war. (*Para. 67*)

44.

CENTRAL INTELLIGENCE AGENCY
Directorate of Intelligence
28 April 1972

INTELLIGENCE MEMORANDUM

SOVIET DEFENSE POLICY
1962-72

I. BASIC OBJECTIVES AND TRENDS

The objectives underlying Soviet military policies can be described today in much the same way as a decade ago: preserving the security of the homeland; maintaining hegemony over Eastern Europe; and fostering an image of strength in support of a strong foreign policy aimed at expanding Soviet influence.

The military policies that support these objectives, however, have shifted markedly. The impulsive policies of Khrushchev, who downgraded the importance of conventional forces and tried to buy a strategic nuclear deterrent cheaply, gave way in the mid-Sixties to more functional concepts of military power under Brezhnev and Kosygin. Soviet military policy was also influenced by fundamental changes in the way the USSR viewed its own power in relation to the other major countries of the world, by its estimate of the external threat, and by the impact of new technology on Soviet weaponry--and on the capabilities of potential enemies.

Trends in Military Policies

In broadest outline, the major trends in Soviet military policies over the past decade have been these:

Note: This memorandum was prepared by the Office of Strategic Research and coordinated within CIA.

44. (continued)

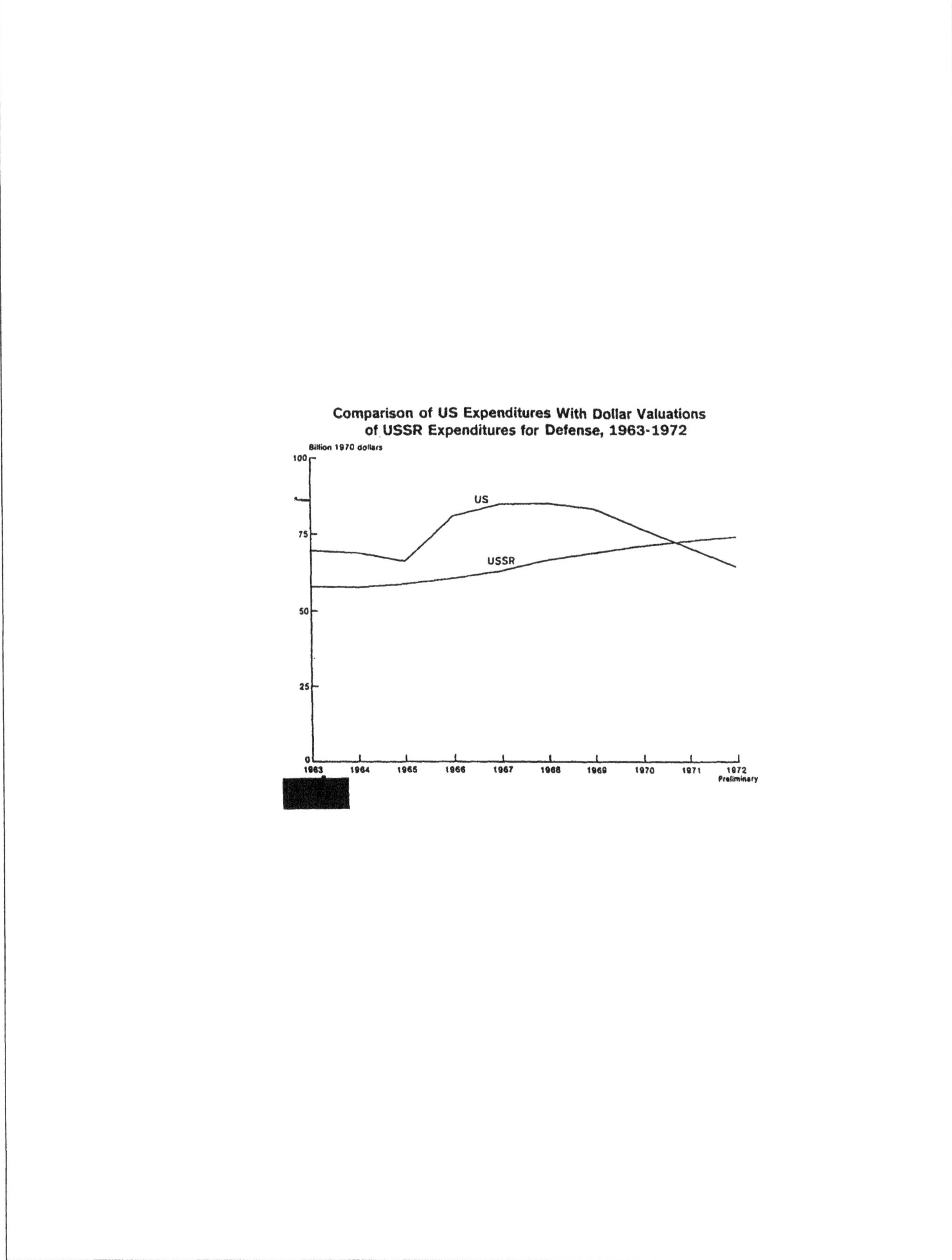
Comparison of US Expenditures With Dollar Valuations of USSR Expenditures for Defense, 1963-1972
Billion 1970 dollars
100
75
50
25
0
US
USSR
1963
1964
1965
1966
1967
1968
1969
1970
1971
1972
Preliminary

TOP SECRET

-- Expansion and improvement of strategic offensive and defensive forces to the point that the Soviets now regard themselves as having achieved rough strategic parity with the US.

-- Continued maintenance of strong ground, air, and missile forces opposite NATO, but with increasing confidence that NATO does not pose an imminent military threat.

-- Growing concern over the possibility of armed conflict with China, and a consequent strengthening of military forces along the border since the mid-Sixties.

-- Development of missile-equipped naval forces increasingly able to operate in distant areas, both to counter Western naval forces and to show the flag.

Trends in Military Spending

These policies led to a gradual increase in military spending. Total Soviet expenditures for military purposes grew from an estimated 18 billion rubles (58 billion dollars) in 1963 to about 22 billion rubles (72 billion dollars) in 1971, an increase of about 22 percent.* The graph opposite shows the trend in Soviet military spending and compares it to US expenditures over the years.

The year-to-year changes in Soviet military expenditures have been shaped mainly by the Soviet drive to catch up with the US in strategic arms. Much of the rapid growth between 1966 and 1970 resulted from increases in outlays for strategic attack and defense programs, and particularly for military research and development. A decline in strategic attack expenditures--reflecting a leveling

** The ruble figures are estimates of what the USSR pays for its military forces and programs. The dollar figures are estimates of what the Soviet forces and programs would cost if purchased and operated in the US.*

-2-

TOP SECRET

44. (continued)

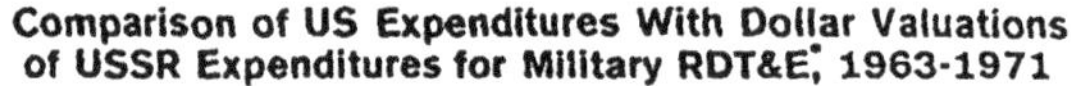
Comparison of US Expenditures With Dollar Valuations
of USSR Expenditures for Military RDT&E,* 1963-1971

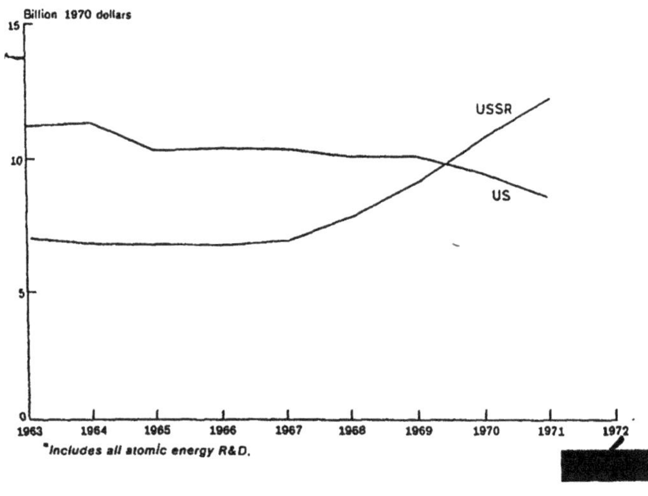
Billion 1970 dollars
15
10
5
0
USSR
US
1963
1964
1965
1966
1967
1968
1969
1970
1971
1972
*Includes all atomic energy R&D.

off in ICBM deployment--was primarily responsible for the low growth rate of about 1 percent in 1971. Soviet defense expenditures for 1972 are expected to reach about 22.5 billion rubles (74 billion dollars), about 2 1/2 percent more than in 1971.

Since 1967, the most dynamic element in Soviet defense spending has been military research and development. It has climbed sharply and in 1971 accounted for over 15 percent of the total dollar valuation of the Soviet defense effort. Historically the US has outspent the Soviets in this area, but since 1969 this relationship has been reversed as a result of continued growth of the Soviet effort while US spending on military R&D declined. (See Graph)

<u>Trends in Military Manpower</u>

Soviet military manpower has increased substantially over the past decade, moving from a total of about 3 million in 1962 to over 3.9 million this year. The increase resulted largely from the growth of ground forces to reinforce the border opposite China, and from the expansion of strategic forces.

US military manpower has shown a markedly different trend and is now about 1 1/2 million men below the Soviet total. Manpower for strategic forces has declined steadily, while general purpose forces peaked during the height of the Vietnam War and then declined. (Table 4 of the Annex compares US and Soviet military manpower trends.)

II. STRATEGIC FORCES

In the aftermath of the Cuban missile crisis and the failure of Khrushchev's effort to improve the USSR's strategic position at one stroke, Soviet leaders saw the building of a significant deterrent force as their most pressing military requirement. It was evident to them that their small force of ICBMs, heavy bombers, and missile submarines was being grossly outnumbered by US missile and bomber deployment programs, and that their strategic defenses were becoming outmoded. Their response was

-3-

44. (continued)

Operational US and USSR ICBM Launchers

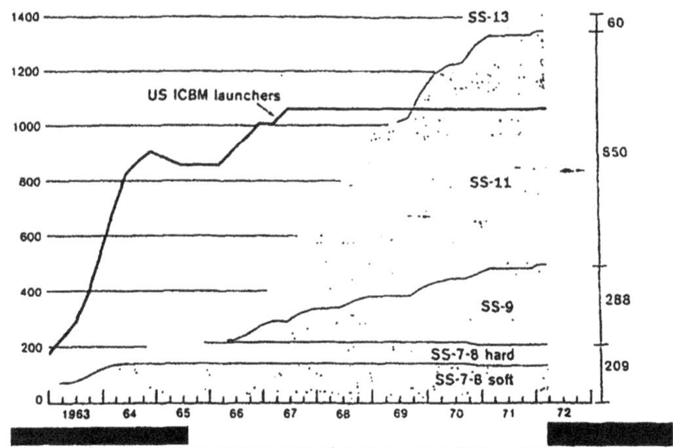

The chart shows the estimated number of Soviet operational ICBM launchers as of early 1972. The completion of all known standard silos has provided the Soviets with a total of 1,407 operational launchers at their ICBM complexes. Because of the uncertainty surrounding the purpose and construction timing of the new silo program, it is not reflected in the chart. The chart also excludes the 120 ICBM launchers at Pervomaysk and Derazhnya, which are believed to be intended for use against targets in Western Europe.

Operational US and USSR SLBM Launchers

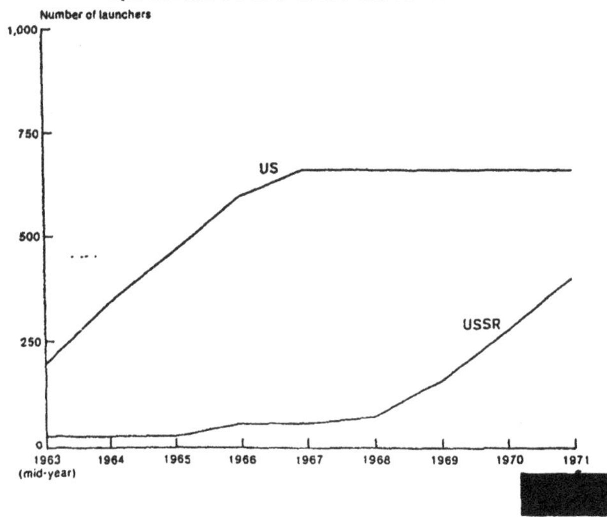

to undertake a massive effort to redress this growing imbalance by deploying large, survivable strategic attack forces and improving their strategic defenses.

Intercontinental Attack Forces

At the end of 1962, the Soviet intercontinental attack forces was composed of some 200 heavy bombers, 54 soft ICBM launchers, and less than a hundred short-range submarine-launched ballistic missiles. The only expansion under way was in the ICBM force, and that was moving slowly. The US, in contrast, had a bomber fleet of over 600 B-52s, 175 Atlas and Titan ICBMs, and 9 Polaris missile submarines carrying 16 missiles each. Moreover, the Minuteman ICBM was on the verge of large-scale deployment, and Polaris submarine production was continuing.

Several new Soviet weapons systems were already in research and development at that time, and the decision was made to embark on a sustained high-priority deployment effort centering on three of them: the large, high-yield SS-9 ICBM; the relatively small SS-11 ICBM; and the 16-tube Y class ballistic missile submarine. Bombers were retained as part of the force mix, but there was to be no effort to match the US bomber fleet numerically.

In the decade to follow, the Soviets worked a dramatic improvement in their strategic posture relative to the US. US deployment programs leveled off in the mid and late Sixties, and the Soviets began to catch up. The graphs opposite illustrate this trend for the ICBM and missile submarine forces.

ICBM Force Developments. By the end of 1968, the Soviets had reached virtual parity with the US in numbers of operational ICBMs, most of them now in hardened silos, and by the time SALT began in late 1969 they were moving well ahead. In the fall of 1970, there was a major switch in the ICBM deployment program. Construction of additional standard silos was abruptly halted, and a few groups of silos were even abandoned before they were finished. Instead, the Soviets introduced two new types of silos designed

-4-

TOP SECRET

for increased hardness, one probably intended for a large new missile and the other for a variant of the small SS-11. Over the next several months the Soviets began construction on 91 of the new-type silos, but in the summer of 1971 they stopped adding more and have not done so since.

Missile Submarines. The Y-class submarine construction program came later than the ICBM programs, but was well under way by 1968. Production reached a rate of 8 units a year in 1970. Since then, production has begun shifting from the standard Y class to a modified version which will carry a larger missile but will have 12 rather than 16 launch tubes. If production continues at current rates, the operational Y-class fleet would equal the US fleet of 41 modern ballistic missile submarines in 1974. Because of the reduced number of launch tubes in the new version, however, it would be another year before the Soviets caught up in total modern submarine missile launchers.

R&D Programs. While pursuing these deployment programs, the Soviets have continued to develop new offensive weaponry. There is evidence, for example, that preliminary tests of a new ICBM larger than the SS-9 began in late 1971, and other new missile projects appear to be in the offing. In addition, a 3,000-mile missile for the submarine force has been tested extensively, and it will soon be at sea on the new version of the Y-class submarine.

One significant feature of Soviet missile development so far has been the absence of any flight test programs for multiple independently targeted re-entry vehicles (MIRVs). The large new ICBM is a good candidate to be the first Soviet missile with MIRVs, but in this area the Soviets lag considerably behind the US, whose Minuteman III and Poseidon MIRV systems are already operational. Thus, while catching up with the US in total numbers of missile launchers, the Soviets have begun to fall behind again in another important measure of strategic attack capability--the number of separate targets that each side could attack. The US now has a commanding lead in this respect, and that lead is likely to grow at least through the mid-1970s.

-5-

TOP SECRET [redacted]

Expenditures for Strategic Attack. In dollar terms, the Soviets have spent about the same amount on intercontinental attack forces in the 1963-71 period as the United States. The Soviets, however, have also maintained a substantial effort on peripheral attack forces which have no exact counterpart in the US, and when these expenditures are included overall Soviet expenditures on strategic attack for the 1963-71 period were about one-third more. Since US spending for intercontinental attack forces peaked before 1963, while Soviet spending did not reach its peak until 1969, these comparisons understate the long-term US effort to some extent. (The graphic opposite page 7 shows the trends in US and Soviet expenditures for strategic attack.)

Strategic Defense

Defense of the homeland from strategic attack has historically had a high priority in Soviet military planning, claiming a much higher share of resources than do strategic defenses in the US budget. In 1962, PVO Strany, the Soviet strategic defense organization, could already boast that it was numerically the largest air defense organization in the world, having some 7,500 SAM launchers and 4,500 interceptor aircraft. Moreover, construction had begun on ABM defenses around Moscow.

But the massive Soviet investments in missiles, aircraft, and radars were being undermined by changing US offensive capabilities. New US weapons and tactics--low-altitude penetration of bombers carrying long-range standoff weapons, and penetration aids and MIRVs on ballistic missiles--posed problems not satisfactorily solved to this day. The story of PVO Strany during the past decade is one of a vigorous but imperfect effort to upgrade its forces to counter the fast-paced changes in the US offense.

Air Defense Improvements. Unlike the US, the Soviets have added steadily to their air-defense weaponry in recent years. Since 1964 they have introduced five new types of fighter-interceptors, and production is continuing on two of them. The air-defense missile force has also continued to expand

-6-

TOP SECRET [redacted]

44. (continued)

Comparison of US Expenditures With Dollar Valuations of USSR Expenditures
for Strategic Attack and Strategic Defense, 1963-1971

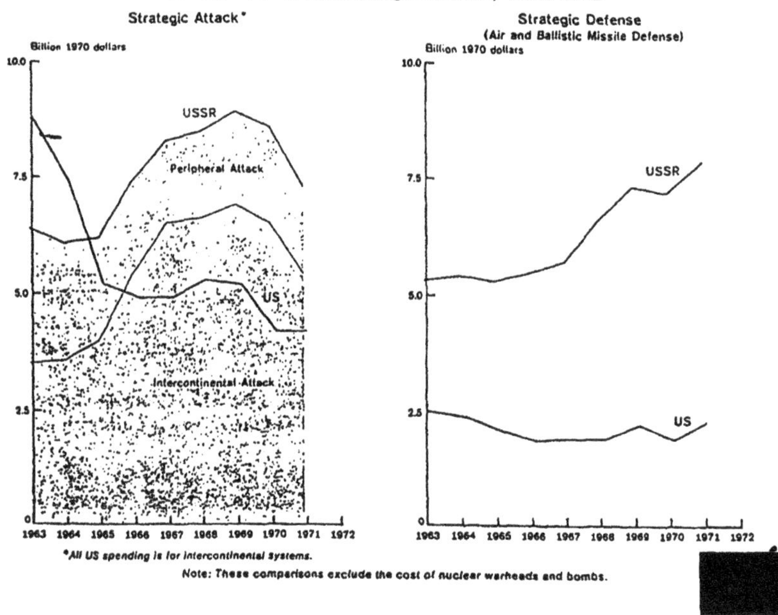

*All US spending is for intercontinental systems.

Note: These comparisons exclude the cost of nuclear warheads and bombs.

and improve. Deployment programs are still in progress for the long-range SA-5 system and the SA-3 system designed for low-altitude defense. New radars, communications systems, and hardened control facilities have also been added. These improvements have plugged many gaps in Soviet air defenses, but they have not closed off the threat of low-altitude penetration by attacking bombers.

ABM Developments. The decision to begin deploying ABMs around Moscow in 1962 gave the Soviets an early start, but it saddled them with a system based on technology that was soon to be overtaken by offensive innovations. The dish-type radar used for target tracking, for example, is capable of engaging only a few targets at a time. The Soviets apparently soon recognized that the system could be overcome by multiple warheads and penetration aids, and between 1964 and 1967 they abandoned half of the ABM sites begun around Moscow.

In 1967, the Soviets began experimenting with new types of ABM radars capable of handling many targets simultaneously, and a year later, work started on a prototype for a completely new ABM system using this kind of radar. The new system is cheaper than the cumbersome Moscow system and could be deployed in much shorter time (construction of the sites at Moscow took about 7 years). The range of this system appears to be considerably less than that of the Moscow system, and it could be used for local defense of key target areas or possibly ICBM fields. Meanwhile, new ABM missiles have been undergoing tests since late 1970.

So far, none of the new ABM equipment has been put into operational use. Satellite photography has not revealed any evidence of operational ABM deployment in the Soviet Union beyond the Moscow area.

Expenditures for Strategic Defense. Soviet expenditures for deploying and operating their strategic defenses, as valued in dollars, have been nearly three times those of the US during the past decade. (The graph opposite shows the trends for both countries.) This difference is accounted for largely by the USSR's larger commitment to air defense--a reflection of the fact that the Soviets are confronted by a much larger bomber threat than is the US. The total expenditures of the two countries on deployment of ABM systems have been about same. In the ABM field, of course, expenditures on R&D in both countries have greatly exceeded the deployment and operating expenses incurred so far, but it has not been possible to make meaningful comparisons of ABM R&D spending.

Soviet Strategic Concepts and Perceptions

The way the Soviets have developed, deployed, and operated their strategic forces says several things about how they view the utility of these forces:

-- They consider these forces primarily as a deterrent. The major effort has been on programs which assure the ability of these forces to absorb a US strike and still be able to return a devastating blow.

-- They nevertheless plan for the possibility that deterrence might fail. They give high priority to strategic defenses, and they apparently target their strategic attack forces primarily against military-related installations rather than population and industry per se. In their doctrine, the preferred use of strategic attack forces is to pre-empt--that is, to launch an all-out strike against the enemy's forces when the enemy clearly is about to launch his own nuclear attack. A "launch-on-warning" strategy has also been advocated by some Soviet military writers, but others have warned of the risks involved.

-- They do not contemplate launching a sudden, bolt-from-the-blue, first strike on the US, nor do they expect one on themselves. They have not acquired forces with the necessary combination of accuracy, yield, and numbers to be effective in this role, and there is abundant evidence that they do not maintain their strategic forces in a state of constant alert. (One of the enduring tenets of their

doctrine is that any general war would be preceded by an extended buildup of tensions that would allow time for preparation.)

Soviet strategic doctrine also appears to reject the feasibility of graduated nuclear warfare. In their writings and statements on the subject, Soviet strategists are consistently skeptical that it is possible for two nuclear powers to exercise restraint once nuclear weapons have been employed.

The Soviet leadership has probably concluded that for the foreseeable future neither the US nor the USSR will be capable of acquiring a strategic superiority sufficient to ensure success in confrontation or a victory other than a Pyrrhic one in a nuclear war. Nevertheless, there are those in Moscow who believe that the US is striving to obtain some relative advantage in terms of political-military leverage and actual warfighting capabilities. The US doctrine of "strategic sufficiency" and emphasis on MIRV programs have been interpreted in some Soviet quarters as pointing in this direction. There are also voices calling for the USSR to strive for a measure of advantage.

There is probably no unanimous view in the Kremlin, however, as to how the strategic relationship should be measured. One senior member of the Soviet SALT delegation complained that some Soviet military men still tend to think as though they are counting "rifles and cannons" and pay too little attention to qualitative factors in looking at the strategic equation. At the same time, there is evidence that the Soviets perform sophisticated war-gaming analysis in much the same way as the US does. Whatever the measures, it is clear that the Soviets attach great importance to maintaining a position of "strategic equality" with the US and having it recognized by the US and other nations.

Soviet Motives at SALT

The Soviet decision to enter SALT in mid-1968 was induced not only by the evolution of a rough numerical parity between the two opposing strategic arsenals, but also by a number of interrelated economic and political considerations. As SALT has progressed over the first seven rounds, Soviet interest in an arms limitation agreement has come into sharper focus.

One of Moscow's primary interests has been to stabilize the US-Soviet strategic relationship and to gain US recognition of the principle of "equal security with no military advantage for either side." Although the strategic forces of the two sides are asymmetrical, the Soviets apparently believe them to be comparable in terms of overall capabilities, and undoubtedly appreciate that this acknowledgement at SALT would buttress their claim for a role in world affairs equivalent to that of the United States.

Moscow's decision to enter SALT also reflected its desire to limit certain aspects of US-Soviet competition through negotiation. The negotiating record has indicated, however, that the Soviets did not enter SALT with the intent of ending strategic competition between the two countries. Rather, they have attempted to narrow the focus of this competition and limit it chiefly to the qualitative area of research and development. They have also insisted that force modernization be allowed to continue, at least under the terms of an interim agreement.

In spite of the Soviet buildup in strategic forces over the past decade the share of GNP allocated to defense fell to about 6 percent in 1971. This declining military burden indicates that purely economic considerations have not forced the Soviets to seek a SALT agreement. The Soviets may, nevertheless, hope to realize some savings in terms of high-quality physical and human resources--assets that are needed to modernize the civilian economy and boost productivity.

III. GENERAL PURPOSE FORCES

Forces Opposite NATO

The structure and posture of Soviet and Warsaw Pact theater forces at the time of the 1962 Cuban missile crisis reflected Soviet doctrine which had evolved in the late Fifties and early Sixties. This doctrine was based on the belief that any war between NATO and the Warsaw Pact would immediately escalate to nuclear war.

In the Pact strategy for nuclear war in Europe, the mission of the ground forces was to exploit massive nuclear strikes delivered throughout the depth of the theater by advancing rapidly across Western Europe. Ground and tactical air forces were equipped to provide greater mobility and concentrated, short term combat power. The ground forces were entirely mechanized and provided with massive numbers of tanks. The number of tactical aircraft was reduced, and equipment modernization programs emphasized air defense and tactical nuclear delivery capabilities. This focus on nuclear warfare resulted in a decline in conventional firepower.

By 1968, the Soviet view of war in Europe had undergone a significant change. In response to the NATO flexible response strategy, Pact planners have come to believe that the initial period of a war with NATO could be fought without the use of nuclear weapons. They still cling to the view that an unsuccessful NATO conventional offensive--or a breakthrough by a Warsaw Pact counteroffensive--would compel NATO to resort to tactical nuclear weapons. The Soviets see the conventional phase, therefore, as only a prelude to nuclear war. The Soviets believe moreover, that NATO does not intend to restrict a European conflict to the use of tactical nuclear weapons only and that a limited nuclear response on the part of the Pact would only offer the West the opportunity to deliver a massive and decisive strategic nuclear strike.

Soviet acceptance of a possible nonnuclear phase of hostilities has led to some changes in force structure. Division artillery, for example, has been increased by about 50 percent since 1967. Pact tactical aircraft, however, continue to be characterized by relatively small payloads, despite some improvements in current Soviet fighters.

For this reason the Soviets plan to use medium bombers for large-scale conventional bombing in the initial phase of a war with NATO. At the same time, the Soviets have continued to develop their tactical nuclear capabilities, increasing their tactical nuclear missile forces by about one-third.

Aside from these changes in combat support, Soviet theater force organization has not diverged significantly from the pattern established in the early Sixties. This organization emphasizes the shock power, mobility, and protection against nuclear effects of the tank, and is intended for a relatively short, fast moving offensive. The Soviets hope to conduct a conventional offensive using essentially the same tactics as for nuclear war.

Forces Opposite China

Deteriorating Soviet-Chinese relations have been responsible for significant changes in Soviet theater forces during the past decade. Since 1965 the Soviets have tripled their ground forces opposite China, and the buildup is continuing. There are now some 37 to 42 Soviet divisions and 370,000 men deployed in the border area. About 11 of these divisions are at or near combat strength.

The pattern of the ongoing buildup suggests that the Soviets intend eventually to have 42 to 48 divisions and close to 1,100 aircraft opposite China. At full strength, this force would have about 780,000 troops. Such a force probably would enable the Soviets to seize and hold indefinitely the most important peripheral regions of China such as Manchuria, Inner Mongolia, or large parts of Sinkiang.

It is clear that the Soviets are preparing for the possibility of tactical nuclear warfare against Chinese forces. Almost every division along the border has nuclear-capable tactical rockets, and there are four brigades equipped with 160-mile-range tactical ballistic missiles. In addition, the Soviets have deployed the 500-mile Scaleboard and

300-mile Shaddock mobile missile systems with ground forces in the area. Ultimately the Soviet forces along the border will probably have about the same proportion of tactical nuclear weapons as the forces opposite NATO.

Some Soviet strategic missiles and bombers are almost certainly targeted against China also.

Naval Forces

The requirement for anticarrier forces was the major influence on the development of the Soviet general purpose naval forces from the mid-Fifties through the mid-Sixties. Subsequently the emphasis broadened to include improvement of antisubmarine capabilities and expansion of out-of-area operations.

Anticarrier Forces. The Soviets decided to counter Western carrier forces primarily with anti-ship cruise missiles, rather than building their own carriers. By 1962 the Soviet Navy already had a large force of missile-armed medium bombers and had begun deploying cruise missile submarines. During the early and mid-Sixties the cruise missile submarine force was built up rapidly, and the naval air forces received new types of missiles and aircraft. Long-range cruise missiles also were fitted on a number of new major surface combatants.

Antisubmarine Warfare. During the last half of the Sixties the Soviets deployed a variety of new systems with improved ASW capabilities, while continuing to strengthen the anticarrier forces as well. The new weapons systems included helicopter carriers, long-range ASW aircraft, and two new classes of nuclear-powered submarines.

Despite these efforts, the Soviet Navy has made little progress in ASW. It has not solved the problem of initial detection of submarines, either through use of ASW forces or by an ocean surveillance system. As a result, current Soviet ASW forces do not pose a serious threat to the US ballistic missile submarine force. Furthermore, this same deficiency leaves Soviet naval surface forces vulnerable to Western attack submarines.

44. (continued)

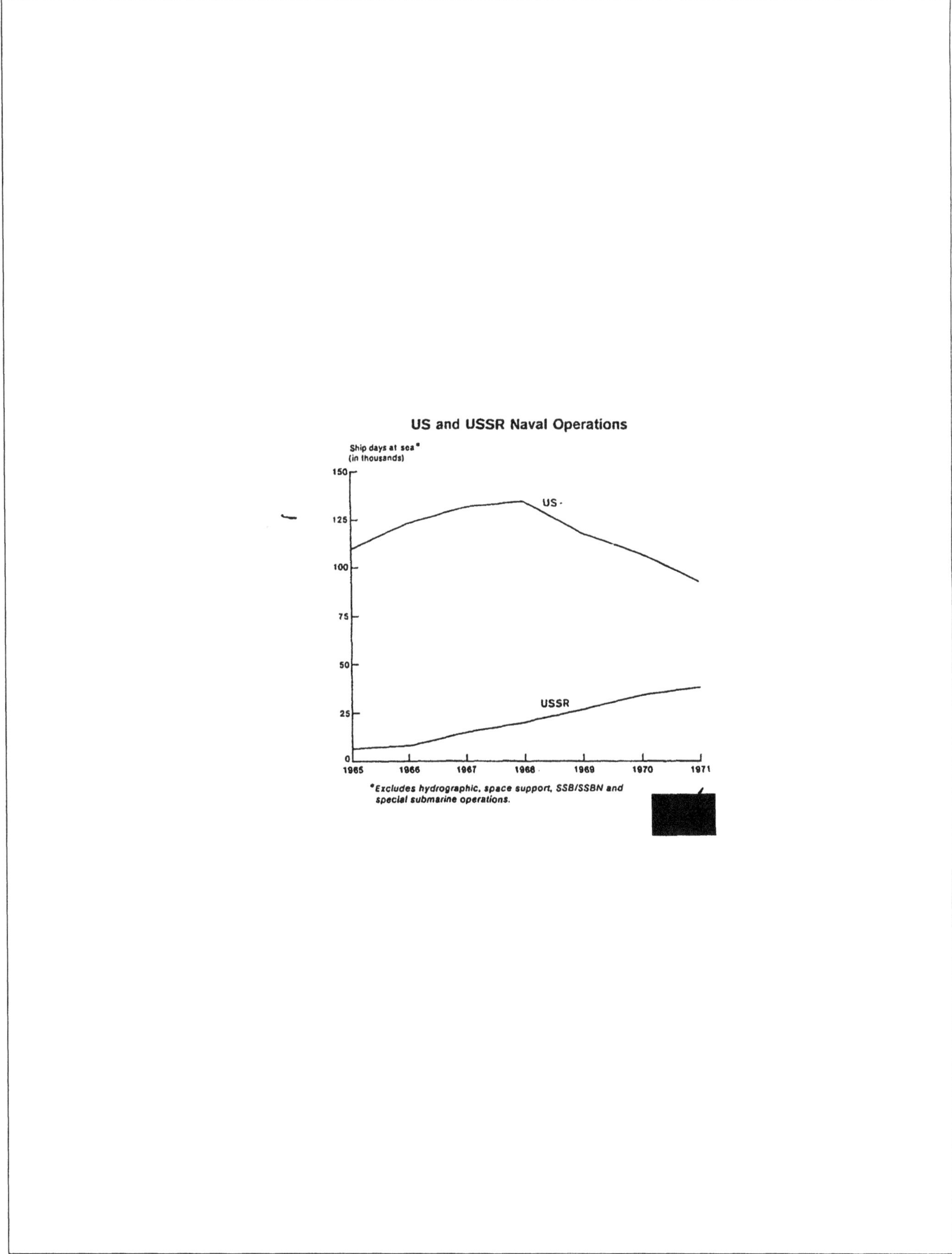
US and USSR Naval Operations
Ship days at sea*
(in thousands)
150
125
100
75
50
25
0
US
USSR
1965
1966
1967
1968
1969
1970
1971
*Excludes hydrographic, space support, SSB/SSBN and special submarine operations.

Out-of-Area Operations. Concurrently with the ASW programs, the Soviet Navy undertook a major effort to operate its forces in distant waters. In the early Sixties the Navy rarely ventured outside its coastal waters, even during major exercises. As late as 1965, Soviet surface combatants, attack submarines, and naval auxiliaries spent only about 6,000 ship-days on out-of-area operations. During the last half of the Sixties, however, Soviet naval operations expanded rapidly. The graph opposite shows this trend and compares it with US naval operations.

The 1962-71 period also saw an expansion of Soviet naval activity into new operating areas. The Soviet Mediterranean Squadron, for example, was first established in 1964 and grew into a major force in 1967. Soviet naval forces established a presence in the Indian Ocean in 1968, began a series of deployments to the Caribbean in 1969, and in 1970 began what has become a small continuous presence off of West Africa.

Naval air operations have expanded also. In 1965, the naval air forces received new reconnaissance aircraft and began to conduct long-range missions over the open ocean. In 1968, a Soviet naval air squadron was established in Egypt, and in 1970 naval reconnaissance aircraft began to make brief visits to Cuba.

Shipbuilding. During the 1962-1971 period, the Soviets built more major naval ships than the US, but their ships were generally smaller. In contrast to US practice, the Soviets have shown a preference for relatively small multi-purpose ships, with an emphasis on speed and firepower at the expense of range, endurance, and sustained combat capability. The only major area in which they have surpassed the US is in numbers of attack submarines, as shown in the following table:

44. (continued)

Comparision of US Expenditures With Dollar Valuations of USSR Expenditures for General Purpose Forces, 1963-1971

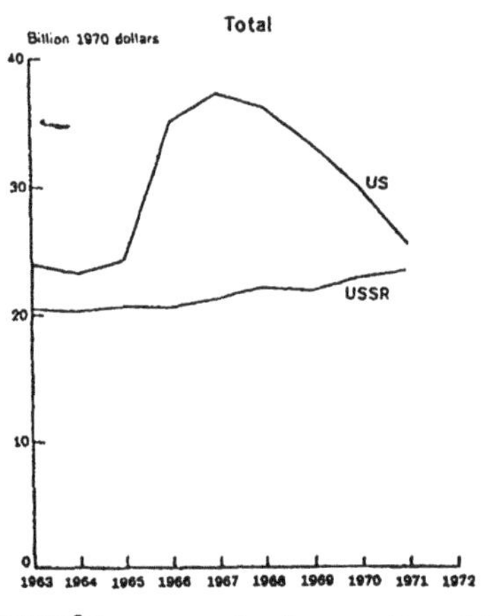

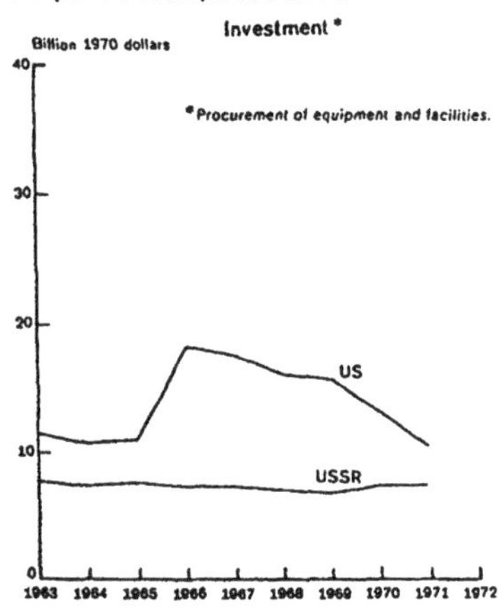

Note: These comparisons exclude the cost of nuclear warheads and bombs.

TOP SECRET [redacted]

Number and Tonnage of Major Naval Ships Commissioned, 1962-1971

	Number		Thousand Tons	
	US	USSR	US	USSR
Major Surface Combatants	83	92	564	291
Attack Submarines	42	117	154	428
Major Amphibious Ships	45	11	634	38
TOTAL	170	220	1,352	757

The Soviet Navy does not have a major mission of projecting forces ashore, as does the US Navy, nor is it as concerned with protecting extended sea lines of communications. As a result, the Soviet Navy has been able to concentrate its main efforts on systems designed to attack and destroy other naval forces.

Expenditures for General Purpose Forces

Soviet spending on general purpose forces has grown slowly during the past decade but has remained well below US expenditures in this category. (The graphs opposite illustrate this trend.) Before the US made large-scale commitment in Vietnam, US expenditures for general purposes forces averaged about 15 percent above the dollar valuation of counterpart Soviet spending. During the height of the Vietnam conflict--1965-69--US spending was about 65 percent higher. Since then US expenditures in this category have dropped sharply, and in 1971 they were less than 10 percent above the Soviet total.

-15-

TOP SECRET [redacted]

44. (continued)

~~TOP SECRET~~ [redacted]

TABLE 1
SOVIET INTERCONTINENTAL ATTACK FORCES

	End 1962	End 1968	1 April 1972
ICBM Launchers			
SS-6	4	--	--
SS-7	50	197	190
SS-8	--	23	19
SS-9	--	168	288
SS-11			
At ICBM Complexes	--	580	850
At MR/IRBM Complexes**	--	--	120
SS-13	--	--	60
Total	54*	968*	1,527*
Ballistic Missile Submarines (Launch tubes in parenthesis)			
G class**	23(69)	22(66)	22(70)
H class	9(27)	9(27)	9(30)
Y class	--	4(64)	25-27(400-432)
Total	32(96)*	35(157)*	56-58(500-532)
Heavy Bombers			
Bear	100	110	110
Bison	100	90	85
Total	200	200	195

* *These totals are for operational ICBMs and ballistic missile submarines, and they do not include others under construction at the times indicated. At the end of 1968, for example, some 330 additional ICBM silos (60 of them for the SS-9) were under construction and 13 additional 16-tube Y class submarines were under construction or fitting out. As of 1 April 1972, there were 91 new-type ICBM silos under construction and 15 Y class submarines under construction or fitting out.*

***These probably are intended primarily for attack against targets in Europe and Asia.*

CURRENT US INTERCONTINENTAL ATTACK FORCES

ICBM Launchers	
Minuteman	1,000
Titan	54
	1,054
Ballistic Missile Submarines	
Polaris/Poseidon	41 (656 launch tubes)
Strategic Bombers	
B-52	450
FB-111	74
	524

~~TOP SECRET~~ [redacted]

TOP SECRET [redacted]

TABLE 2
SOVIET STRATEGIC DEFENSE FORCES

AIR DEFENSES	End 1962	End 1968	April 1972
Interceptor Aircraft			
Subsonic	3,325	1,575	885
Supersonic	1,260	1,775	2,230
	4,585	3,350	3,115
Surface-to-Air Missile Launchers			
SA-1 (at Moscow only)	3,276	3,276	3,276
SA-2	4,020	4,500	4,380
SA-3	220	480	988
SA-5	--	360	1,332
	7,516	8,616	9,976
ABM DEFENSES			
Engagement Radars (Moscow)	--	3	8
Launchers (Moscow)	--	24	64
Hen House Ballistic Missile Early Warning Radars	--	2	6
Regional ABM Radars (Moscow)	--	1	2

CURRENT US STRATEGIC DEFENSE FORCES

AIR DEFENSES	
Interceptor Aircraft	
F-101, F-102, F-106 (including Air National Guard)	593
Surface-to-Air Missile Launchers	
BOMARC	84
Nike Hercules (including Army National Guard)	755
	839

ABM DEFENSES	
Ballistic Missile Early Warning Radars (BMEWS)	3
Over-the-Horizon Radars	9
SLBM Warning System Sites	8
Satellite Early Warning Systems	2 satellites 2 ground stations

TOP SECRET [redacted]

44. (continued)

TOP SECRET [redacted]

TABLE 3
SOVIET NAVAL GENERAL PURPOSE FORCES

	End 1962	End 1968	April 1972	Current US Totals	
Major Surface Forces					
Aircraft carriers	-	-	-	17	
Helicopter carriers	-	1	2		
Cruisers - CL and CLG	14	12	15	9	
Cruisers - CLGM (1)	1	8	11	28	frigates
Destroyers	107	81	82	122	
Escorts	79	104	112	68	
	201	206	222	244	
Submarine Forces					
Cruise Missile - nuclear	5	35	40	-	
- diesel	11	26	28	-	
Total Cruise Missile	16	61	68	-	
Torpedo Attack - nuclear	8	18	28	56	
- diesel	253	234	182	38	
Total Torpedo Attack	261	252	210	94	
	277	313	278	94	
Naval Air Forces					
Missile carriers	265	270	275	See footnote (2)	
Reconnaissance/bomber	165	355	360		
Patrol/ASW aircraft	80	85	135		
ASW helicopters	110	175	235		
	620	885	1,005	2,500	

(1) *These ships--the Kynda and Kresta classes--are commonly identified as light cruisers because of their surface-to-surface missiles, but they are about the same size as a US guided missile frigate. They are less than half the size of a US light cruiser.*

(2) *The US Navy's air arm cannot be compared meaningfully to Soviet Naval Aviation because of the major differences in missions and equipment. The Soviets, for example, have no naval fighter aircraft, while the US has no long-range missile carriers comparable to the Soviet types.*

TOP SECRET [redacted]

44. (continued)

~~TOP SECRET~~ [redacted]

TABLE 4

USSR AND US MILITARY MANPOWER

	1962		1968		1972	
	USSR	US	USSR	US	USSR	US
Strategic Attack	174,000	263,000	325,000	169,000	363,000	150,0
Strategic Defense	415,000	149,000	459,000	102,000	529,000	52,0
Ground Forces*	1,219,000	860,000	1,485,000	975,000	1,562,000	580,0
Tactical Air Forces	223,000	155,000	240,000	345,000	259,000	215,0
Navy	340,000	405,000	369,000	460,000	385,000	340,0
Command & Support	548,000	924,000	673,000	1,460,000	694,000	1,018,0
Research & Development	45,000	54,000	53,000	42,000	53,000	35,0
Military Security Forces	225,000	-	225,000	-	225,000	-
Total Active Military Manpower	3,061,000	2,810,000	3,704,000	3,550,000	3,931,000	2,340,00

*Includes Soviet Naval Infantry and US Marines.

~~TOP SECRET~~ [redacted]

Summary of Conclusions

Four principal questions relating to Soviet nuclear war doctrine are treated in this paper. The conclusions of the paper on these and a number of subordinate questions are summarized below.

1. *What purposes do the Soviets see their nuclear forces as serving?*

The main objectives underlying Soviet strategic policy may be described in broad terms as similar to those of a decade ago: to protect the security of the homeland, to deter nuclear war but to wage war successfully should deterrence fail, to project an image of military strength commensurate with the position of a great world power, and to support foreign policy aims if only by checking strategic forces of potential opponents.

-- *What is the relative weight of such factors as deterrence, considerations of prestige or influence, and use of nuclear weapons in war?*

It is difficult to separate these factors and assign each an exact ranking of significance. The pattern of development, deployment, and operation of the strategic forces, however, suggests how the Soviets view the utility of these forces. (1) Deterrence is a key objective. The major effort has been on programs which assure the ability of these forces to absorb a US strike and still return a devastating blow. (2) The Soviets nevertheless plan for the possibility that deterrence may fail, although they do not contemplate launching a sudden first strike on the US or expect one on themselves. (3) Their strategic buildup over the past decade shows that they are unwilling to remain in a position of marked strategic inferiority relative to the US. They apparently consider that their larger policy aims would be prejudiced by such a position.

-- *What is the implication of the Soviets' forgoing an ABM defense as a result of the ABM Treaty?*

- 3 -

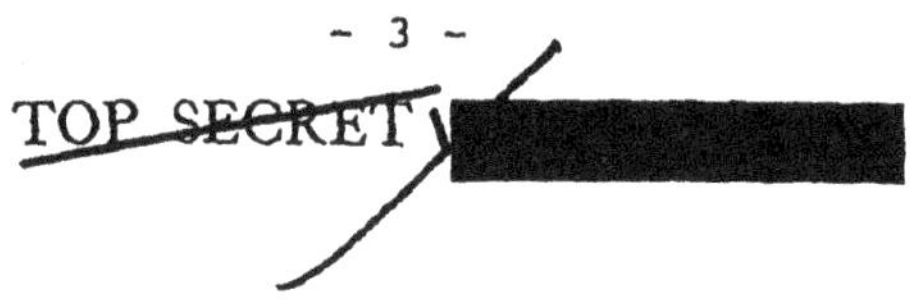

TCS 1164/73

Soviet agreement to this treaty probably reflects a desire to limit competition in an area where the US had significant technical advantages and stood to lengthen its lead. In this regard, the Soviets would believe that they gave up little and gained substantial benefits.

The ABM Treaty, however, introduces a new consideration into Soviet planning for aerospace defense: the potential effectiveness of the extensive Soviet air defense network is undermined in the absence of a complementary ABM defense. If the treaty remains in effect over the long term, Soviet air defenses will be susceptible to disruption by a precursor missile attack. This consideration may affect future air defense system procurement. It may have already done so, in view of the absence of new strategic air defense weapons systems at test ranges for the past several years, although the evidence is inconclusive at this point.

A second implication of the treaty is that the USSR has limited the use of active defenses to deter or counter third-country missile attacks outside of Moscow and has chosen to rely primarily on the deterring influence of a superior offensive arsenal.

2. *How do the Soviets decide how much is enough?*

The ultimate objectives and intentions underlying Soviet strategic arms programs will continue to be a subject of uncertainty, given a dynamic strategic environment characterized by continuing competition on both sides, each attempting to prevent the other from achieving a measurable advantage, and in the absence of arms control agreements sufficiently comprehensive to restrain that competition.

Soviet spokesmen have often stated in recent years that the USSR's basic aim is to maintain a condition of "equal security" in relation to the US. This concept is not capable of precise definition. Possession by the Soviets of an assured deterrent

- 4 -

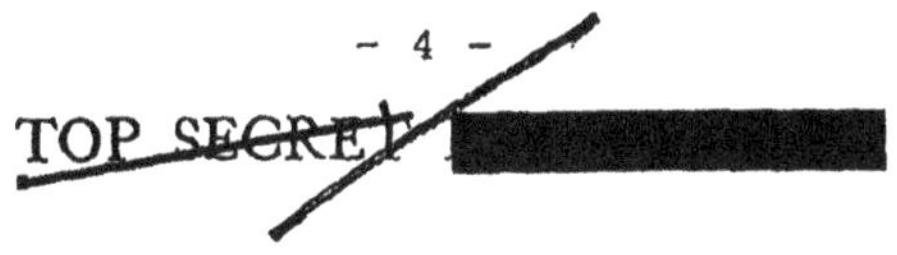

TCS 1164/73

capability, even though clearly recognized by the US, is evidently not "enough" if the deterrent forces stand in marked quantitative inferiority to those of the US. Similarly, the lag behind the US in significant qualitative aspects of strategic weaponry, such as MIRV technology, is probably also unacceptable.

Even if the intention is only to strive to maintain a relationship of rough strategic equality with the US, Soviet arms programs are bound to be vigorous and demanding. This is in part because of existing asymmetries, which may appear to the Soviets to justify certain quantitative advantages for the USSR, for example in land-based ICBMs, to maintain "equal security." Ongoing US development and deployment programs are probably also seen as requirements for offsetting action by the USSR. The Soviets would like to have a margin of strategic advantage over the US in some form, but we do not know what particular weapon programs the Soviets would consider most likely to afford them a useful advantage over the US or how they might assess the risks and costs of such programs in view of possible US reactions.

-- *Is there any doctrinal or conceptual limit on force size or composition? Or are the limitations the result of such practical considerations as cost, technology, and estimates of US reaction?*

There is a growing body of evidence that Soviet decisions on force goals involve a complex interplay of many factors beyond rational and objective considerations of strategic needs. The political leadership has the final say on those matters it considers, but it operates in the presence of other influences, including competing policy positions, special interest groups, Kremlin politics, bureaucratic pressures, and technological and economic constraints. Decisions are worked out on an incremental basis, and choices are susceptible to change from one year to the next. The decisionmaking process itself is veiled in secrecy, and evidence is often lacking on the substance and influence of positions taken by key institutions and individuals.

- 5 -

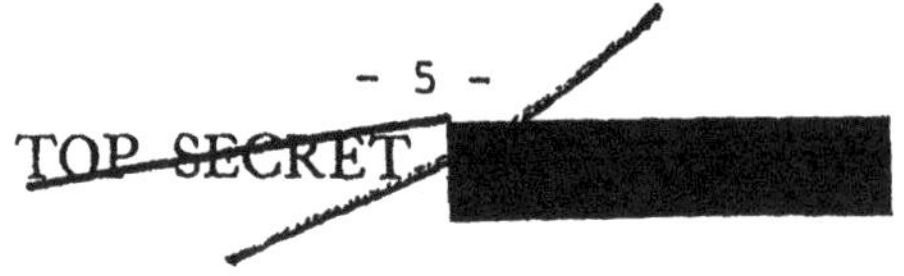

TCS 1164/73

Consequently we do not know precisely what conceptual criteria may govern Soviet force size and composition. It is possible, however, to circumscribe in a rough way the range of choices available in the light of major factors that the Soviets must take into account in planning for the future of their strategic forces. These factors include the provisions of strategic arms limitation agreements and the manner in which these agreements alter or appear to alter the strategic, political, and economic conditions confronting the USSR; the leadership's sense of stability or change in its strategic relationship with the US, including interaction in research and development; the pace and scope of technological change; economic capabilities; and the Chinese military threat.

-- *What is the impact of SALT on Soviet strategic doctrine?*

The ABM Treaty reflects a change from Soviet doctrine emphasizing active air and missile defenses against all threats. Otherwise, there is no evidence available at present to indicate whether or how the strategic arms limitation agreements have affected Soviet strategic doctrine.

3. *How would the Soviets envision using nuclear weapons?*

-- *Do they see using them at all? For initiation, retaliation, preemption?*

There is good evidence that the Soviets do not consider a sudden first strike to be a workable strategy. The Soviets have not deployed counterforce weapons in sufficient numbers to make a first-strike damage limiting strategy feasible. At the same time, the Soviets evidently do not anticipate a sudden first strike by the US. Their propaganda continues to cite the threat of a US surprise attack, but the observed day-to-day readiness posture of their strategic forces indicates that the Soviets do not, in fact, expect such an attack.

- 6 -

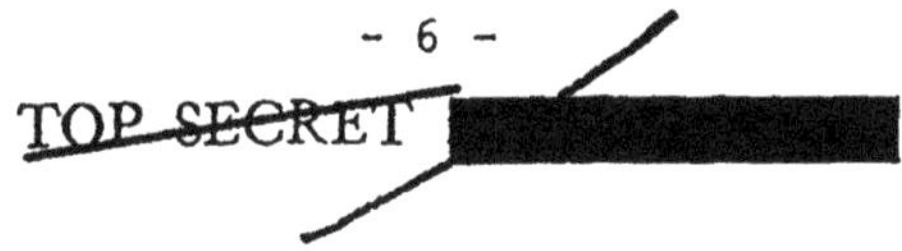

TOP SECRET

TCS 1164/73

Excluding a sudden first-strike strategy, the Soviet leadership has considered three strategic options: preemption, launch-on-warning, and retaliation.

Preemption is often presented in Soviet military writings as a desirable strategic option, but these discussions fail to address such factors as the US early warning systems and massive retaliatory capabilities. Given the immense risks involved, the Soviets probably would not attempt to translate this theoretical concept into a practical option.

Launch-on-warning evidently has been considered as a strategic option, but it is rarely mentioned by the Soviets. The concept may be seen as having a certain psychological value in reinforcing deterrence, but as a policy it would present command and control problems. The Soviet leadership is unlikely to delegate the authority to launch a nuclear attack or to accept the unpredictable risks of accidental or unauthorized launch inherent in such a policy.

Retaliation is the oldest declared Soviet strategy and the one most frequently advocated by the top party and government officials. None of the Soviet statements about preemption and launch-on-warning have come from the upper levels of the civilian leadership. The Soviet strategic buildup over the past decade has made retaliation a thoroughly credible doctrine. The assumptions underlying the leadership's view of retaliation, as reflected in the Soviet position at SALT, are that the US and USSR possess more than enough nuclear weapons to bring about a world-wide catastrophe, that the side attacked first would retain a retaliatory force capable of annihilating the attackers's homeland, and that a war between the US and USSR would be disastrous for both.

-- *Do the Soviets see using nuclear weapons for devastation in retaliation or for military effect? What military effects would be valued most?*

Both counterforce and countervalue targets are incorporated in Soviet planning. The basic targets

- 7 -

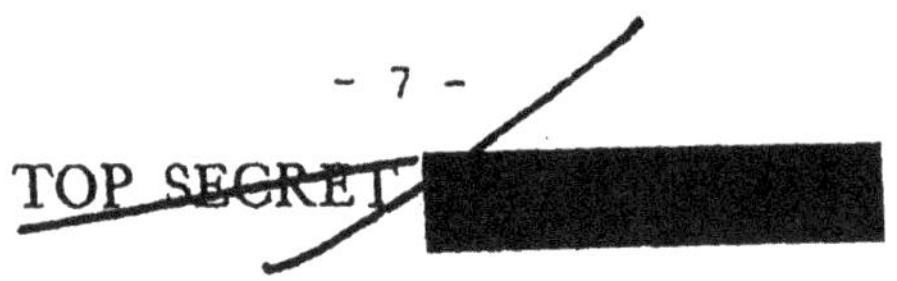

TOP SECRET

are identified as missile launch sites, nuclear weapons production and storage facilities, other military installations, systems for controlling and supporting strategic forces, and military-industrial and administrative centers. Explicit references to the destruction of enemy population, as such, are notably omitted from available Soviet listings of strategic targets. The list obviously implies, however, the direct targeting of major American cities and therefore massive civilian fatalities.

-- *Do the Soviets envision use of nuclear weapons all at once or in some escalatory fashion? Is there any evidence of Soviet thinking about war bargaining, i.e. efforts to use nuclear weapons to create circumstances for bargaining, de-escalation?*

In the context of intercontinental warfare, there is no indication in available materials that the Soviets accept the feasibility of limited strategic nuclear warfare or war bargaining. At least in public they have consistently rejected the possibility that either the US or the USSR would be able to exercise restraint, once nuclear weapons had been employed against its homeland. Despite these disclaimers, the Soviet strategic arsenal could support a strategy of controlled strategic attack, raising the possibility that such a contingency may be included in Soviet targeting and attack planning.

In the context of warfare in Europe, Soviet doctrine on escalation has been modified since the mid-Sixties. An earlier position that any war involving NATO and the Warsaw Pact would automatically escalate to theater-wide nuclear war has been altered to allow for an initial conventional phase. Soviet writings and Warsaw Pact exercises have paid increasing attention to the importance of having armed forces equipped and trained for conventional as well as nuclear tactical warfare. Current Pact planning for a war in Europe recognizes the possibility of both a conventional or nonnuclear phase and a nuclear strike phase. Pact planners apparently believe that successful conventional operations by the Pact would force NATO to resort to nuclear weapons, and they emphasize the importance of the timing of their initial use.

- 8 -

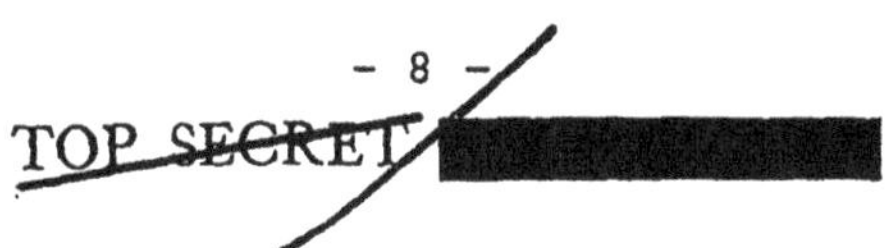

TCS 1164/73

Soviet military writers have given little attention to the concept of controlled nuclear war in Europe. They emphasize the decisiveness of an initial nuclear attack and the need for effective coordination. The first salvo of intermediate- and medium-range ballistic missiles by the Strategic Rocket Forces evidently would be the signal for nuclear strikes by other Warsaw Pact forces.

For the Soviet political leadership, a broader range of options is likely to exist than is evident in Pact exercises and documents. Authorization for the scale of fighting to be pursued, the use of nuclear weapons, and the scope of permitted nuclear operations would rest with the political leaders. Under actual combat conditions they could decide to employ nuclear forces in a more carefully controlled manner than indicated in military writings and exercises.

4. *How do the Soviets see the relation between their intercontinental and theater forces?*

-- *Is there any way of judging which the Soviets might believe more likely to be used? Is there any evidence of Soviet views as to coupling or decoupling?*

We do not have good evidence on how the Soviets view the possibility of an intercontinental exchange between the US and the USSR if theater nuclear warfare erupts in Europe. The Soviets would presumably prefer to avoid a level of combat that would involve massive strikes on their own country. Their willingness to escalate to global nuclear warfare might depend largely on what they expected the US response would be to events in Europe.

Until the mid-Sixties Soviet declaratory doctrine held that a war between NATO and the Warsaw Pact would automatically escalate to theater-wide nuclear war in Europe and possibly to global nuclear war. Some Soviet military writers have continued to express skepticism that a European conflict could be kept limited. At the same time, other Soviet military writings have

- 9 -

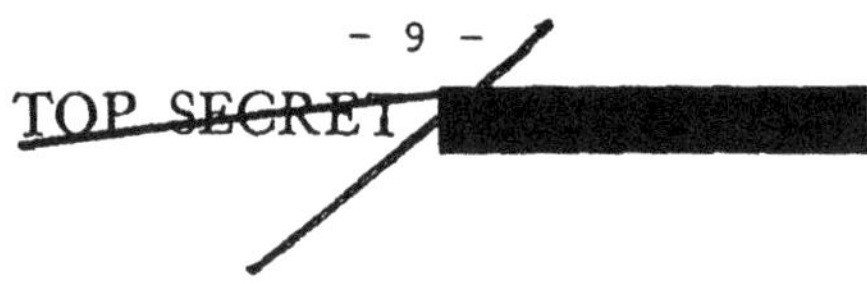

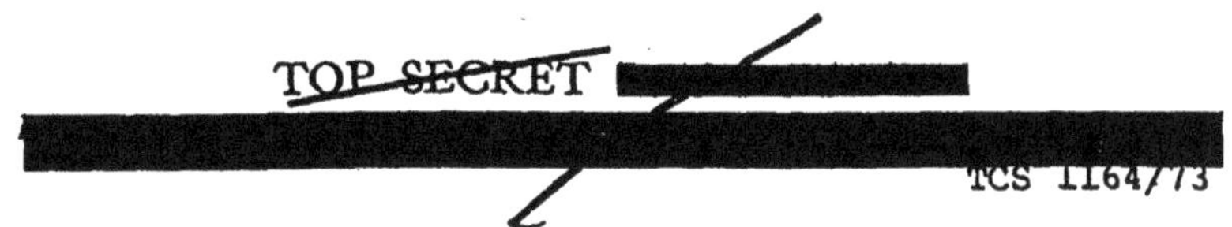

paid increased attention to the possibilities of limiting a war in Europe. In view of the modification of their doctrine on escalation, Soviet planners may have become more willing to consider decoupling a war in Europe from a direct US-USSR intercontinental confrontation.

- 10 -

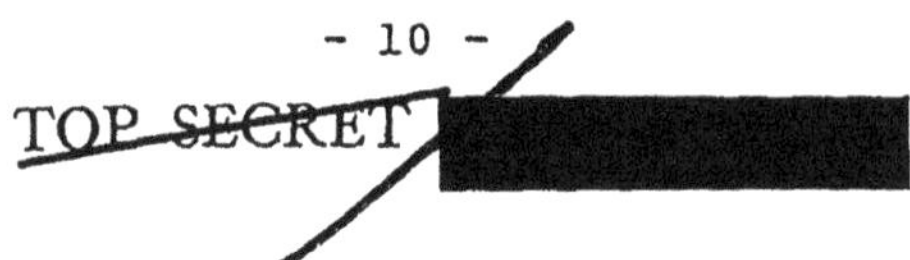

46.

THE TRACK RECORD

IN STRATEGIC ESTIMATING

An Evaluation of the Strategic
National Intelligence Estimates, 1966-1975

6 February 1976

Robert L. Hewitt
Dr. John Ashton
Dr. John H. Milligan

~~TOP SECRET~~

74

46. (continued)

CONCLUSIONS

1. The intelligence community, as judged by the findings in its national estimates, has a good record of detecting and determining major characteristics and missions of new weapons systems soon after testing begins and usually well before IOC. ?

a. This capability has improved since 1966 with the development of higher resolution photography and improved SIGINT capabilities. ?

b. However, the community was not always right from the outset: *Minutiae ↓*

-- The SS-N-8 was considered to have a 3,100 nm range (3,500 nm maximum) until it demonstrated 4,200 nm in November and December 1972 (IOC was in April 1974). Lacking firm data, the analysts misjudged how close to 100 percent to propellant capacity was being used.

-- There was initial confusion about the size and functions of some of the new hardened missile silos introduced in the early 1970s.

-- Not until the early 1970s was it determined that some SS-11 silos which began deployment in 1967 were oriented to provide previously lacking coverage of China, and that others *for what purposes* were oriented to cover Europe, the Mediterranean and South Asia. All, however, can be used against the US and are so counted.

- 1 -

Silly section: "Good record" but . . . ! Softens a[nd] [illegible] excuse fundamental errors & contrives [to] reflect them

~~TOP SECRET~~ [redacted]

c. There were also persistent problems and disagreements over three weapon systems which appeared well suited for one sort of mission but at least marginally capable of performing another mission of more serious concern to the US. These were the SS-9 Mod 4, the SA-5, and the Backfire bomber.

-- In all three cases, the limitations of available evidence left uncertainties about detailed system performance, despite the sophisticated analytical techniques employed by the intelligence community. Thus there were questions, some of them still not resolved, about how much of a capability in the second category really existed, and hence about Soviet intentions in designing and building the systems.

2. The intelligence community has also been generally successful in monitoring the deployment of new weapon systems and the introduction of major modifications in existing ones, despite some initial difficulties in determining the scope and pace of deployment. There have been recurring minor uncertainties and disagreements about how many silos are under construction, how many submarines are in the building shed, and the like. These uncertainties have been reduced but not eliminated with the advent of better, more precise sensors.

a. The principal problems arose during the mid-1960s, before the full scope of the ICBM buildup and the pace of Y-class submarine production were clear.

~~TOP SECRET~~

3. The Community's record in perceiving likely Soviet force goals over the longer run, on which direct evidence was usually lacking.

a. The most obvious shortcoming was the failure of the earlier estimates to foresee the degree to which the Soviets would not only catch up to the US in number of ICBMs but keep right on going. There was a similar early failure to recognize that the Soviets would want -- and demand in negotiating the Interim Agreement in 1972 -- more than the 15-50 modern ballistic missile submarines which the estimates took to represent rough parity with the US.

-- The estimators appear to have been overimpressed with the magnitude of the problems and uncertainties the Soviets faced in achieving and then retaining full equality with the US and to have overestimated Soviet concern about provoking new US deployments or force improvements. At the same time, they evidently underestimated the strength and persistence of the political, institutional, and probably most of all military pressures for continuation of the buildup -- probably in part because of doubt that a push much past equality would be of real military value.

b. On the other hand, the NIEs overestimated Soviet willingness to deploy ABMs in defense of key target areas beyond

- iii -

46. (continued)

Moscow, even though they identified the weaknesses and shortcomings of the Moscow system, and interpreted failure to complete it as evidence of Soviet discontent with the system, and recognized that there were probably divided counsels over the desirability of further deployment, even with an improved system. A key consideration appears to have been past evidence of Soviet willingness to deploy new and expensive strategic defense systems which had major weaknesses and shortcomings.

c. Deployment goals were more easy to gauge with defensive systems like the SA-5, where the coverage provided by existing air defense systems provided useful precedents, and with air defense interceptors, whose production runs normally fall within certain limits and which are usually deployed to known airfields. Even so, the NIEs for a time overestimated SA-5 force goals and misjudged actual force goals of two interceptors.

d. In the last few years, there have been no discernable problems about estimating force levels in the NIEs. The 1972 SALT accords removed many uncertainties by placing quantitative limits on certain categories, while in others, such as current SAM systems, the Soviets seem to be at or close to completion of deployment. The task was eased by the switch in 1970 from an attempt to define force goals by a single set of low-high numbers to the use of alternative projections illustrating what the Soviets might accomplish under various assumptions.

- iv -

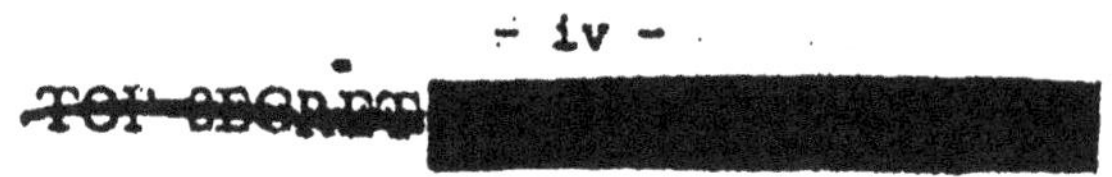

7. The estimative record in foreseeing qualitative improvements in Soviet strategic systems is mixed. For the most part, they appear to have been successful in identifying major requirements the Soviets would probably seek to satisfy through new or improved weapon systems, though not exactly when or in what form the improvement would appear. In particular, they foresaw the development by the early or mid-1970s of MIRVed ICBMs with improved accuracy and hard target kill capability. They also foresaw the introduction of longer range SLBMs than those of the Y-class. In the various fields of strategic defense, they appear to have identified correctly the problems the Soviets faced and the most promising lines of development.

a. However, there have been some surprises. While anticipating greater Soviet emphasis on the survivability of their ICBMs, they did not foresee -- before construction actually began -- that the Soviets would undertake the very extensive remodeling of silos and construction of new launch control facilities now going on. More important, they failed to foresee that the Soviets would greatly increase the throwweight of their new missiles and introduce new launch techniques with some. Although the throwweight issue was examined in the context of possible SALT constraints, no one anticipated that the Soviets might greatly increase missile volume without increasing silo diameter.

b. In addition, the Soviets have thus far failed to make a number of advances which analysis in the estimates indicated would be necessary or desirable -- e.g., the development of quieter submarines with a capability for covert trail of US submarines. *Why not? Very significant*

8. In terms of the threat to the Triad, the record can be summarized as follows:

a. The threat to Minuteman from Soviet hard target MIRVs has been overestimated in terms of how soon high accuracy would be obtained, if the current estimates are correct, but was underestimated in terms of throw weight and number of RVs. Although the key consideration remains accuracy, the early availability of additional RVs will move up the date when there will be enough to threaten Minuteman survivability.

b. The threat to US bombers and ASMs penetrating Soviet territory has grown about as the estimates indicated, with the Soviets continuing to make incremental improvements in virtually all phases of air defense, but not the drastic improvements in low level intercept capabilities that were required. Although it is now judged that the Soviets may be able to overcome current deficiencies by the early 1980s, it remains uncertain whether this will provide an effective operational capability under actual combat conditions. There is no indication that the ?

- vi -

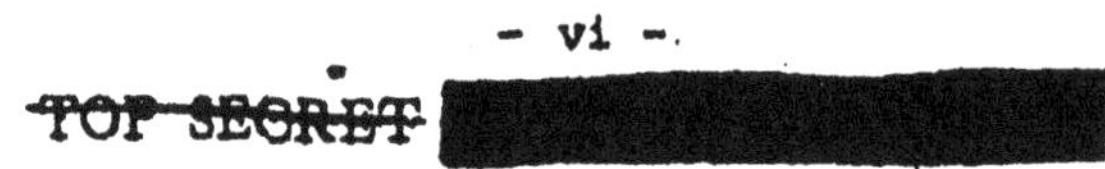

Soviets are developing a depressed trajectory mode of operation for submarine-launched ballistic missiles, so that they could be used against US bomber bases with reduced warning time. ?

c. Soviet ABM capabilities did not develop as expected; improved systems have been slower to develop, additional deployment at Moscow or elsewhere failed to take place and deployment is now severely limited by treaty.

d. Soviet ASW capabilities against US SSBNs have remained very low as was estimated, despite vigorous Soviet ASW programs. ?

9. With respect to the effectiveness of the NIEs in depicting Soviet motivations, goals, and expectations over the past decade, it is probably impossible to provide an evaluation that will satisfy everyone. However, in terms of the intelligence community's present perceptions and judgments, the only particular shortcomings we would note are the following:

a. In retrospect, it is evident that the estimates of the mid and late 1960s failed to convey an adequate sense of the determination of the Soviets to build up sizable force and warfighting capabilities, however long it took. Perhaps there was temporary uncertainty in Moscow about what courses of action to follow and how the US might respond, as those estimates suggest. It now looks as though the Soviets adopted ambitious

- vii -

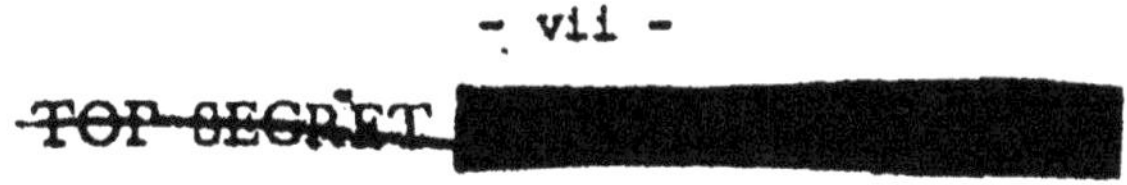

strategic force goals and moved steadily forward without much concern that the US might feel it necessary to step up its own programs in turn.

b. NIE 11-8-72 gives the impression that Soviet acceptance of the 1972 SALT accords involved greater Soviet interest in a stabilized strategic relationship with the US and a greater concern to avoid actions which might jeopardize detente than proved to be the case -- although it estimated that new weapon programs would be "vigorous and demanding," and presented force projections comparable to or in some cases more ambitious than the modernization programs now in progress. They must be kidding!

b. In fact the Soviets have taken a highly competitive view of the strategic relationship with the US; have evidently considered a high level of force development activity as quite consistent with "detente," and appear to have looked on arms control primarily as a means of constraining US force development rather than as a means of curtailing the overall competition and thus achieving greater stability. God

10. One final point is that, just as the strategic situation has changed greatly over the past decade, so have the scope and contents of the estimates. The estimates of the mid and late 1960s were relatively short and general in nature, with details about

- viii -

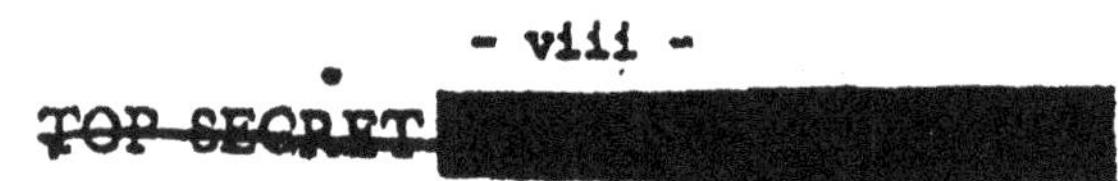

how future Soviet forces might develop relegated to supplementing documents like the NIPP. More recently they have included greatly expanded and more explicit treatments of the evidence and analysis underlying key judgments and more on the organizational aspects and operational implications of the capabilities being built up. The content and focus of the estimates have since varied in some degree from year to year, depending on the observed progress of Soviet programs, on what topics were considered most pertinent and important, and on the availability of new analytical studies. Beginning in 1974 the NIE 11-3 and NIE 11-8 series have been combined in a single document, so that all aspects of Soviet strategic policy and activities are considered together.

11. How effective these changes have been in improving the usefulness of the estimates is for the customer to say. With respect to the estimative track record, however, it is pertinent to note that the analysts whose work is reflected in the estimates have had to address increasingly complex questions and in answering them have been under heavy pressure to be explicit about the nature and extent of their evidence, how their conclusions were arrived at, and how much confidence can be placed in them. Moreover, while there remain important limits on how much can be learned about Soviet strategic weapons and about Soviet strategic plans and policies, there have been important improvements in both the quality and quantity of information available to US intelligence.

- ix -

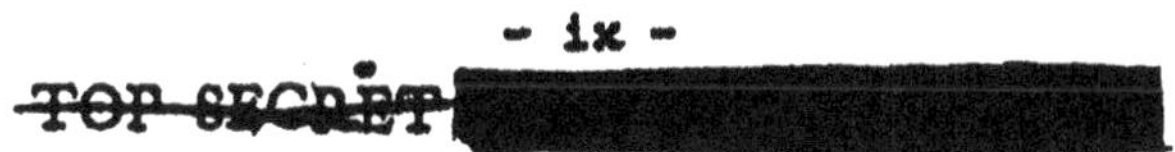

47.

KEY JUDGMENTS

The USSR's invasion of Afghanistan in December 1979 provided a rare opportunity to test the efficacy of the US warning system in situations involving substantial movements of the Soviets' armed forces outside their borders. Moreover, it afforded a chance to examine the behavior of the Soviet military in preparing for such an undertaking and to determine what implications this might have for the Intelligence Community's capacity to provide warning in other situations, especially one involving a Warsaw Pact move against NATO.

From the outset, it was recognized that the conclusions of this study could not be pressed too far. Both the performance of the Intelligence Community in providing warning of the invasion of Afghanistan and the applicability to other theaters of the lessons learned in that situation are very much affected by the particular circumstances involved. In contrast to a Soviet move against NATO, the situation for which the US warning system is largely designed, the invasion of Afghanistan required only a fraction of the USSR's military assets, was not opposed at the outset, did not involve a certainty of confrontation with US forces, and occurred in a region where US intelligence collection capabilities were limited.

These limitations notwithstanding, the examination of the Soviet approach to invading Afghanistan and the Intelligence Community's success in giving prior notice of this event have yielded some valuable lessons:

— Despite the unique circumstances surrounding this operation, the Soviets' behavior was essentially in keeping with US estimates of their doctrine for mobilization and the initiation of hostilities. This finding is important because the success of any warning system is dependent on the extent to which an adversary's behavior conforms to expectations.

— The system of warning indicators that is set up to detect potentially important changes in the Soviet/Warsaw Pact military posture provided a structured approach to and a sound evidentiary base for the Intelligence Community's conclusion that the USSR was preparing to introduce substantial forces into Afghanistan. The fact that the system worked in this unique situation provides increased assurance of its usefulness in other theaters, particularly in the NATO area.

- The US intelligence collection system proved equal to the task of providing analysts with sufficiently detailed, accurate, and timely data to allow them to reach essentially correct conclusions about the military activities in the Soviet Union with respect to Afghanistan. Of particular note was the synergy of signals and imagery intelligence in this collection effort and the quality of the data collected, despite limitations on the resources available.
- The Intelligence Community's analysts met their basic responsibility in a situation of this sort by providing sufficient prior reporting to assure that no key policymaker should have been surprised by the invasion. The analysts were unable to forecast precisely the timing or the size of the Soviets' move, but gave warning at least 10 days beforehand that the USSR was prepared to invade.

In conclusion, the examination of the early phases of the Soviet military intervention in Afghanistan provides a basis for greater confidence in US intelligence estimates of Soviet doctrine with respect to initiating hostilities and in the capacity of the US Intelligence Community to provide warning of such hostilities.

48.

Intelligence Forecasts of Soviet Intercontinental Attack Forces: An Evaluation of the Record

Summary

Information available as of 1 March 1989 was used in this report.

The US Government's primary projections of Soviet intercontinental attack forces have been published annually in National Intelligence Estimates (NIEs). These projections have contained cases of both intelligence successes and failures.

During the early 1960s, the Intelligence Community took seriously Khrushchev's boast that ICBMs would be "turned out like sausages" and, in the absence of confirmation from overhead photography, substantially overestimated the number of ballistic missiles that would be deployed. After the first overhead imagery became available, few ICBMs were found to be deployed and the Intelligence Community's projections were scaled back accordingly. By then the Soviets had largely completed deployment of medium-range ballistic missiles opposite Europe and had solved the technical problems they had encountered with their early ICBMs. The Soviets were thus ready to begin a massive buildup in their ICBM force, which the NIEs published during the mid-1960s did not anticipate.

Once the magnitude of the Soviet buildup became clear, the NIEs depicted large uncertainties about the Soviet Union's ultimate strategic force levels. These uncertainties began to diminish after the Strategic Arms Limitation Talks (SALT) began. By 1971 the SALT ceiling on total numbers of strategic nuclear delivery vehicles (SNDVs), coupled with assumptions regarding Soviet willingness to remain within the agreed constraints, became the "governor" for SNDV force projections. Because SALT reduced uncertainty about the future, throughout the 1970s the Intelligence Community's projections of SALT-limited forces accurately reflected the number of SNDVs in the Soviet force.

With the acquisition of MIRV technology in the early 1970s, Soviet strategic forces began to expand rapidly in terms of the number of deployed RVs. The Intelligence Community predicted well in advance when the Soviets would field MIRVed ICBMs and in 1970 began to include in its projections estimates of the total number of weapons deployed on delivery vehicles. The high and low projections made from 1970 to 1977 successfully bracketed the actual number of nuclear weapons in the Soviet force. The accuracy of the record in the early 1970s was due to a combination of correct estimates of the numbers of MIRVs on ICBMs and

SOV 89-10031
April 1989

of the rate at which these missiles would be deployed. In the mid-1970s, however, the accuracy of the overall record was fortuitous because it was the product of two offsetting errors:

- The projected number of RVs per missile deployed on submarine-launched ballistic missiles proved to be about half the number the Soviets deployed.
- The projected rate of modernization with new missiles carrying MIRVs was much greater than that which the Soviets actually achieved.

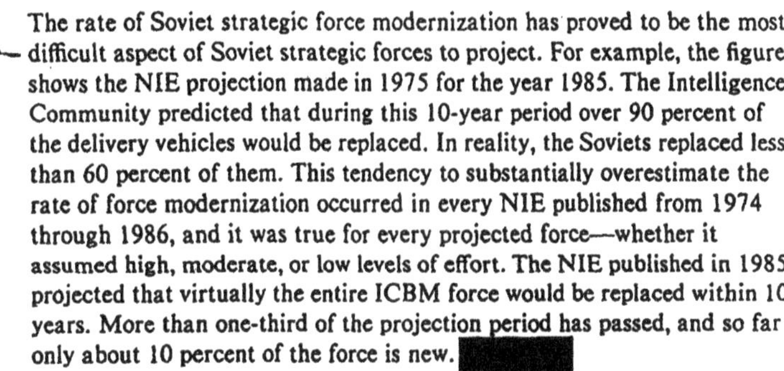
The rate of Soviet strategic force modernization has proved to be the most difficult aspect of Soviet strategic forces to project. For example, the figure shows the NIE projection made in 1975 for the year 1985. The Intelligence Community predicted that during this 10-year period over 90 percent of the delivery vehicles would be replaced. In reality, the Soviets replaced less than 60 percent of them. This tendency to substantially overestimate the rate of force modernization occurred in every NIE published from 1974 through 1986, and it was true for every projected force—whether it assumed high, moderate, or low levels of effort. The NIE published in 1985 projected that virtually the entire ICBM force would be replaced within 10 years. More than one-third of the projection period has passed, and so far only about 10 percent of the force is new.

The overestimates of force modernization have had two components. The date of initial operational capability (IOC) of a weapon system often was predicted to occur earlier than the actual date, and the rate of deployment was projected to be faster than it actually was. Of the 17 weapon systems that have been predicted to reach IOC since 1970, the Intelligence Community predicted that 10 would become operational earlier than they did, six were projected accurately, and one was projected to reach IOC later than it did. There are three reasons the projected IOC dates were often early:

- The Intelligence Community did not correctly understand Soviet military requirements.
- The Soviets slowed some weapon programs to conform to arms control limits.
- Some programs had serious (and expensive) technical problems.

48. (continued)

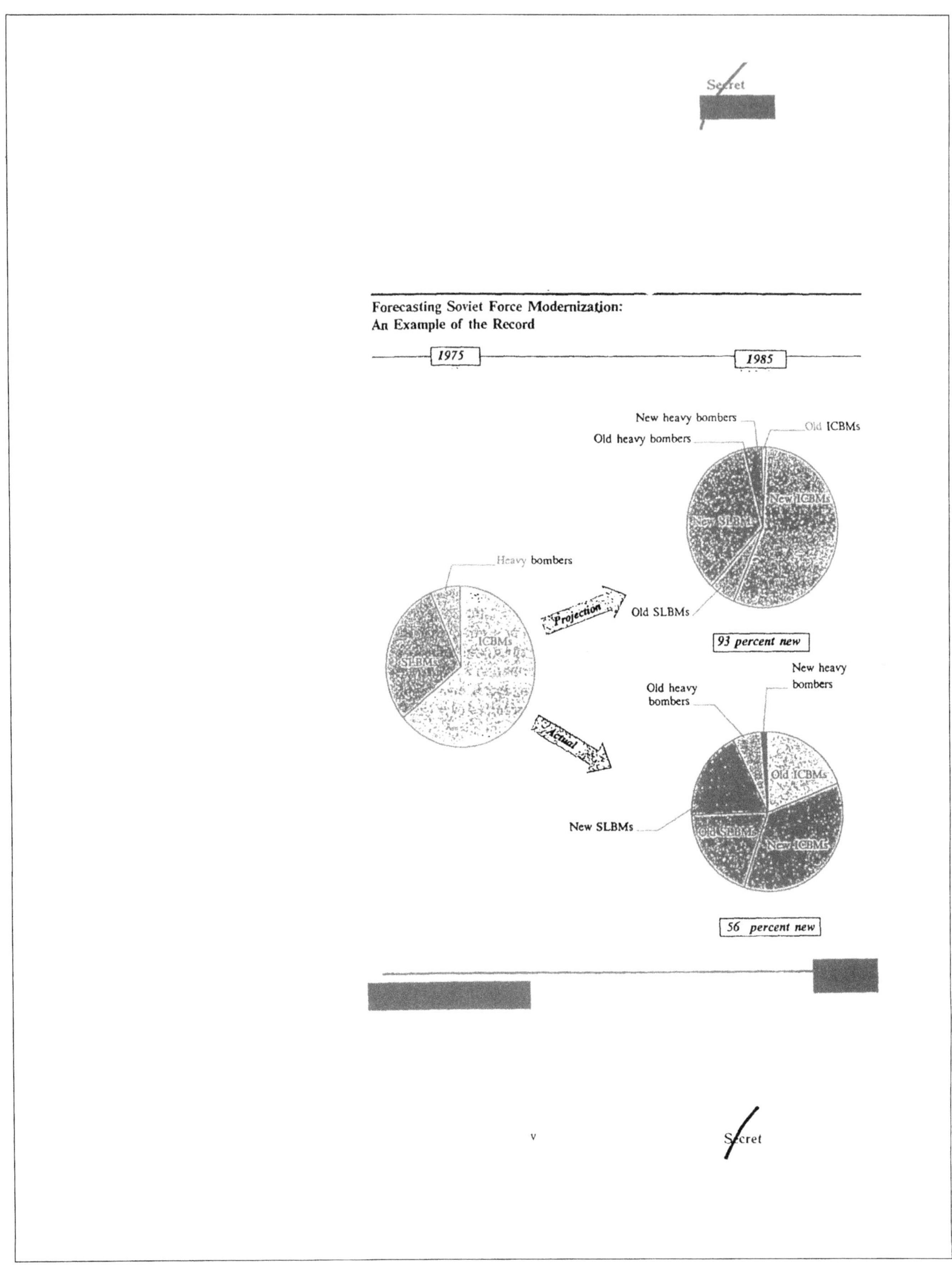
Secret
Forecasting Soviet Force Modernization:
An Example of the Record
1975
1985
New heavy bombers
Old ICBMs
Old heavy bombers
New ICBMs
New SLBMs
Heavy bombers
Projection
Old SLBMs
93 percent new
ICBMs
SLBMs
New heavy
bombers
Old heavy
bombers
Actual
Old ICBMs
New SLBMs
Old SLBMs
New ICBMs
56 percent new
v
Secret

Overestimates of deployment rates also contributed to the overall record on force modernization. Analysts used the rapid Soviet missile buildup in the late 1960s as a guide for future deployment rates, but that rate of deployment was never approached again. Examination of deployment rates also revealed that sometimes, when the follow-on to a weapon system was projected to arrive too soon after the original weapon system was fielded, the Intelligence Community anticipated the arrival of the follow-on by rapidly phasing in and phasing out the original weapon in the projections.

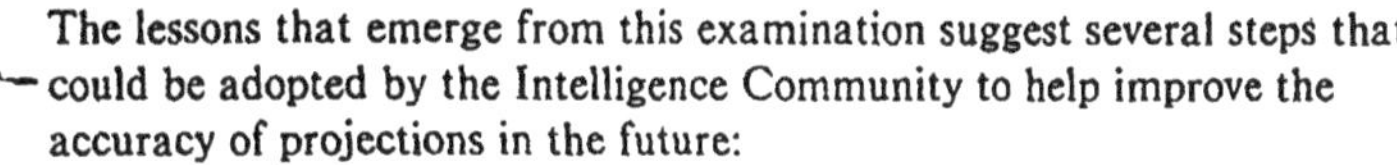

The lessons that emerge from this examination suggest several steps that could be adopted by the Intelligence Community to help improve the accuracy of projections in the future:

- *Institutionalize evaluations of the projections record by making them part of the annual Community product.* This is perhaps the simplest step to take, but, for it to succeed, the most recent projection must be evaluated in terms of all projections that were made over the last 10 years. Comparing last year's projection with this year's projection does not provide enough information to indicate trends in the forecasting record. Moreover, making incremental adjustments to a projection based upon changes that have occurred over the last year can mask fundamental trends and thereby prolong misperceptions.

- *Continue to develop measures for the projections to more sharply define the key changes that occur in the force.* The need to periodically evaluate and measure forces from a different perspective is a direct result of the changing technologies, functions, and capabilities embodied in military forces. Today the major Soviet weapon families—ICBMs and SLBMs—are reaching technological maturity. Although further improvements in accuracy and survivability are likely, if Soviet strategic delivery systems start to evolve in an entirely different direction—for example, by carrying advanced conventional munitions rather than nuclear payloads—the rate of modernization might no longer be a major focus of interest. Other measures of force capability would be needed to correctly depict force modernization.

vi

- *Continue to examine the full range of factors bearing on force developments, the assumptions regarding the direction of force developments, and the magnitude of the effect of such factors.* Evaluating the many competing factors that the Soviets weigh in setting their procurement goals has been a perennial problem in making the force projections. Crediting one factor as having a central influence on force projections, especially for an extended period of time, obscures the roles that other factors play. Economic difficulty is one example of a factor that was given little weight in the past, but has now become important. In the current situation in the USSR, where traditional approaches are being swept aside and Gorbachev's national security policy is the subject of intense debate, the relative weights of the factors that influence future forces need to be carefully scrutinized each time a new projection is developed.

- *Continue to look at the potential for discontinuities in the future—not only highlighting which weapon systems might change more often or to a greater degree than others, but also examining the implications of major economic and political events.* Discontinuities are often the most imponderable of all analytical problems associated with developing projections. Defining "low" and "high" force projections in terms of a range of specific political, economic, or military developments—instead of as representations of different levels of effort—would help anticipate the consequences of these potential developments.

49.

Secret

The Development of Soviet Military Power: Trends Since 1965 and Prospects for the 1980s

Summary: The Past, Present, and Future of Soviet Military Power

The Soviet Military Effort Under Brezhnev

For more than two decades, the USSR has been engaged in a major buildup of its military forces. In the Khrushchev era the emphasis was on strategic nuclear programs, but since Brezhnev came to power in 1964 there has been an across-the-board expansion and modernization of all the Soviet forces. Among the many factors underlying this buildup, the most basic is the attitude of the Soviet leaders that military might is a necessary and effective instrument of policy in an inherently unstable world. This attitude has been embodied in and reinforced by an ambitious military doctrine that calls for forces structured to fight and win future conflicts and by a political and economic system that gives priority to military requirements

Taken together, these conditions have imparted a considerable momentum to the Soviet military effort. Thus, despite changes in the international environment, Brezhnev's detente policy, and Strategic Arms Limitation agreements, the overall pace of the Soviet military buildup has remained steady during the Brezhnev years. Annual Soviet military spending has nearly doubled in real terms and now consumes over one-eighth of GNP; military manpower has increased by one-third to more than 5 million; [1] defense research and development facilities have more than doubled in size; and weapon production facilities have expanded by nearly 60 percent

The number of Soviet strategic nuclear weapons delivery vehicles has increased from a few hundred in 1965 to about 2,500 today, overturning the previous US quantitative superiority. (The United States has just over 2,000 delivery vehicles.) The accuracy of the newest Soviet weapons now exceeds that of US systems, creating a major threat to US fixed, land-based missiles. These improvements have enhanced the capability of Soviet forces to fight a nuclear war. Moreover, by hardening their land-based missile launchers and putting a greater number of ballistic missiles on submarines, the Soviets have made their strategic forces so survivable that even after absorbing a US attack they could destroy most of the US population and most US military and economic targets in a retaliatory strike

[1] This figure includes about 1 million men who fulfill roles that the United States would not consider related to national securit·

Soviet planners also emphasize defense against strategic weapons, but their defenses cannnot prevent similar devastation from a US retaliatory strike:

- The Soviets have introduced systems to detect and defend against ballistic missiles, but technical limitations and treaty constraints render them largely ineffective against a large-scale US missile attack.
- They have expanded and improved their air defense network (the world's largest), giving it a good capability against high-flying aircraft but only limited effectiveness against low-altitude penetration.
- Defense against missile-launching submarines is poor despite its high priority in naval planning, because the search and detection capabilities of Soviet forces are insufficient to locate submarines in the open ocean.
- Continuing attention to civil defense has provided protection for virtually all political leaders, most key workers, and about 10 percent of the urban residents; but the rest of the population would be dependent on evacuation, and economic and military facilities are still vulnerable

The Soviets have eliminated the West's former edge in short- and medium-range nuclear delivery systems in Europe. The number of Soviet tactical surface-to-surface missiles there has increased by a third, and the number of aircraft capable of delivering nuclear weapons in Central Europe has more than tripled. The Soviets have broken the monopoly held by NATO since the 1960s in nuclear artillery and have introduced other new tactical delivery systems with improved ranges, accuracy, readiness, and destructive power. They may also have nuclear landmines. With these improvements, Soviet theater forces are now in a better position to match any NATO escalation of a European conflict from one level of nuclear war to another, without using long-range theater nuclear systems based in the USSR.[2] Those systems have also been improved by deployment of the SS-20 intermediate-range ballistic missile with three independently targetable warheads and of the Backfire bomber with improved payload and air defense penetration capabilities

To the extent that Soviet intercontinental nuclear forces now check those of the United States and Soviet gains in theater nuclear forces have offset those of NATO, the balance of conventional forces in Europe has become increasingly significant. In the conventional area, the Soviets expanded their

[2] The Soviets would hope to confine a NATO–Warsaw Pact war to European territory, avoiding the use of systems based in the Soviet Union so as not to invite retaliatory attacks. Nevertheless, they doubt that nuclear escalation in such a war could be held within bounds.

already large ground and theater air forces during the 1965-80 period and introduced modern systems, some of them equal or superior to those of NATO:

- Total ground forces manpower increased by nearly 50 percent, while the number of major weapons in a division increased by about a third and artillery firepower more than doubled.
- The number, variety, and capability of air defense systems available to tactical commanders increased rapidly, with deployment of all-weather missile-equipped interceptor aircraft and mobile air defense missiles and guns.
- The latest Soviet tanks (now common to most first-line Soviet units in Eastern Europe, but not yet widely deployed among units in the USSR) have armor that provides good protection against the most advanced antitank weapons.
- New tactical aircraft deployed in the 1970s have increased ninefold the weight of ordnance that Soviet theater air forces could deliver against targets in NATO's rear areas (the Benelux countries and parts of France, for example). More accurate bombing systems (radars, laser rangefinders, and computers) and precision munitions have improved Soviet capabilities against point targets and largely eliminated NATO's rear areas as sanctuaries in conventional wai

On the other hand, the Warsaw Pact's military potential is affected by its political cohesion and its will to use force. Pact performance on the field of battle would be heavily influenced by the attitudes and effectiveness of the non-Soviet armies, which have been assigned major roles in both combat and support. These armies are less modern than that of the USSR. More important, the solidarity and enthusiasm that they would exhibit in combat against NATO are open to serious question

The Soviets also maintain large forces opposite China. Since the late 1960s, the number of Ground Forces divisions along the Sino-Soviet border has doubled and their total manpower has more than tripled. Expansion of Soviet tactical aviation forces since the late 1960s has also been directed primarily at Chin

In the early 1960s, the Soviet Navy was a coastal defense force with limited capabilities for operations in the open ocean, but it is being transformed into an outward-looking force deploying heavily armed surface ships, high-speed submarines, and advanced aircraft. The number of ships has changed little, but the proportion of large surface combatants and nuclear-powered submarines is growing. Qualitatively, Soviet naval forces remain vulnerable to air and submarine attack; nuclear-powered submarines are noisier (and thus easier to detect) than their Western counterparts; and capabilities for distant combat operations—such as the landing of troops and provision of carrier-based air support—are extremely limited. But their numerous missile-equipped surface ships, submarines, and aircraft enable the Soviets to control their own coastal waters and to contest the use of open-ocean areas by the West

To support the expanded combat capabilities of their forces, the Soviets have introduced space systems for communications, intelligence collection, navigation, and other military functions. They now have an average of about 90 satellites operational at any given time, of which about 70 percent are military and another 15 percent have both military and civilian uses. The Soviets have also introduced new procedures and systems for controlling military operations. These include an increase in the operational authority of the General Staff, creation of new intermediate levels of command, introduction of mobile and hardened command posts, and deployment of new communications systems. These measures have improved the flexibility, reliability, security, and survivability of command

As their military power has grown at the intercontinental, theater nuclear, and conventional levels, the Soviets have increasingly used military instruments to achieve political gains, especially in the Third World. Soviet exports of military equipment to the Third World have increased rapidly since their beginning in the mid-1950s. During 1980, some $14 billion worth of hardware was sold to the Third World, and in 1979 nearly 15,000 Soviet advisers were in Third World countries—more than four times as many as in 1965. Operations of naval ships outside home waters increased sixfold between 1965 and 1970, fluctuated for several years, and increased sharply again during 1979 and 1980. Soviet naval ships now make several hundred visits to Third World ports each year

Military involvement in Third World conflicts has become more active and direct:

- In the late 1960s and early 1970s, Soviet air and air defense forces were used in defensive roles in the Middle East.
- In the mid-to-late 1970s, Soviet logistic support transported Cuban intervention forces to Angola and Ethiopia and sustained them there.
- In 1979, Soviet combat ground and air units invaded Afghanistan—the first direct involvement of Soviet ground forces outside the Soviet Bloc

To support their growing military involvement overseas, the Soviets have improved the ability of their forces to project power:

- The lift capability of primary Soviet amphibious ships has more than tripled since 1965. These ships can transport some 10,000 to 12,000 men (but they are spread out among four fleet areas). Merchant ships, some of which have been specifically designed to support naval operations, are also available.

- The firepower, mobility, and air defense capabilities of the six combat-strength airborne divisions have improved with the deployment of more modern weapons.

- By introducing heavy transport aircraft, the Soviets have doubled their airlift capacity (but their capabilities remain inferior to those of the United States)

The Soviets have not developed many forces specifically for overseas invasion. They rely instead on general purpose forces designed principally for use in Europe but also suitable for operations in more distant areas to which they can deploy without opposition. Most areas of vital interest to them are close to the USSR, however, and thus Soviet requirements for long-distance intervention forces are less demanding than those of the United States

Factors Affecting Future Military Programs
As the Soviet leaders formulate their defense plans for the future, they face major external and domestic uncertainties:

- The fluid international situation dictates a prudent defense posture, and the Soviets' perceptions of emerging military threats argue especially for continued qualitative improvement in forces.

- On the other hand, to maintain even a modest rate of economic growth, those leaders must allocate more resources to capital investment and must improve labor productivity, in part by providing a rising standard of living.

This dilemma could cause political tension, particularly at a time of leadership transition.

These uncertainties make it particularly difficult to forecast Soviet policies. We have sufficient information on each of the factors involved, however, to make fairly informed judgments about their probable impact on the development of Soviet military power in the 1980s and to examine the possible effects of discontinuities in policy

In the international arena, the Soviets are concerned by the prospect that the United States will augment its defense effort, by China's opening to the West, and by the possibility that US opposition to Soviet global aspirations will increase. They are troubled by instability on their borders—an insurgency in Afghanistan that they have been unable to suppress, an unpredictable regime in Iran whose fundamentalist Islamic ideology could spread to Muslim minorities in the USSR, and a major threat to Communist Party control in Poland. They probably view the 1980s as a decade of heightened competition, in which they will run a greater risk of military confrontation with the United States and of actual combat with major powers

While they see increasing tension, the leaders and planners also see foreign nations making military efforts that threaten to undercut the strengths of Soviet forces and exacerbate their weaknesses. These threats, as well as deficiencies that the Soviets currently perceive in their own military capabilities, make continued pursuit of new weapon programs essential from the perspective of the Soviet planners. They see the possible US deployment of the M-X missile, for example, as a dual threat:

- Its survivability (from deployment on mobile launchers or in multiple shelters) could force the Soviets to expend all of their ICBM weapons against the M-X alone, were they to undertake a massive counterforce strike.
- Its accuracy increases the risk that the United States could neutralize the Soviets' land-based ICBMs, which provide nearly 75 percent of the weapons and warheads on their intercontinental nuclear delivery vehicles.

The Soviets also consider NATO's plan to deploy advanced ballistic and cruise missiles in Europe as part of a US strategy to threaten Soviet ICBMs and to reduce Soviet capabilities for theater war in Europe

Many other military developments are a cause of concern to Soviet planners:

- They foresee that new Western ballistic missile submarines, with their greatly enlarged patrol areas, will further tax their inadequate antisubmarine capabilities.
- They are watching China's lengthening nuclear reach and the upgrading of French and British strategic forces.
- They regard NATO's programs for armor and antiarmor systems, precision munitions, and nuclear weapons as substantial and technologically challenging.
- They believe they must accelerate their efforts to compete with NATO in tactical aircraft and air defenses.
- They are worried about the antisubmarine capabilities of the West and the vulnerability of their ships to air and submarine attack.
- They see the widespread deployment of cruise missiles on US ships as reducing their capabilities in ship-to-ship warfare and—if the long-range Tomahawk cruise missile is deployed—as introducing a new strategic threat to Soviet territory.
- Finally, instability on their borders and US plans to form a rapid deployment force have increased Soviet concern about military developments in areas near the USSR

As they attempt to react to the wide array of situations they perceive as either promising or threatening, Soviet policymakers will face a far more constrained resources picture than in the 1960s and 1970s:

- Soviet economic growth, which has been declining since the 1950s, has slowed to a crawl in the past several years. The real average annual growth in GNP in 1979 and 1980 was a little over 1 percent—the worst in any two-year period since World War II.

- In the 1980s, developing energy and demographic problems probably will hold GNP growth to an average of 2 percent or less—only half the rate at which defense expenditures have been growing.

- If military spending is allowed to follow its past trend, its share of economic output could increase from about one-eighth now to over one-sixth in 1990.

Secret

- More importantly, this increased military burden would reduce significantly the share of the annual increment to GNP that can be distributed among civilian claimants to ease the political tensions that arise from competition for resources. Military programs—especially those for nonstrategic forces—divert key resources from the production of critically needed equipment for agriculture, industry, and transportation

The problems of Soviet leaders in allocating resources could be further complicated by a political succession. Soviet President Brezhnev is 74 and in poor health, and most of his colleagues are also in their seventies, many of them also ailing. The departure of these men could affect military policy, but probably not immediately. The process of Soviet national security planning and decisionmaking is highly centralized, secretive, and resistant to fundamental change. It is strongly influenced by military and defense-industrial organizations, represented by men who have held their positions for many years, providing a continuity of plans and programs. Because of this momentum, and the political clout of the men and institutions that support defense programs, we doubt that Soviet emphasis on military power would decrease in the early stages of a leadership succession

The attitudes of the senior leaders are another buffer against any quick change of direction. If Brezhnev leaves the scene soon, the chances are that he would be replaced by one of the current group, most of whom share his general policy views. The two most likely candidates are party secretaries Kirilenko (who has expressed views somewhat more conservative than Brezhnev's on national security policy) and Chernenko (who has always been very close to Brezhnev). Eventually, of course, the interim leader will be replaced by a younger man; but among the younger Politburo members who appear to be candidates, most also seem to favor a continued high priority on defense. The effect of a political transition is inherently unpredictable, however, and we cannot exclude the possibility that major policy changes could result

In contrast to the imponderables of the economic and political environments, we have a good capability to identify most future Soviet weapon systems. The forces of the 1980s will be equipped primarily with systems already in the field and secondarily with those now entering production or in late stages of development. (Because it takes a decade or more to develop and test modern weapon systems, few of those now in early stages of development could be introduced in significant numbers in the 1980s.) We believe that we have identified about 85 percent of the new systems likely to be introduced

Secret

xx

in this decade. Knowing Soviet military requirements and the amount of available development and production resources, we can postulate others. These identified and postulated systems, plus existing systems, will make up well over 90 percent of the weapons in the field in 1990

Soviet Military Power in the 1980s

Taking these factors into account, we can project in broad outline the prospects for further development of Soviet military power in the 1980s. We have made several projections. The most detailed (our baseline projection) is the one most consistent with currently available evidence. It assumes that pressures in favor of continuing the current policies—pressures from external challenges, from the Soviets' ambitious military doctrine, and from the powerful institutions that support defense programs—will offset to a large extent any inclination toward change that might arise from the leaders' growing economic concerns. The baseline projection allows for adjustments to defense expenditures—provided they do not significantly affect military capabilities

Because changes in political and economic conditions could lead to discontinuities in policy, we present three alternative projections: two that require an acceleration in the growth of military spending and one that requires an absolute reduction. We consider all of these to be less likely than the baseline projection but present a discussion of them intended to suggest reasonable limits to the options open to Soviet policymakers

Baseline Projection. For our baseline projection we estimate—on the basis of the weapon production and development programs we have identified—that the Soviets will continue their policy of balanced force development. Within the outlines of this continuity, however, we expect them to increase their emphasis on strategic forces that can survive a US attack, on strategic defense, and (to a lesser extent) on forces for the projection of Soviet power to distant areas. Manpower constraints will limit increases in the size of forces, but improvements will continue rapidly as new weapons become available. Improvements in Soviet military forces will lead to growing capabilities in many areas—including some areas of traditional Western strength

We expect the Soviets to carry out programs aimed at maintaining or increasing their lead over the United States in most measures of intercontinental nuclear attack capability and at upgrading their nuclear war-fighting capabilities. They will continue to improve the accuracy of their ICBMs and

~~Secret~~

will develop a variety of payload options for responding to US deployment of new ICBMs. As a result, the Soviet ICBM force—with or without the SALT II Treaty—will have the theoretical potential to destroy most of the warheads on US land-based missiles throughout the decade. This potential will be greatest in the early 1980s, before the United States can deploy a new ICBM. But even in that early period, US forces could conduct a massive retaliatory strike

To maintain survivable strategic forces in the face of a potential threat to their own fixed, land-based missiles, we expect the Soviets to increase the capability of their submarine-launched ballistic missiles and possibly (especially in the absence of SALT constraints) to deploy land-mobile ICBMs. They may introduce a new strategic bomber or an aircraft to carry long-range cruise missiles, and they may already be testing a sea-launched strategic cruise missile

Should strategic arms control negotiations be resumed, these weapon developments could complicate monitoring—an already difficult US intelligence task. Land-mobile strategic weapons and cruise missiles cannot be counted with high confidence. As a result, monitoring strategic arms control agreements will be much more difficult in the 1980s than it was in the 1970s

Air defense improvements have been identified at Soviet test ranges, and some are now entering deployment. These include new surface-to-air missiles and interceptor aircraft with radars that enable them to detect and engage low-flying targets. These defenses could make penetration of Soviet airspace much more difficult for large manned bombers of current types. The small size and low flight altitudes of modern cruise missiles present a more complicated problem, however, and we project that Soviet defenses will be less effective against these new systems during the 1980s

The Soviets continue their antiballistic missile (ABM) programs, but the technical difficulties of detecting, identifying, and intercepting ballistic missiles have kept progress slow. Moreover, the deployment constraints of the 1972 ABM Treaty severely limit the effectiveness of defenses against missiles. (Should the Soviets abrogate the treaty, they could deploy ABM defenses widely in the latter half of the decade.) We expect continuing Soviet interest in antisatellite defenses and in high-technology systems for strategic defense. Possible developments in the late 1980s could include a space-based antisatellite laser system and a few laser air defense weapons. Continuing

~~Secret~~

xxii

Secret

will develop a variety of payload options for responding to US deployment of new ICBMs. As a result, the Soviet ICBM force—with or without the SALT II Treaty—will have the theoretical potential to destroy most of the warheads on US land-based missiles throughout the decade. This potential will be greatest in the early 1980s, before the United States can deploy a new ICBM. But even in that early period, US forces could conduct a massive retaliatory strike

To maintain survivable strategic forces in the face of a potential threat to their own fixed, land-based missiles, we expect the Soviets to increase the capability of their submarine-launched ballistic missiles and possibly (especially in the absence of SALT constraints) to deploy land-mobile ICBMs. They may introduce a new strategic bomber or an aircraft to carry long-range cruise missiles, and they may already be testing a sea-launched strategic cruise missile

Should strategic arms control negotiations be resumed, these weapon developments could complicate monitoring—an already difficult US intelligence task. Land-mobile strategic weapons and cruise missiles cannot be counted with high confidence. As a result, monitoring strategic arms control agreements will be much more difficult in the 1980s than it was in the 1970s

Air defense improvements have been identified at Soviet test ranges, and some are now entering deployment. These include new surface-to-air missiles and interceptor aircraft with radars that enable them to detect and engage low-flying targets. These defenses could make penetration of Soviet airspace much more difficult for large manned bombers of current types. The small size and low flight altitudes of modern cruise missiles present a more complicated problem, however, and we project that Soviet defenses will be less effective against these new systems during the 1980s

The Soviets continue their antiballistic missile (ABM) programs, but the technical difficulties of detecting, identifying, and intercepting ballistic missiles have kept progress slow. Moreover, the deployment constraints of the 1972 ABM Treaty severely limit the effectiveness of defenses against missiles. (Should the Soviets abrogate the treaty, they could deploy ABM defenses widely in the latter half of the decade.) We expect continuing Soviet interest in antisatellite defenses and in high-technology systems for strategic defense. Possible developments in the late 1980s could include a space-based antisatellite laser system and a few laser air defense weapons. Continuing

Secret

Soviet naval programs will continue to emphasize open-ocean forces and the deployment of air power to sea. These programs will improve the Navy's capabilities to contest areas of the open ocean with the West. Ships and submarines with a new, long-range cruise missile are being introduced to offset Western gains in shipborne defenses. The Soviets are producing nuclear-powered attack submarines at an increasing rate, and the submarines introduced in this decade probably will be quieter (and harder to detect and track) than current models

Another naval development has important implications for Soviet military power—we have evidence of activities that probably are related to a program for a new aircraft carrier. It could be introduced in the late 1980s and probably would carry standard fighter or attack aircraft and be nuclear-powered. (The Soviets have helicopter carriers and ships that carry short-range, vertical and short takeoff and landing aircraft, but this could be their first attack aircraft carrier.) It would improve the Navy's air defenses and—more importantly—it could inaugurate a capability for projection of air power in distant areas. The USSR could not achieve a large-scale capability in the 1980s—only one or two carriers could be available—but this could emerge as a major theme in the 1990s and later

We expect other improvements in Soviet forces for power projection, besides the aircraft carrier. Introduction of a new class of landing ships—if it occurs in the 1980s—would increase the troop-lift capability of the Navy. The Soviets are reportedly working on a large transport aircraft, similar in size to the US C5A. If they produce such an aircraft, their airlift capabilities by 1990 could be substantially improved

In the 1980s, the Soviets will continue to improve their military space and command and control systems. We expect them to place in orbit new military space stations, to be used for intelligence purposes, and new unmanned satellites for real-time photographic reconnaissance and the detection of missile launches. We also expect further improvements in command and control, with emphasis on mobile systems and on the use of computers

With these new forces and capabilities, we expect the Soviets to maintain a high level of activity in the Third World to achieve both military and political goals. They may be willing to use their own forces more actively in the Third World, even if the activity brings a greater risk of confrontation with Western powers

If the Soviets carry out the programs that we have identified, their defense expenditures will continue to increase in real terms throughout the 1980s. The precise rate of increase is difficult to predict. It could be as high as 4 percent a year, if no constraints are imposed by arms control agreements and if the Soviets do not alter the support structure of their armed forces. A rate of 4 percent would increase the military drain on the economy and the potential for internal political problems

In an attempt to address these problems, the Soviets might try to reduce the growth of their defense spending to, say, 2 percent or less. To accomplish this they could:

- Cut back the current production of some systems while continuing development of follow-ons.
- Stretch out new production programs and postpone the target dates for force modernization.
- Attempt to improve efficiency in the military and the defense industries.

They could even take advantage of the limited financial savings that arms control agreements would permit by deploying fewer weapons—but their past actions suggest that they would procure forces to the limits of any such agreements.[3]

If the Soviets chose to make adjustments, they could spread them out among all of the military services, minimizing the impact on the rate of modernization of the forces as a whole. These changes could be risky from the point of view of the military, but might be attractive to political leaders with a broader perspective. We believe adjustments sufficient to hold the growth in spending down to 2 percent would not significantly alter the major judgments of our baseline projection

Alternative Projections. More radical changes in Soviet military policy are possible. Currently available evidence provides no clear indications that they are in the offing, but the interaction of political, economic, and technological forces in the 1980s could conceivably lead to major discontinuities.

[3] Arms control agreements could also reduce uncertainty about Western military programs and thus enable the Soviets to avoid some of the costs of hedging against uncertainty

One possibility is that the Soviets will reduce the level of military expenditures absolutely (rather than merely reducing the rate of increase). We believe this to be unlikely in the near term. Their dim view of the international environment would argue against such cuts, and the guidelines they have published for their next Five-Year Plan imply continued growth in defense spending. We have not detected any evidence that the Soviets are considering reductions

Nevertheless, reductions cannot be excluded as a long-run possibility; and, as one alternative projection, we have examined the consequences of a cut in defense expenditures. We believe that to reduce expenditure levels in real terms the Soviets would have to alter the roles and missions of some of their armed forces. They probably would spread the cuts among all the military services—making them somewhat deeper in general purpose forces, especially ground forces. General purpose forces are larger than strategic forces and they take up more of the defense budget and use more of the energy, manpower, and key material resources needed by the civilian economy. Production of general purpose weapon systems competes directly with production of equipment for transportation, agriculture, and manufacturing. (The resources devoted to production of strategic weapons, on the other hand, are more specialized and less readily transferable to important civilian uses.

Another alternative projection considers the possibility that the Soviets will increase defense spending more rapidly than in the past, to support a stepped-up military competition. This effort (focused on either strategic or conventional forces) could expand the forces and improve capabilities more rapidly than is forecast in our baseline projection. The range of program options is broad enough to permit a major increase in defense spending, and Soviet military-industrial capacity is large enough to sustain it. Such an increase would affect the distribution of economic resources significantly, however (especially if it were in conventional forces), and its political consequences could be extremely serious:

- The Soviets' ability to increase investment resources critical to long-term economic growth would be reduced substantially.
- Per capita consumption might decline in real terms late in the decade.
- Key sectors of the economy would be disrupted.

We do not know at what point the Soviets would find an increased defense burden to be unacceptable. This would depend on the international environment and the outlook of the leaders in power. Judging by their past behavior, we believe that they would prefer, if possible, to keep defense expenditures within their current growth rate, while still pursuing their military goals.

- The Soviets probably will seek to constrain US programs and to reduce their uncertainty about future US capabilities by urging further arms control negotiations.
- They will also attempt, through propaganda and diplomacy, to undermine Western cohesiveness on security issues and to slow the pace of West European defense programs.

The Soviets' incentives for such actions will increase as their economic growth slows in the 1980s. But Soviet leaders place a high premium on military power and will not, for economic reasons alone, accept constraints on defense programs that they consider vital to their interest

Background and Structure of This Report

This report is based on a major interdisciplinary research effort carried out by the National Foreign Assessment Center during the 1979-80 period. It surveys the development of Soviet military power in the Brezhnev era—a period of relative economic prosperity and political stability—and outlines its probable evolution in the 1980s, when declining economic growth, a leadership succession, and a complex international environment will pose difficult choices for Soviet political and military leaders. To improve our understanding of these choices, more than 40 individual research projects were undertaken by the Offices of Central Reference, Economic Research, [ ] Political Analysis, Scientific and Weapons Research, and Strategic Research. [ ]

Beginning with a discussion of the Soviet military buildup under Brezhnev and of the factors underlying it, the paper then discusses the forces that will affect Soviet power and policies in the 1980s. These ideas underlie our baseline projection for the period through 1990 (page 73). Finally, several alternative courses of action that the Soviets could follow are outlined, as well as the conditions and constraints that bear on Soviet behavior and the clues that could alert us to changes in Soviet military policy

49. (continued)

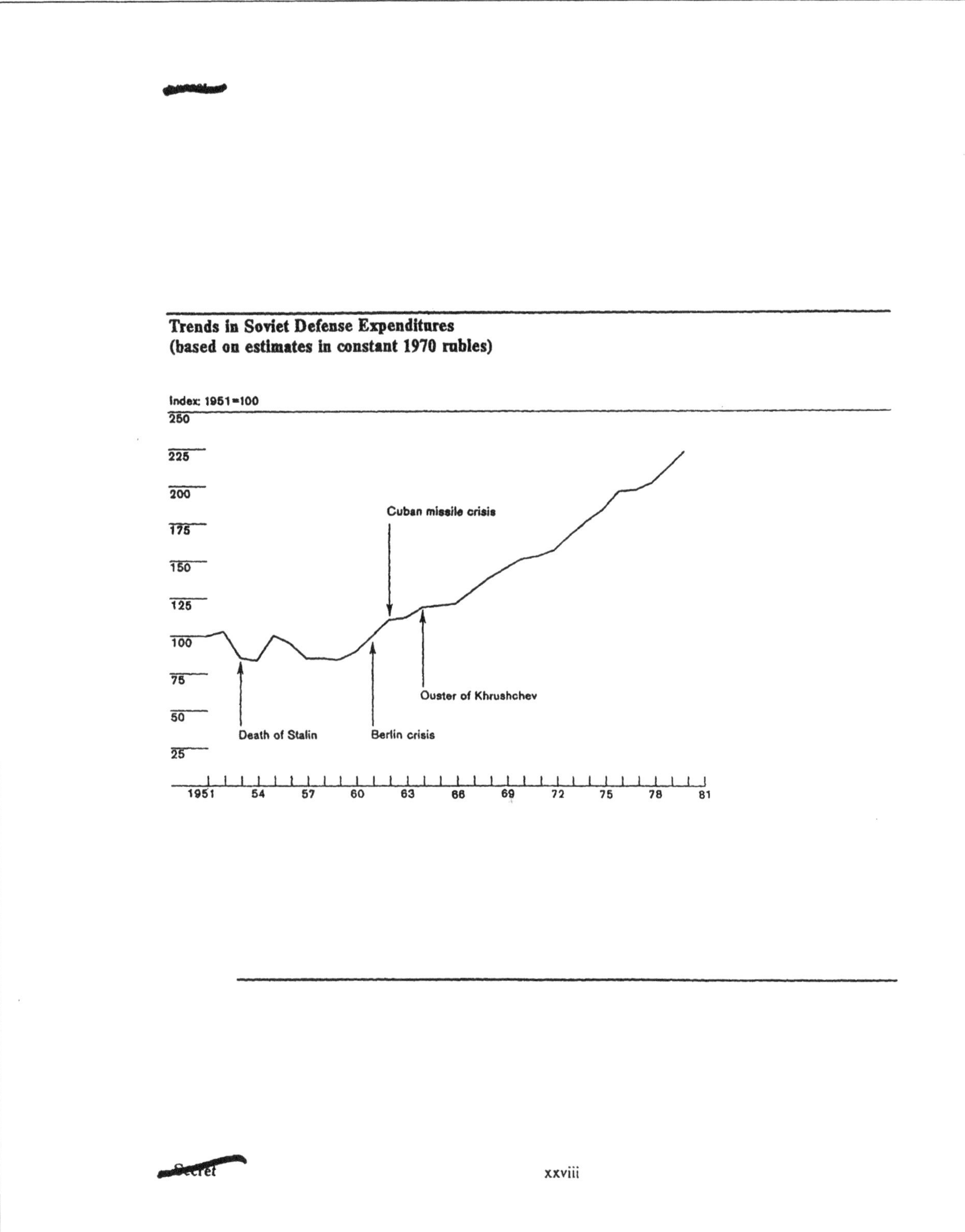

**Trends in Soviet Defense Expenditures
(based on estimates in constant 1970 rubles)**

www.ingramcontent.com/pod-product-compliance
Lightning Source LLC
Chambersburg PA
CBHW050409110426
42812CB00006BA/1841
* 9 7 8 1 7 8 0 3 9 3 7 7 3 *